THE MOUNTAIN BIKER'S GUIDE
TO ARIZONA

Dennis Coello's America by Mountain Bike Series

THE MOUNTAIN BIKER'S
GUIDE TO ARIZONA

*Dennis Coello's America by
Mountain Bike Series*

Sarah L. Bennett

Foreword and Introduction
by Dennis Coello, Series Editor

MENASHA
RIDGE
PRESS

Copyright © 1993 by Sarah L. Bennett
All rights reserved
Printed in the United States of America
Published by Menasha Ridge Press and Falcon Press
First Edition, second printing 1994

Library of Congress Cataloging-in-Publication Data
Bennett, Sarah L.
    The mountain biker's guide to Arizona / Sarah L. Bennett :
foreword and introduction by Dennis Coello, series editor.
        p.   cm. — (Dennis Coello's America by mountain bike
series)
    ISBN 1-56044-199-2
    1. All terrain cycling—Arizona—Guidebooks.
2. Guidebooks—Arizona.   3. Trails—Arizona—
Guidebooks.   I. Title.   II. Series: America by mountain bike
series.
GV1045.5.A6B46   1993
796.6'4'09791—dc20   93-17462
                                                           CIP

Photos by the author unless otherwise credited
Maps by Tim Krasnansky
Cover photo by Bob Allen

Menasha Ridge Press
3169 Cahaba Heights Road
Birmingham, Alabama 35243

Falcon Press
P. O. Box 1718
Helena, Montana 59624

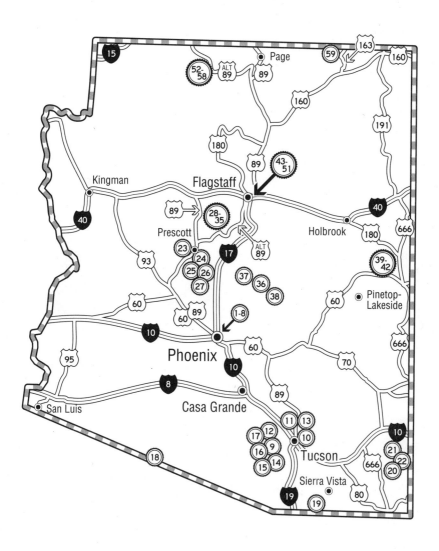

Table of Contents

List of Maps

AMERICA BY MOUNTAIN BIKE *MAP LEGEND*

Ride trailhead　　　　　　　**Steep grade**

Primary bike trail	Direction of travel	(arrows point downhill)	Optional bike trail	Other trail	Hiking trail

Interstate highways (with exit no.)	U.S. routes	Arizona state routes	Other paved roads	Unpaved, gravel or dirt roads (may be 4WD only)

U.S. Forest Service roads	Phoenix ◉ Flagstaff **Cities**	Greaterville ◉ Oracle **Towns or settlements**	Dam Lake	River, stream or canal

0　½　1 MILES **Approximate scale in miles**	**N** True North	CAMPGAW MTN **Parklands**	International Border	State Border

✈ Airport	⊥ Fire tower or lookout	⚖ Museum
▼ Archeological site or ruins	⊞ Food	⚲ Observatory
·) Archery range	⊠ Gate	♦ Park office or ranger station
▲ Campground	♦ House or cabin	🗇 Picnic area
≡ Cattle guard	⊟ Lodging	♦ Port of Entry
‡ Cemetery or gravesite	🌄 Mountain or butte	╱ Power line or pipeline
♦ Church	🌄 Mountain pass	♦ Ranch or stable
ϟ Cliff, escarpment or outcropping	△ Mountain summit 3312 (elevation in feet)	🏊 Swimming Area
♦ Drinking water	🔥 Military test site	‖ Transmission towers
	✕ Mine	⌣ Tunnel

Acknowledgments

Many, many thanks are due to the people who assisted me in my four months on the road gathering information for this project. The interest and enthusiasm I received from friends and strangers alike was overwhelming. Whether it was a shower and a bed, a meal, directions, or simply a smile and a slap on the back, it was the generosity of these people that enabled me to continue along the trails. Without their help I doubt this book would have been possible.

My gratitude and respect also go out to the men and women who work for our National Forest Service, and those who have the difficult task of managing a wide range of public interests and demands upon our wildlands. We have these people to thank for building and maintaining most of the roads and trails in this book. They deserve special acknowledgement for the work they are doing to accommodate the growing number of mountain bikers that will visit our national forests in the future. These folks need our input and deserve our cooperation.

The riders with whom I shared the trails, and who appear in the pages of this book, are deeply appreciated for their love of fat tires and the outdoors, and their spirit of adventure. I am convinced that their concern for all these things will keep the sport growing in the right direction.

And last but not least, I would like to thank my editor and friend, Dennis Coello, for offering me this project, and the opportunity to spend so many months in the beautiful American Southwest.

Foreword

Welcome to *America by Mountain Bike,* a twenty-book series designed to provide all-terrain bikers with the information necessary to find and ride the very best trails everywhere in the mainland United States. Whether you're new to the sport and don't know where to pedal, or an experienced mountain biker who wants to learn the classic trails in another region, this series is for you. Drop a few bucks for the book, spend an hour with the detailed maps and route descriptions, and you're prepared for the finest in off-road cycling.

My role as editor of this series was simple: First, find a mountain biker who knows the area and loves to ride. Second, ask that person to spend a year researching the most popular and very best rides around. And third, have that rider describe each trail in terms of difficulty, scenery, condition, elevation change, and all other categories of information which are important to trail riders. "Pretend you've just completed a ride and met up with fellow mountain bikers at the trailhead," I told each author. "Imagine their questions, be clear in your answers."

As I said, the *editorial* process—that of sending out riders and reading the submitted chapters—is a snap. But the work involved in finding, riding, and writing about each trail is enormous. In some instances our authors' tasks are made easier by the information contributed by local bike shops or cycling clubs, or even by the writers of local "where-to" guides. Credit for these contributions is provided in each chapter, and our sincere thanks goes to all who have helped.

But the overwhelming majority of trails are discovered and pedaled by our authors themselves, then compared with dozens of other routes to determine if they qualify as "classic"—that area's best in scenery and cycling fun. If you've ever had the experience of pioneering a route from outdated topographic maps, or entering a bike shop to request information from local riders who would much prefer to keep their favorite trails secret, or know how it is to double- and triple-check data to be positive your trail info is correct, then you have an idea of how each of our authors has labored to bring about these books. You and I, and all the mountain bikers of America, are the richer for their efforts.

Dennis Coello
Salt Lake City

P.S. You'll get more out of this book if you take a moment to read the next few pages explaining the "Trail Description Outline." Newcomers to mountain biking might want to spend a minute as well with the Glossary, so that terms like *hardpack, single-track,* and *windfall* won't throw you when you come across

A beautiful Sonoran desert evening in the Santa Catalina Mountains.

them in the text. "Topographic Maps" will help you understand a biker's need for topos, and tell you where to find them. And the section titled "Land-Use Controversy" might help us all enjoy the trails a little more. Finally, though this is a "where-to," not a "how-to" guide, those of you who have not traveled the backcountry might find "Hitting the Trail" of particular value. All the best.

Preface

Before I agreed to do this project I had spent little time in the Southwest. One brief weekend trip to Tucson and a rafting adventure through the Grand Canyon was all I knew of Arizona. I had found the area surrounding Tucson to be rugged, wild country, intimidating when glimpsed through a mixture of dust and shimmering heat. The desert flora was exotic and other-worldly to me, and the imagined creatures that crept among the spiny giant cactus were downright unnerving. I found myself straining my ears to hear the buzz of the rattlesnake which I knew was nearby. Anxiety overwhelmed me as I pedaled under the scorching rays of the Sonoran sun, and I began to feel the confidence gained over years in the outdoors slip away.

These first impressions and sensations are probably not all that different from those that most strangers to this country experience when first venturing into the desert Southwest. While they are not wholly incorrect they are not completely accurate, either. For there is a slightly different set of rules by which one must play in this part of the world. But these rules are easy to learn and will enhance your respect for the life-forms able to flourish in this generally arid environment. By following a few simple guidelines you will free yourself from danger and will be prepared to explore some of the most beautiful wilderness this country has to offer.

In the almost eight months I spent traveling across the southwestern states— riding, camping, and doing research for this book—I was constantly amazed at the rich variety of the flora and fauna, the climate, the people, and also the history of the region. My earliest impressions of the Southwest were quickly diffused by cool days in the pines, by rides across lush, green meadows rimmed with aspen and fir, and by getting caught in cold, pelting rainstorms that stung my hands and face. From the Lower Sonoran Desert to the high alpine environment of the San Francisco Peaks, this land is full of the unexpected. It holds unlimited opportunities for mountain biking, camping, and sightseeing throughout the year.

And now for some information to help you ride Arizona safely and appreciate the state more completely:

THE WEATHER

Of all the concerns people have when considering travel in the desert Southwest, it is the thought of hot, dry weather that causes the greatest anxiety. The weather can be extreme in this part of the country and does play a very important part in the safety and enjoyment of exploring by mountain bike. It is important to remember, however, that the extreme variations in elevation and terrain through-out these states provide comfortable temperatures for biking (if you know where to find them) during every month of the year. There are few states in this country that offer so much rideable terrain year-round.

Riding at elevations below 5,000 feet in summer months is difficult, for there tends to be little cooling at night. In the spring and fall months the days can really heat up in the lower deserts, but the nights cool off sufficiently to make early morning and evening riding very pleasant. The temperatures for riding in these lower elevations are just about perfect during the winter months when higher elevations are impassable due to snow.

If you are coming from another part of the country and are unaccustomed to the strength of the desert sun and the aridity, you will need several days to ac-climate yourself to these conditions. The dry air, heat, and elevation will at first take a substantial toll on your strength and endurance, so start out slowly. A bad sunburn, high exertion, and low liquid intake can combine to create a number of very dangerous situations. The warning signs and dangers of these heat-related conditions should be recognized. (See "Desert Health and Safety" on page xx.)

Arizona, while generally considered to be a desert state, has a bonafide mon-soon season. During late summer and fall, weather patterns begin to change in the southwestern deserts, as moisture begins pumping into the upper and middle levels of the atmosphere from the Gulf of Mexico, sending humidity levels soar-ing. This moist warm air rises as it travels over the hot desert creating beautiful towers of billowing cumulo-nimbus storm clouds, which can lash out violently with lightning, hail, and torrential rains.

Within an eight- to twelve-week window beginning sometime in mid-July and running through September, cycles of cloud building and storms can become a daily routine. By mid- to late afternoon it is a good idea to be off of high or ex-posed places and close to shelter, due to the tremendous amount of electricity generated by these storms. Also avoid driving through, or camping in, arroyos (water-carved gullies or drainages) at this time of year. Arroyos can become raging torrents in a matter of seconds. While these thunderstorms tend to be isolated, they can wreak havoc on your outing, so get an early start if afternoon thunderstorms are predicted.

The higher altitudes, besides receiving the lion's share of summer thunder-storms, are always places where you should be prepared for rapid temperature changes. It is a good idea to carry a weatherproof shell along on your ride, espe-cially if you are riding in the mountains. Snowfall in the higher ranges is not uncommon in the late spring or early fall months. Here too it is prudent to be aware of the signs of hypothermia which you will find outlined in "Desert Health and Safety."

THE LAND

The land that lies within the borders of Arizona can be thought of as a giant wedge which starts high in the north and runs out to lower elevations in the south. Elevations range from 70 feet near Yuma, Arizona, to 12,633 feet atop Humphrey's Peak in the San Francisco Peaks north of Flagstaff. Within the state, the sixth largest in the union, there exists such a variety of geological and geographical features that one can't help but be awestruck by the continually changing face of the land.

The northern half of Arizona is dominated by the Colorado Plateau, a giant uplifted landmass ranging from 5,000 to 8,000 feet above sea level, and extending into northern New Mexico and southern portions of Utah and Colorado. Long broad mesas, sculpted red rock formations, and deep canyons characterize the landscape of the Colorado Plateau. In places the plateau's crust has given way to powerful volcanic events that have created the San Francisco Peaks and the White Mountains in Arizona. Many of the mesas (flat-topped hills or mountains) in this region are capped by a resistant basaltic layer, which once flowed like a syrupy liquid from these peaks over large expanses of this country. The Colorado Plateau terminates along the well-defined Mogollon (pronounced *MUGGY-own*) Rim in Arizona, which extends as a series of sheer cliffs across long stretches of the state's mid-section.

Most of the southern half of Arizona is included in a region referred to in geological terms as "basin and range." This is true desert country, with broad, barren expanses interrupted only by small, isolated mountain ranges, which have been thrust upward as fault blocks. Some of these small ranges have peaks over 10,000 feet and are called "islands in the sky." Because these cooler, wetter peaks are surrounded by extremely dry desert floor they have become much like islands surrounded by ocean, where certain species of plants and mammals have been trapped and developed characteristics peculiar only to their specific mountain home.

Many of these ranges once contained small but rich lodes of gold, silver, and copper ore, which drew people by the thousands to this part of the country in the mid-1800s. Very few of these sites are mined today, but the efforts of those old-timers have left most of these small ranges crisscrossed with mining roads and dotted with stone ruins. We have them to thank for the backbreaking work that created these roads which are so well suited to mountain biking.

FLORA AND FAUNA

The plant and animal life of this region is as rich and varied as any area of North America. Six of the world's seven life zones exist in Arizona due to the 12,000-

foot elevation variable and the climate extremes. Life zone data is based on the Merriam system which combines elevation and rainfall. The varied landscapes of Arizona are therefore home to everything from Gila monsters, scorpions, diamondback rattlers, and javelina in the Lower Sonoran Desert, to black bear, cougar, and elk in the higher Transition and Canadian Zones of the Kaibab Plateau and the San Francisco Peaks.

The variety of plant life in this region is equally astounding, from the majestic saguaro cactus in the Sonoran Desert, to fall's brilliant golden stands of aspen along the Mogollon Rim. The Sonoran Desert in bloom is a spectacle of such magnificent beauty that it must be seen to be believed, and even then it's hard to believe. Brilliant waxy blossoms snuggled into the spiny crowns of these seemingly inert giants tell of a land full of surprises. Cacti and their blossoms in the Sonoran Desert come in a rainbow of colors, shapes, and sizes, and within the short span of a few weeks in April and May they cover the desert floor like dancers on parade. These beautiful pointed desert dwellers, who have managed to eke out a living for centuries on the baked plains of the Sonora, look tough but are in fact extremely fragile. Their root systems are shallow and wide, which has made them easy targets for vandals who like to push them over. These cacti are unique to this part of the world. They are found only in the Sonoran Desert of Mexico and Arizona. They are both menacing and beautiful and deserve our respect.

The elegant shapes of fragrant piñon and juniper trees that dot the rolling hills of the central highlands fall into the Upper Sonoran life zone category. These highlands are the foothills of the Colorado Plateau, which is blanketed by thick stands of ponderosa pines which characterize the Transition Zone. Because ponderosas tend to grow straight, tall, and close together, they are very appealing to the lumber industry and have been logged extensively throughout northern and central Arizona. Some of the only old-growth ponderosas surviving are to be found on the Kaibab Plateau, where they are protected inside Grand Canyon National Park. Once again the industries that harvest the land's resources have left widespread road systems on which mountain bikers can travel quickly and easily into remote country. Don't hesitate to ask the forest ranger about logging practices in an area you may be riding. Remember, these forests belong to all of us and it is important for us to educate ourselves—and once having done so to express our viewpoint to those who make decisions for us.

The mixed spruce, fir, and aspen forests that are found throughout the Canadian and Hudsonian Zones above 8,000 feet make for classic alpine riding conditions in the mountains of Arizona. These higher climes receive most of the moisture that falls on the Southwest, and they remain nice and cool during the heat of the summer months. This high country is steep and sensitive to trail traffic, and it's where you'll find the bulk of the land designated as Wilderness Area. Wilderness Areas are off-limits to all mechanized vehicles, and that includes mountain bikes. It is important that we acknowledge this restriction and the fact that there are some places mountain bikes just don't belong.

THE PEOPLE

The area that is now Arizona has been inhabited for the last 20,000 years, beginning with a nomadic band of Paleo-Indians who left behind only a few spear points to tell of their travels. Scientists now believe that these were some of the first ancestors of the native North Americans who crossed over from Asia during the last ice age. Small bands continued to migrate through the area until they learned agricultural skills, which allowed them to establish more permanent settlements. Many of these small settlements grew into bustling societies that erected beautiful stone cities and developed extensive trade networks with Mexico and South America.

Anglo peoples as well have a long and colorful past in the region. More than a hundred years before the Pilgrims set foot in North America the Spanish had penetrated deep into the New World, bringing armies, missionaries and priests to Christianize its native inhabitants. This culturally rich region, now known as Arizona, has assimilated the best of all worlds.

In the mountains of central New Mexico and eastern Arizona, discoveries of prehistoric campfire sites littered with bones and crude spear points have often been found in caves. The evidence found at these sites reveals that the first inhabitants of the Southwest successfully hunted such animals as the wooly mammoth and giant ground sloth, animals that have been extinct for some 10,000 years. A change in the climate forced the big animals into extinction by turning the grasslands and forests into desert. Until about 500 B.C. small bands of people survived by hunting rabbits, grouse, and other small game, and by gathering what seeds, berries, and roots they could find. At this time squash and beans were introduced and agriculture became the main source of subsistence. These first farming cultures lived in pithouses and manufactured the earliest pottery for storing and cooking beans and grains.

With the success of farming, these small communities began to grow. Above ground stone houses were built, new religions were developed, new crafts were created, and new trade was established. Gradually distinct cultural groups emerged: the Anasazi of the Colorado Plateau, the Mogollon of the central highlands, and the Hohokam of the southern deserts. These cultures flourished from A.D. 500 to A.D. 1100, at which time they mysteriously began to disappear. Drought, disease, and pressure from tribes moving into the area are all possible reasons for their demise. The natives left behind hundreds of beautifully constructed stone houses and complex irrigation and road systems. Riders traveling in Arizona will miss a unique experience if they fail to visit a few of the many ruins scattered throughout the state.

The very first Europeans to enter the Southwest were supposedly a small group of Spaniards who survived the sinking of their ship somewhere in the Gulf of Mexico in 1527. The next ten years were spent traveling west and then south to Mexico, where they told stories of having seen seven huge cities constructed of gold and turquoise. The viceroy of New Spain (which is now Mexico) promptly organized an exploration party led by the missionary Fray Marcos de Niza. He discovered the stone city of the Zuni Pueblo just over the border from Arizona in present-day New Mexico, where most of his party was killed by frightened and defensive Indians. He returned with news of his discovery, which encouraged Francisco Vasquez de Coronado to organize another exploration party. With more than three hundred soldiers and over one thousand Mexican Indians, Coronado explored the Southwest for nearly two years, roaming the territory between the Grand Canyon and Kansas. He found only the stone houses of the Pueblo, who were less than happy to see these intruders in their homeland.

The first real effort to colonize the American Southwest was made in 1598 by Don Juan de Oñate. His expedition failed due to his cruelty to the native Indians and his followers' dissatisfaction with the dry climate. The next attempt at colonization and rule was made by Don Pedro de Peralta, who set up operations in what is now Santa Fe. He appointed himself, with the blessing of the King of Spain, as the governor of New Mexico. At this point the effort to Christianize the Indians of Arizona and New Mexico had begun in earnest. The Spanish were extremely harsh in trying to convert the Indians, many of whom were either tortured or killed when they refused the faith. There were a number of bloody revolts by the region's Indians, which only briefly gained them their freedom, but eventually all were subdued under Spanish rule.

During the next 200 years the Spanish empire declined, and in 1821 Mexico won its independence. Anglos began filtering into what is now Arizona and New Mexico—trapping, prospecting, and trading. Brigham Young sent Mormon pioneers from the north who began to settle the region. After the discovery of precious minerals throughout the hills of Arizona the tide of settlers became enormous, and towns gained a permanent foothold.

The region that is now Arizona was won by the United States in the Mexican-American War of 1847–48. The southernmost strip of Arizona was added to the territory by the Gadsden Purchase of 1853; statehood was declared in 1912. And mountain bikes were introduced in the eighties.

DESERT HEALTH AND SAFETY

Water, Water, Water

The single most important item riders can take with them into the desert is water. Bikers exerting themselves in an arid climate, in high temperatures, need tremendous quantities of water to remain healthy and to keep functioning properly. Remember, don't let thirst regulate your water intake; by the time you first sense you are thirsty you are already experiencing a fluid deficit. For long rides in hot weather you will want to carry some kind of fluid or drink mix that is high in salt, potassium, and glucose. These will help to replace electrolytes which then aid the body in metabolizing fuel into energy.

Heat-related stress and illness

Heat cramps: These are muscle spasms that occur during long periods of exposure to heat and dehydration. They are caused by the constriction of blood vessels to the muscles in response to heat, and by the loss of bodily salts that results from sweating. If heat cramps are ignored, a more serious situation can occur. Relief of these symptoms includes drinking plenty of water and restoring salt and electrolytes to your system. Increasing fluid, salt, and electrolyte intake before a ride will help prevent this condition from developing.

Heat exhaustion: This is a condition caused by stress to your circulatory system combined with a reduction of blood volume in your body due to extensive fluid loss. Symptoms of heat exhaustion include dizziness, nausea, headaches, and a general feeling of weakness. Your pulse rate becomes weak and rapid and you lose the ability to perspire. Anyone who experiences these symptoms should stop exercising immediately, find a cool spot in which to rest, and consume large amounts of fluids. Some of these symptoms may appear hours after getting out of the sun and completing your ride, as the body struggles to recuperate.

Heatstroke: This is the most dangerous of all heat-related conditions and requires immediate action. Heatstroke is what happens when the internal body temperature has risen so high that the body loses its ability to control sweating, heart rate, and the reactions that protect the internal organs. Symptoms of heatstroke include the inability to sweat, hot and dry skin, and a dangerously high internal body temperature. Someone who is suffering from heatstroke can suffer disorientation, hallucinations, and seizures. Heatstroke causes excessive strain on the circulatory system, which can result in permanent liver, heart, or kidney damage. It may also cause damage to the central nervous system and result in permanent disabilities. If left untreated it can result in complete circulatory collapse and death—it *is* a serious medical emergency. Action you can take while waiting for medical help includes finding a cool place for the victim, submerging the person in a cold stream if possible, or rubbing water over the skin. Riders on the trail need to listen to their bodies and monitor each other for signs of the heat cramps and heat exhaustion which can lead to heatstroke if untreated.

Keeping the desert sun off your skin is another very important measure you can take toward preventing any of these heat-related problems from developing. A loose white or light-colored button-down shirt, a hat or visor to keep the sun off your face, and lots of sunscreen will help prevent a damaging sunburn and will aid your body in its fight to stay cool.

Timing your rides so that you are not out in the hottest part of the day or during the hottest season of the year will also help prevent heat stress. Early morning and evening are excellent times for riding. You may even want to do half your ride in the morning and half in the evening, with a siesta in a cool spot planned

This is Arizona! Lockett Meadow in the San Francisco Peaks.

for the afternoon. Spring and fall are the best times for enjoying the desert, but even then temperatures in the middle of the day can climb to 90 degrees and above. Stopping frequently to drink and snack in the shade is the best strategy for avoiding stress to your system from the desert heat.

Cold

At the other end of the spectrum is a condition that develops from exposure to cold. It is called hypothermia, and despite what you may think it can strike in the middle of summer, even in the desert. Getting caught out after dark, or in a rainstorm at high elevations without the proper clothing to protect you from the elements, can result in this life-threatening situation.

Hypothermia: This is a condition that is caused by an alarming drop in the body's core temperature. Symptoms of hypothermia include slurred speech, poor coordination, mental dullness and confusion, sleepiness, and a loss of color in the face and extremities. Immediate action is required to reduce further heat loss. Ingesting hot fluids, or increasing surface heat by means of a fire or by using the body heat of another person, are steps that can be taken to increase the body's temperature. Dry clothing, sleeping bags, quilts, tarps, or anything that will hold in heat should be applied after wet clothing is removed. It is always a good idea to bring an extra layer for warmth *and* a weatherproof shell when riding at higher elevations, or on a day when foul weather is predicted.

Food

Another element important to enjoying long hours in the saddle is food. Eating enough of the right kinds of foods to maintain energy levels throughout the day is not difficult, but there are a few important things to remember.

First, excitement of a great ride, especially when combined with high temperatures, can often lead to a decreased appetite. Eating throughout the day, however, is very important and should not be left until hunger strikes. As with thirst, once you sense that you are hungry you are already experiencing a depletion in your body's fuel. But in the case of food, fuel replenishment is not instantaneous.

Plan ahead, before the ride, by eating carbohydrates which can be easily metabolized into polysaccharides, or sugars. This group includes bread, cereals, rice, and pasta. But eat normally; there's really no need for "carbo-loading" in recreational riding. And then take breaks—every two hours or so—throughout the day's ride, to snack on the kinds of trail food which will sustain a high energy level.

I have included this information not to scare you, but to assist you in enjoying Arizona completely and safely. Riding the high desert and mountains of this fascinating state does require a few precautions. But once those are taken you can look forward to unparalleled scenic beauty—and mountain biking at its best.

Sarah L. Bennett

Introduction

TRAIL DESCRIPTION OUTLINE

Information on each trail in this book begins with a general description that includes length, configuration, scenery, highlights, trail conditions, and difficulty. Additional description is contained in eleven individual categories. The following will help you to understand all of the information provided.

Trail name: Trail names are as designated on USGS (United States Geological Survey) or Forest Service or other maps, and/or by local custom.

Length: The overall length of a trail is described in miles, unless stated otherwise.

Configuration: This is a description of the shape of each trail—whether the trail is a loop, out-and-back (that is, along the same route), figure-eight, trapezoid, isosceles triangle . . . , or if it connects with another trail described in the book.

Difficulty: This provides at a glance a description of the degree of physical exertion required to complete the ride, and the technical skill required to pedal it. Authors were asked to keep in mind the fact that all riders are not equal, and thus to gauge the trail in terms of how the middle-of-the-road rider—someone between the newcomer and Ned Overend—could handle the route. Comments about the trail's length, condition, and elevation change will also assist you in determining the difficulty of any trail relative to your own abilities.

Condition: Trails are described in terms of being paved, unpaved, sandy, hard-packed, washboarded, two- or four-wheel-drive, single-track or double-track. All terms that might be unfamiliar to the first-time mountain biker are defined in the Glossary.

Scenery: Here you will find a general description of the natural surroundings during the seasons most riders pedal the trail, and a suggestion of what is to be found at special times (like great fall foliage or cactus in bloom).

Highlights: Towns, major water crossings, historical sites, etc., are listed.

General location: This category describes where the trail is located in reference to a nearby town or other landmark.

Elevation change: Unless stated otherwise, the figure provided is the total gain and loss of elevation along the trail. In regions where the elevation variation is not extreme, the route is described in a more general manner of flat, rolling, or as possessing short steep climbs or descents.

Season: This is the best time of year to pedal the route, taking into account trail condition (for example, when it will not be muddy), riding comfort (when the weather is too hot, cold, or wet), and local hunting seasons.

Note: Because the exact opening and closing dates of deer, elk, moose, and antelope seasons often change from year to year, it is suggested that riders check with the local Fish and Game department, or call a sporting goods store (or any place that sells hunting licenses) in a nearby town. Wear bright clothes in fall, and don't wear suede jackets while in the saddle. Hunter's-orange tape on the helmet is also a good idea.

Services: This category is of primary importance in guides for paved-road tourers, but is far less crucial to most mountain bike trail descriptions because there are usually no services whatsoever to be found. Authors have noted when water is available on desert or long mountain routes, and have listed the availability of food, lodging, campgrounds, and bike shops. If all these services are present, you will find only the words "All services available in. . . ."

Hazards: Special hazards like steep cliffs, great amounts of deadfall, or barbed-wire fences very close to the trail are noted here.

Rescue index: Determining how far one is from help on any particular trail can be difficult due to the backcountry nature of most mountain bike rides. Authors therefore state the proximity of homes or Forest Service outposts, nearby roads where one might hitch a ride, or the likelihood of other bikers being encountered on the trail. Phone numbers of local sheriff departments or hospitals have not been provided because, again, phones are almost never available. Besides, if a phone is reached the local operator will connect you with emergency services.

Land status: This category provides information regarding whether the trail crosses land operated by the Forest Service, Bureau of Land Management, a city, state, or national park, whether it crosses private land whose owner (at the time the author did the research) allowed mountain bikers right of passage, and so on.

Note: Authors have been extremely careful to offer only those routes that are open to bikers and are legal to ride. However, because land ownership changes over time, and because the land-use controversy created by mountain bikes still has not subsided totally, it is the duty of each cyclist to look for and to heed signs warning against trail use. Don't expect this book to get you off the hook when you're facing some small-town judge for pedaling past a "Biking Prohibited" sign erected the day before. Look for these signs, read them, and heed the advice. And remember there's always another trail.

Maps: The maps in this book have been produced with great care, and in conjunction with the trail-following suggestions will help you stay on course. But as every experienced mountain biker knows, things can get tricky in the backcountry. It is therefore strongly suggested that you avail yourself of the detailed information found in the 7.5 minute series USGS (United States Geological Survey) topographic maps. In some cases, authors have found that specific Forest Service or other maps may be more useful than the USGS quads, and tell how to obtain them.

Finding the trail: Detailed information on how to reach the trailhead and where to park your car is provided here.

Sources of additional information: Here you will find the address of a bike shop, governmental agency, or other source from which trail information can be obtained.

Notes on the trail: This is where you are guided carefully through any portions of the trail that are particularly difficult to follow. The author also may add information about the route that does not fit easily into the other categories.

ABBREVIATIONS

The following road-designation abbreviations are used in the *America by Mountain Bike* series:

CR	County road
FR	Farm route
FS	Forest Service road
I-	Interstate
IR	Indian route
US	United States highway

State highways are designated with the appropriate two-letter state abbreviation, followed by the road number. *Example:* UT 6 = Utah State Highway 6.

Postal Service two-letter state code:

AL	Alabama	ME	Maine
AK	Alaska	MD	Maryland
AZ	Arizona	MA	Massachusetts
AR	Arkansas	MI	Michigan
CA	California	MN	Minnesota
CO	Colorado	MS	Mississippi
CT	Connecticut	MO	Missouri
DE	Delaware	MT	Montana
DC	District of Columbia	NE	Nebraska
FL	Florida	NV	Nevada
GA	Georgia	NH	New Hampshire
HI	Hawaii	NJ	New Jersey
ID	Idaho	NM	New Mexico
IL	Illinois	NY	New York
IN	Indiana	NC	North Carolina
IA	Iowa	ND	North Dakota
KS	Kansas	OH	Ohio
KY	Kentucky	OK	Oklahoma
LA	Louisiana	OR	Oregon

PA	Pennsylvania	VT	Vermont
RI	Rhode Island	VA	Virginia
SC	South Carolina	WA	Washington
SD	South Dakota	WV	West Virginia
TN	Tennessee	WI	Wisconsin
TX	Texas	WY	Wyoming
UT	Utah		

TOPOGRAPHIC MAPS

The maps in this book, when used in conjunction with the route directions present in each chapter, will in most instances be sufficient to get you to the trail and keep you on it. However, these maps cannot begin to provide the detailed information found in the 7.5 minute series USGS (United States Geological Survey) topographic maps. Recognizing how indispensable these are to bikers and hikers alike, many bike shops and sporting goods stores now carry topos of the local area.

But if you're brand new to mountain biking you might be wondering "What's a topographic map?" In short, these differ from standard "flat" maps because they indicate not only linear distance, but elevation as well. One glance at a topo will show you the difference, for "contour lines" are spread across the map like dozens of intricate spider webs. Each contour line represents a particular elevation, and each topo has written at its base a particular "contour interval" designation. Yes, it sounds confusing if you're new to the lingo, but it truly is a simple and wonderfully helpful system. Keep reading.

Let's assume that the 7.5 minute series topo before us says "Contour Interval 40 feet," that the short trail we'll be pedaling is two inches in length on the map, and that it crosses five contour lines between its beginning and end. What do we know? Well, because the linear scale of this series is two thousand feet to the inch (roughly 2¾ inches representing a mile), we know our trail is approximately four-fifths of a mile long (2" × 2,000'). But we also know we'll be climbing or descending 200 vertical feet (5 contour lines × 40 feet each) over that distance. And the elevation designations written on occasional contour lines will tell us if we're heading up or down.

The authors of this series warn their readers of upcoming terrain, but only a detailed topo gives you the information that enables you to pinpoint your position exactly on a map, steer you toward optional trails and roads nearby, plus let you know at a glance if you'll be pedaling hard to take them. It's a lot of information for a very low cost. In fact, the only drawback with topos is their size—several feet square. I've tried rolling them into tubes, folding them carefully, even cutting them into blocks and photocopying the pieces. Any of these systems is a pain, but no matter how you pack the maps you'll be happy they're along.

Major universities and some public libraries also carry topos; you might try photocopying the ones you need to avoid the cost of buying them. But if you want your own and can't find them locally, write to:

USGS Map Sales
Box 25286
Denver, CO 80225

Ask for an index while you're at it, plus a price list and a copy of the booklet *Topographic Maps*. In minutes you'll be reading them like a pro.

A second excellent series of maps available to mountain bikers is distributed by the United States Forest Service. If your trail runs through an area designated as a national forest, look in the phone book (white pages) under the United States Government listings, find the Department of Agriculture heading, and then run your finger through that section until you find the Forest Service. Give them a call and they'll provide the address of the regional Forest Service office, from which you can obtain the appropriate map.

LAND-USE CONTROVERSY

A few years ago I wrote a long piece on this issue for *Sierra Magazine* and called literally dozens of government land managers, game wardens, mountain bikers, and local officials, to get a feeling for how ATBs were being welcomed on the trails. All that I've seen personally since, and heard from my authors, indicates there hasn't been much change. Which means we're still considered the new kid on the block, that we have less right to the trails than horses and hikers, and that we're excluded from many areas including:

a) wilderness areas
b) national parks (except on roads, and those paths specifically marked "bike path")
c) national monuments (except on roads open to the public)
d) most state parks and monuments (except on roads, and those paths specifically marked "bike path")
e) an increasing number of urban and county parks, especially in California (except on roads, and those areas specifically marked "bike path")

Frankly, I have little difficulty with these exclusions, and would in fact restrict our presence from some trails I've ridden (one time) due to the environmental damage and chance of blind-siding the many walkers and hikers I encountered along the way. But these are my personal views. They should not be interpreted as those of the authors and are mentioned here only as a way of introducing the land-use problem and the varying positions on it which even mountain bikers hold.

You can do your part in keeping us from being excluded from even more trails by riding responsibly. Many local and national off-road bicycle organizations have been formed with exactly this in mind, and one of the largest—NORBA, the National Off-Road Bicycle Association—offers the following code of behavior for mountain bikers:

1. I will yield the right of way to other non-motorized recreationists. I realize that people judge all cyclists by my actions.
2. I will slow down and use caution when approaching or overtaking another person and will make my presence known well in advance.
3. I will maintain control of my speed at all times and will approach turns in anticipation of meeting someone around the bend.
4. I will stay on designated trails to avoid trampling native vegetation and minimize potential erosion to trails by not using muddy trails or short-cutting switchbacks.
5. I will not disturb wildlife or livestock.
6. I will not litter. I will pack out what I pack in, and pack out more than my share whenever possible.
7. I will respect public and private property, including trail use signs and no trespassing signs, and I will leave gates as I have found them.
8. I will always be self-sufficient and my destination and travel speed will be determined by my ability, my equipment, the terrain, the present and potential weather conditions.
9. I will not travel solo when bikepacking in remote areas. I will leave word of my destination and when I plan to return.
10. I will observe the practice of minimum impact bicycling by "taking only pictures and memories and leaving only waffle prints."
11. I will always wear a helmet whenever I ride.

Now, I have a problem with some of these—number nine, for instance. The most enjoyable mountain biking I've ever done has been solo. And as for leaving word of destination and time of return, I've enjoyed living in such a way that I can say, "I'm off to pedal Colorado. See you in the fall." Of course it's senseless to take needless risks, and I plan a ride and pack my gear with this in mind. But for me number nine smacks too much of the "never-out-of-touch" mentality. And getting away from civilization, deep into the wilds, is for many people what mountain biking's all about.

All in all, however, theirs is a good list, and surely we mountain bikers would be liked more, and excluded less, if we followed the suggestions. But let me offer a "code of ethics" I much prefer, one given cyclists by Utah's Wasatch-Cache National Forest office.

Study a Forest Map Before You Ride
Currently, bicycles are permitted on roads and developed trails within the Wasatch-Cache National Forest except in designated Wilderness. If your

route crosses private land, it is your responsibility to obtain right-of-way permission from the land owner.

Keep Groups Small
Riding in large groups degrades the outdoor experience for others, can disturb wildlife, and usually leads to greater resource damage.

Avoid Riding on Wet Trails
Bicycle tires leave ruts in wet trails. These ruts concentrate runoff and accelerate erosion. Postponing a ride when the trails are wet will preserve the trails for future use.

Stay on Roads and Trails
Riding cross-country destroys vegetation and damages the soil.

Always Yield to Others
Trails are shared by hikers, horses, and bicycles. Move off the trail to allow horses to pass and stop to allow hikers adequate room to share the trail. Simply yelling "Bicycle!" is not acceptable.

Control Your Speed
Excessive speed endangers yourself and other forest users.

Avoid Wheel Lock-up and Spin-out
Steep terrain is especially vulnerable to trail wear. Locking brakes on steep descents or when stopping needlessly damages trails. If a slope is steep enough to require locking wheels and skidding, dismount and walk your bicycle. Likewise, if an ascent is so steep your rear wheel slips and spins, dismount and walk your bicycle.

Protect Waterbars and Switchbacks
Waterbars, the rock and log drains built to direct water off trails, protect trails from erosion. When you encounter a waterbar, ride directly over the top or dismount and walk your bicycle. Riding around the ends of waterbars destroys them and speeds erosion. Skidding around switchback corners shortens trail life. Slow down for switchback corners and keep your wheels rolling.

If You Abuse It, You Lose It
Mountain bikes are relative newcomers to the forest and must prove themselves responsible trail users. By following the guidelines above, and by participating in trail maintenance service projects, bicyclists can help avoid closures which would prevent them from using trails.

I've never seen a better trail-etiquette list for mountain bikers. So have fun. Be careful. And don't screw up things for the next guy.

HITTING THE TRAIL

Once again, because this is a "where-to," not a "how-to" guide, the following will be brief. If you're a veteran trail rider these suggestions might serve to remind you of something you've forgotten to pack. If you're a newcomer, they might convince you to think twice before hitting the backcountry unprepared.

Water: I've heard the questions dozens of times. "How much is enough? One bottle? Two? Three?! But think of all that extra weight!" Well, one simple physiological fact should convince you to err on the side of excess when it comes to determining how much water to pack: a human working hard in ninety-degree temperature needs approximately ten quarts of fluids every day. Ten quarts. That's two and a half gallons—*twelve* large water bottles, or *sixteen* small ones. And with water weighing in at approximately eight pounds per gallon, a one-day supply comes to a whopping twenty pounds.

In other words, pack along two or three bottles even for short rides. And make sure you can purify the water found along the trail on longer routes. When writing of those routes where this could be of critical importance, each author has provided information on where water can be found near the trail—if it can be found at all. But drink it untreated and you run the risk of disease. [See *Giardia* in the Glossary.]

One sure way to kill both the bacteria and viruses in water is to boil it for ten minutes, plus one minute more for each one thousand feet of elevation above sea level. Right. That's just how you want to spend your time on a bike ride. Besides, who wants to carry a stove, or denude the countryside stoking bonfires to boil water?

Luckily, there is a better way. Many riders pack along the effective, inexpensive, and only slightly distasteful tetraglycine hydroperiodide tablets (sold under the names of Potable Aqua, Globaline, Coughlan's, and others). Some invest in portable, lightweight purifiers that filter out the crud. Yes, purifying water with tablets or filters is a bother. But catch a case of Giardia sometime and you'll understand why it's worth the trouble.

Tools: Ever since my first cross-country tour in '65 I've been kidded about the number of tools I pack on the trail. And so I will exit entirely from this discussion by providing a list compiled by two mechanic (and mountain biker) friends of mine. After all, since they make their livings fixing bikes, and get their kicks by riding them, who could be a better source?

The following is suggested as an absolute minimum:

tire levers
spare tube and patch kit
air pump
allen wrenches (3, 4, 5, and 6 mm)
six-inch crescent (adjustable-end) wrench

small flat-blade screwdriver
chain rivet tool
spoke wrench

But their personal tool pouches carried on the trail contain, in addition to the above:

channel locks (small)
air gauge
tire valve cap (the metal kind, with a valve-stem remover)
baling wire (ten or so inches, for temporary repairs)
duct tape (small roll for temporary repairs or tire boot)
boot material (small piece of old tire or a large tube patch)
spare chain link
rear derailleur pulley
spare nuts and bolts
paper towel and tube of waterless hand cleaner

First-Aid Kit: My personal kit contains the following, sealed inside double zip-lock bags:

sunscreen
aspirin
butterfly closure bandages
band-aids
gauze compress pads (a half-dozen 4″×4″)
gauze (1 roll)
ace bandages or Spenco joint wraps
Benadryl (an antihistamine to guard against possible allergic reactions)
water purification tablets
moleskin/Spenco "Second Skin"
hydrogen peroxide/iodine/Mercurochrome (some kind of antiseptic)
snakebite kit

Final Considerations: The authors of this series have done a good job in suggesting that specific items be packed for certain trails—like raingear in particular seasons, a hat and gloves for mountain passes, or shades for desert jaunts. Heed their warnings, and think ahead. Good luck.

Dennis Coello
Salt Lake City

Phoenix Area Rides

The city of Phoenix and the surrounding area, or the "Valley of the Sun," as it is often called, sprawls across the Sonoran Desert floor at an elevation of 1,100 feet above sea level. Phoenix is one of the fastest growing metropolitan areas in the country—our tenth largest city. Temperatures average over 100 degrees during the summer months and somewhere around 60 degrees during the mid-winter months. The natural landscape surrounding the city is stark, and the flat desert floor is interrupted by small, rugged mountain ranges. These ranges close to the city are protected as parks, and are managed by the Maricopa County Parks. South Mountain Park is an exception, and at 16,000 acres is the largest municipal park in the country. These parks are well maintained with miles of trails open to mountain bikers. This city's mountain parks, along with a couple of dozen bike shops in the area, support a tough, heat resistant, and extremely enthusiastic brand of mountain bike rider who taught me—a Utah mountain country rider—what working up a good sweat is all about!

The first inhabitants of this valley were the Hohokam Indians (a Pima Indian word that means "used up" or "departed"), who built large, elaborate irrigation canals and were able to grow bountiful crops of cotton, squash, corn, and beans with water they diverted from the Salt River. The Hohokam flourished in this desert, building expansive adobe houses, practicing elaborate religious rituals, and constructing large ball courts. In these sunken ball courts trained athletes played a game requiring tremendous skill before cheering crowds. Anthropologists believe these games were central to Hohokam life and probably had some religious significance. These ancient desert dwellers were so successful that their population reached an estimated 100,000. The Hohokam are credited with introducing cotton to North America and were unmatched in their weaving skills. Like the Anasazi to the north they mysteriously disappeared sometime during the fourteenth century. The Pima and Papago Indians are generally accepted as descendants of the Hohokam. The Heard Museum in Phoenix holds many Hohokam artifacts, as well as art and artifacts from all the ancient and modern Native American tribes of the Southwest, and is well worth a visit while you are in the area. The Casa Grande ruins, the largest and best preserved Hohokam ruins, are interesting, and only a short drive (or longer road ride) from Phoenix.

When white settlers first came to this valley in the late 1860s, they were able to settle and successfully grow their crops in part because of the extensive and well-built irrigation system left behind by the Hohokam. The canals that crisscross the city today, providing such excellent bike transportation across town, are the same canals originally built by the ancient dwellers of the Valley of the Sun. The sandy soils of the Phoenix basin are the deposits of ancient lake beds which continue to be productive for agriculture. Some of the crops produced here include citrus, nuts, and dates.

The rocks of the Phoenix area's surrounding ranges are widely varied and do not show a consistent geologic record. The extremely weathered granite, gneiss, and schist, painted with desert varnish, found in South Mountain Park, is inconsistent with the sedimentary conglomerates of other mountains nearby. This weathered rock is loose and adds a technical element to much of the riding in the Phoenix area. The steep, weathered nature of these small mountain ranges makes for two kinds of riding in this area: difficult, steep, technical riding, and hard-packed gravel desert cruising. There is great riding for the gonzo technical wizard and for those who are looking for a good challenge in order to improve their skills. Then there is the super hardpack riding for those simply wishing to get out into the country for some fresh air and exercise. The routes on the desert floor are not without some technical challenge, however; one must be ready for the frequent arroyos or riverbeds that intersect the trail. These arroyos provide short, steep descents and climbs, and short sections of looser sands and gravel that can be a trick to pedal through.

While the mountains of the Phoenix area may not be huge, the views from atop these rugged little ridge lines and summits stretch for miles across the desert. Far to the north you may see the Bradshaw Mountains near Prescott. Below you to the northwest you can see the suburb of Glendale. To the east the suburbs of Tempe, Mesa, and Chandler sprawl out with the distinctive Four Peaks rising above the extremely rugged Superstition Mountains beyond in the distance. The White Tank Mountains rise to the west and the Little Estrellas Mountains are to the southwest. There are hieroglyphics etched into the rocks of these mountains and many sites in canyons, and on the ridge tops once considered sacred by the ancient Indians of this valley.

A wide variety of plant and animal life inhabits these seemingly barren, rocky slopes. Cholla, saguaro, and ocotillo cacti are to be found, as well as creosote bush, paloverde, and ironwood trees. Occasionally you might catch a glimpse of a javelina, a type of wild pig, in the evening or early morning. All the animals of this desert become active during the cooler hours of the day, including ring-tailed cats, kit foxes, coyotes, bobcat, jackrabbits, and cottontails. There are also healthy populations of rattlesnakes, which will come out to sun themselves in the early mornings, but do their hunting at night. The very rare and very shy black and yellow Gila monster is a large intricately designed lizard. With its poisonous bite, this hill dweller is rarely seen by humans and is, therefore, not much of a threat. A wide variety of birds thrive in this mountain desert environment, including numerous species of hawks, vultures, owls, swallows, doves, woodpeckers, hummingbirds, and quail. This desert is famous for its bird life. Even beginning bird watchers will be delighted with the many rare and colorful species that make this desert their home during certain times of the year. The amount of life that is able to survive in such close proximity to a major urban center is a wonder, and makes a mountain bike outing in these mountain parks much more enjoyable.

It is important to remember that you are close to an urban area here, and therefore will encounter many other trail users. All the mountain parks are heavily used by equestrians; always stop for horses and other pack animals on the trail. Alert riders to your presence well in advance if you are approaching from the rear. On weekends, holidays, and during the early evening hours there will be more crowding, so you will want to plan your ride accordingly. Always lock your car and keep valuable items out of sight. This will prevent a disappointing end to your ride.

Heat, sun intensity, and aridity are factors that need to be figured into every desert outing, and require special consideration in this region. Please refer to the section entitled Desert Health and Safety to review the problems that riding in this region might pose. In the late fall through early spring hot temperatures will be less of a problem, but the threat of dehydration and exposure to sun in the desert are hazards that persist throughout the year.

All services are available in the Phoenix metro area. It is a good place to start your mountain biking adventures, as all the resources for gathering information about Arizona, its riding opportunities, parks, forests, history, and people can be found here. Here are a few information sources to get you started:

Phoenix Metropolitan Chamber of Commerce
34 West Monroe Street, 9th Floor
Phoenix, Arizona 85003
(602) 254-5521

Phoenix & Valley of the Sun Convention & Visitors Bureau
505 North 2nd Street, Suite 300
Phoenix, Arizona 85004
(602) 254-6500

Sun Cyclery
6066 North 16th Street
Phoenix, Arizona 85016
(602) 279-1905
   (also at)
3110 East Cactus
Phoenix, Arizona 85032
(602) 971-0730

Bike Barn
4112 North 36th Street
Phoenix, Arizona 85018
(602) 956-3870

Tempe Bicycle
330 West University Drive
Tempe, Arizona 85281
(602) 966-6896

*Wide World of Maps
2626 West Indian School Road
Phoenix, Arizona 85017
(602) 279-2323

*All topographical maps are available here, plus a complete selection of field guides, guidebooks and other types of maps.

There are of course many more bike shops in the Phoenix metro area. Check the Yellow Pages for the shop nearest you.

RIDE 1   *THE NATIONAL TRAIL*

The National Trail is a very difficult, very technical, single-track trail that covers steep, rocky terrain. This trail will be a good challenge for even very experienced riders. It is best to ride this trail in one direction and then take one of the options given for the way back. Ridden from the Pima Canyon parking area to the San Juan parking area gives a total distance of approximately 12.4 miles one-way. For riders with advanced riding skills who are in excellent shape this ride will take about four hours to complete. There are several options for creating loops, shortening the distance, and avoiding some of the most technical sections of this route. The condition of the trail surface on this ride adds to the technical difficulty. Although some sections are hard-packed desert soils, other sections consist of loose gravel which results from the disintegrating granite of these mountains. You will also encounter numerous rock obstacles which trials riders will love, but others will have to portage their bikes over or around.

Excellent views of the city of Phoenix and the surrounding area can be seen from along this trail, especially when you reach South Mountain Peak and Buena Vista Lookout. The Bradshaw Peaks (to the north and west) and the Superstition Mountains (with their distinctive Four Peaks to the north and east) can be seen on days when the smog permits. There is a lot of bird and animal life to be observed in the park, so keep your eyes peeled. The Hidden Valley Natural Bridge and the ancient Indian petroglyphs are also attractions on this ride. The petroglyphs are tough to find, however, so if you are interested in seeing them you may want to check with the park ranger for specific directions.

General location: The National Trail is located in South Mountain Park, within the environs of the Phoenix metro area.

Elevation change: At both the Pima Canyon parking area, and the San Juan parking area, your approximate elevation is 1,300' above sea level. From there you will climb steadily to 2,350'. Total elevation gain is 1,200'.

Season: Fall through spring months are the best for riding in this low desert

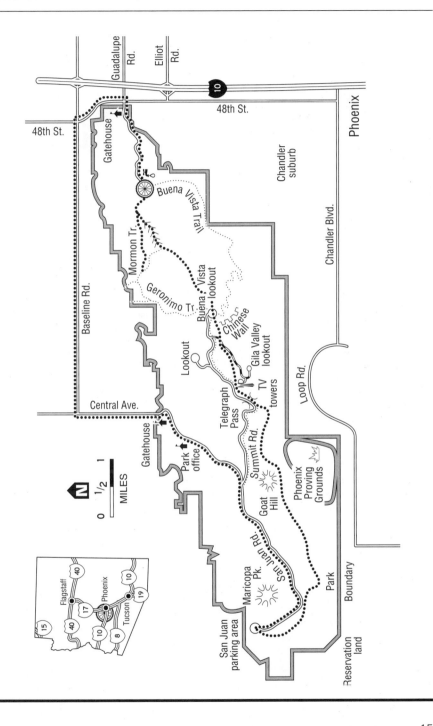

A rider negotiates one of several technically demanding sections of the National Trail in South Mountain Park just outside Phoenix.

region, with the mid-winter month temperatures averaging a comfortable 60 degrees. Riding in the summer months is not recommended except for the later evening and early morning hours. Bring lots of water and protect yourself from those fierce desert rays.

Services: All services are available in Phoenix. Water is available in the park at either of the main parking areas.

Hazards: Trail congestion can be a problem in South Mountain Park. You may encounter equestrian traffic at times, which means you need to make your presence known, then dismount and get off the trail. The extremely technical nature of this ride, with large rock obstacles and drop-offs along the way, is definitely a hazard. A helmet is an absolute must for this ride. Heat is always a hazard when riding in the desert, so be sure to drink lots of fluids before, during, and after your ride.

Rescue index: You are never far away from help in South Mountain Park. You are surrounded by residential areas on all sides of the park and can find park personnel, at most times of the day, at either entrance to the park.

Land status: City of Phoenix Municipal Park. Park hours are from 5:30 A.M. to midnight daily.

Maps: Maps can be obtained from the Parks and Recreation Department of the city of Phoenix, and from the gatehouse keeper or park office through the main gates. USGS 15' quad for Phoenix.

Finding the trail: From downtown Phoenix take I-10 south to the Guadalupe Road exit. Turn left to enter the park at the east entrance. Park at the Pima Canyon parking lot.

To reach the north entrance of the park, take the Baseline Road exit and head west to Central Avenue. Go south on Central Avenue to enter the park from the north through the main gates. You will then follow the main road to the west end of the park where you can park at the San Juan parking area.

From the San Juan parking area, the National Trail takes off from the right side of the parking lot as you enter. To find the trailhead from the Pima Canyon parking lot, ride to the top of the lot and follow a dirt road for a short distance (.25 miles). This dirt road will take you to the marked beginning of the National Trail.

Sources of additional information:

City of Phoenix
Parks and Recreation Department
2700 North 15th Avenue
Phoenix, Arizona 85007
(602) 262-4673

Notes on the trail: You will begin climbing on a good surface, but as the trail winds its way up the ridge of South Mountain you will begin to encounter the rocky outcrops that make this ride both technical and strenuous. Many of these technical spots will have to be portaged by everyone except the most accomplished riders. The Mormon Trail is strongly recommended as a route option on the way up. It leaves the National Trail to the right 1 mile from where the trail begins and rejoins the National Trail near the top via the Geronimo Trail. Stretches between rough spots along this route smooth out and make for some great single-track riding. You will continue following the single-track National Trail west, over some rough terrain, to where it meets Summit Road at the Buena Vista Lookout. You can either take Summit Road down and ride out the north entrance of the park onto Central Avenue, or continue heading west on the National Trail. The National Trail leaves from the west side of the lookout parking lot and then parallels the park's main road atop the ridge for the next 7 miles. The National Trail actually crosses Summit Road and then San Juan Road, before ending at the San Juan parking area. You will want to ride the road back out the north entrance onto Central Avenue, right onto Baseline Road, right onto 48th Street, and right onto Pima Canyon Road, which will take you back to your car.

You may want to experiment with riding this route in the opposite direction, especially if you are unsure about committing yourself to the brutalizing terrain and distance of this ride. The National Trail crosses the paved San Juan Road several times heading in this direction, and will give you the option of riding up on the road instead.

A number of loop options for this trail exist with the various trails and roads that intersect the National Trail. The Mormon Trail can, and should, be taken from the National Trail, approximately 1 mile from where you begin the ride. The Mormon Trail then connects to the Geronimo Trail which will rejoin the National Trail. Summit Road can be ridden down the mountain from the Buena Vista Lookout, and out the main gate onto Central Avenue.

Another option is to take the wild and hazardous Buena Vista Trail down the south side of the mountain, past a rock formation known as the Chinese Wall, then over many rocks and switchbacks to the desert floor where you will head east (with the mountain on your left) back to the Pima Canyon parking lot where you began. There are many trails that crisscross the desert floor on this side of the park.

RIDE 2 DESERT CLASSIC TRAIL

The Desert Classic Trail traverses an area of South Mountain Park that offers easy to moderate riding. This is a great place just to get out and do a little cruising. Riding to the San Juan parking area and back provides a workout of 22 miles. Three hours should be sufficient time for riders with beginning-to-intermediate riding skills to explore this area, if they are in moderate physical condition. There are many, many trails that take off in all directions across hard-packed desert floor. While it is impossible to get really lost, there *are* numerous possibilities for getting sidetracked. Geographical markers will help you find your way around. As you head out from the Pima Canyon parking lot at the east end of the park, the mountains of South Mountain Park rise to your right and the suburb of Chandler sprawls out to the left.

You will be cruising through beautiful Sonoran Desert country on this ride. Many types of cacti, including the tall and stately saguaro cactus, are widely spaced across the hard-packed desert floor. Saguaro cacti usually grow on wind-sheltered areas of the hillsides. Salt bush, creosote, and other desert vegetation grow more densely along drainages, which will alert you to their steep banks and soft gravelly sand. The thicker brush along these drainages is a good place to spot wildlife; coyote, kit fox, javelina, and jackrabbits are a few desert critters you might see darting along ahead of you.

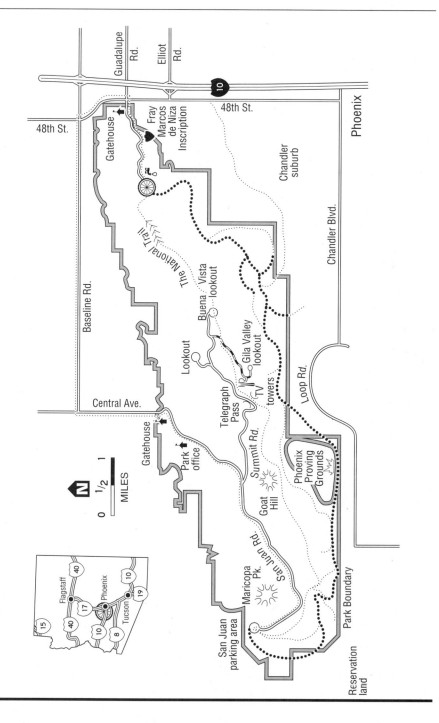

Riders roll out across the desert floor in South Mountain Park on the Desert Classic Trail.

General location: The Desert Classic Trail is located in South Mountain Park, within the environs of the Phoenix metro area.

Elevation change: You will be riding at approximately 1,300' above sea level with little or no elevation change.

Season: Fall through spring months are the best for riding in the Sonoran Desert, with the mid-winter month's temperatures averaging a comfortable 60 degrees. Riding in the summer months is not recommended except for the late evening and early morning hours.

Services: All services are available in Phoenix. Water is available at both of the main parking areas in the park.

Hazards: Arroyos bisect the trail where drainages leave the mountains, creating steep, short embankments. Also, the sand and gravel river bottoms can be a challenge to pedal through.

This area is a maze of trails and while it is hard to get really lost, with the mountains on one side and sprawling suburbia on the other, it is very easy to get unintentionally sidetracked. This trail is not marked and is not officially listed as a trail by park management. This is a good area just to get out on for some exercise, with lots of rideable terrain to explore.

The Chandler area suburbs have been growing rapidly, and housing has recently pushed right up against the park boundary. You may at times find yourself riding right along someone's backyard fence. There are other fences along the route erected by a heavy equipment company that does some testing toward the west end of the park. Access for park users around these fences will allow you to continue your progress. The Gila River Indian Reservation also abuts the park boundary to the west and will be fenced. Getting all the way around to the San Juan area parking lot is a challenge, but is well worth the trouble.

Rescue index: You are never far away from help in South Mountain Park. You are surrounded by residential areas on all sides of the park and can find park personnel, at most times of the day, at either entrance to the park.

Land status: City of Phoenix Municipal Park. Park hours are from 5:30 A.M. to midnight daily.

Maps: Maps can be obtained from the Parks and Recreation Department of the city of Phoenix, and from the gatehouse keeper or park office through the main gates. USGS 15' quad for Phoenix.

Finding the trail: From downtown Phoenix take I-10 south to the Guadalupe Road exit. Turn left, following Guadalupe Road, to enter the park at the east entrance. Park at the Pima Canyon parking lot.

Sources of additional information:

City of Phoenix
Parks and Recreation Department
2700 North 15th Avenue
Phoenix, Arizona 85007

Notes on the trail: Instead of heading uphill to the top of the parking lot and onto the dirt road that takes you to the start of the National Trail, look to your left, behind the big ramada (covered picnic table) for a trail that takes off around the side of the mountain.

You will follow this trail for about the first mile before you begin to encounter several trails branching off in both directions. Many of these trails simply wind around on the desert floor with no particular destination. You will be heading in a west/southwest direction with the peaks of South Mountain to your right and the suburb of Chandler to your left. Follow any of these trails and do a little exploring. It's pretty hard to get lost out here.

Possible options include exiting the park to the south (left) at mile 6 onto 19th Avenue Loop Road, heading east. You will soon pick up Chandler Boulevard. Any route heading east and north from here, through the suburb of Chandler, will eventually get you to 48th Street.

Another possible option exists once you have reached the San Juan parking area; this allows you to do a complete circle of South Mountain and the park. From here you can ride the park road out the north entrance onto Central Avenue. You will then go right onto Baseline Road, right onto 48th Street, and right onto Pima Canyon Road, which will take you back to your car.

RIDE 3   *PEMBERTON TRAIL*

This trail is an easy-to-moderate 15.5-mile loop, marked as Trail B, which traverses a good portion of McDowell Mountain Regional Park. The trail is a hard-packed single-track with only a few sections of loose gravel and rock. This is a fun cruise across the desert floor that should take two to three hours to ride.

As close as you are to a thriving metropolis, you feel like you're almost in the middle of nowhere. This is classic Sonoran hill country, with low rocky hills that cap gently sloping fluvial plains and are covered with the many types of cacti and vegetation typical of this region. The variety of bird life in this part of the country is extraordinary, and this park hosts a substantial number of birds during certain times of the year. An early morning out at McDowell Mountain Park is anything but quiet, and can seem like a concert with the many songbirds that come here to feast on the insects, flowers, and fruits of this desert.

General location: McDowell Mountain Regional Park, 15 miles northeast of Scottsdale, Arizona.
Elevation change: Where the ride begins, from the Horse Staging area, you are at an elevation of 1,850' above sea level. From there you make a gradual climb to the northwest corner of the park where you have reached the elevation of 2,500'. The return leg of this loop is a gradual descent back to the Horse Staging Area. The pitches on this ride are very gradual. Total elevation gain is 650'.
Season: Fall through spring months are the best for riding, with the mid-winter month's temperatures averaging a comfortable 60 degrees. Riding in the summer months is not recommended except for the later evening and early morning hours.
Services: All services are available in Phoenix. Water is available at the park. Camping is also available at the park for $8 a night, showers included. The park is closed in summer.
Hazards: All the hazards of exerting yourself in a desert environment exist here. Try to plan your rides around the hottest hours of the day. While good geographical markers exist, you may still want to carry a compass and a park map. Trails are well marked. These trails are a favorite for equestrians, so smile and say hello and give them the right of way.
Rescue index: McDowell Mountain Regional Park is somewhat remote. In the event of an emergency, help should be sought first at the park campground; a park employee oversees the campgrounds and is often available. Your next option for help is the town of Fountain Hills just a few miles from the entrance to the park.
Land status: Maricopa County Park.
Maps: Maps for McDowell Mountain Regional Park are available from Maricopa County Parks and Recreation Department. USGS quads are McDowell and McDowell Peak.

RIDE 3 *PEMBERTON TRAIL*

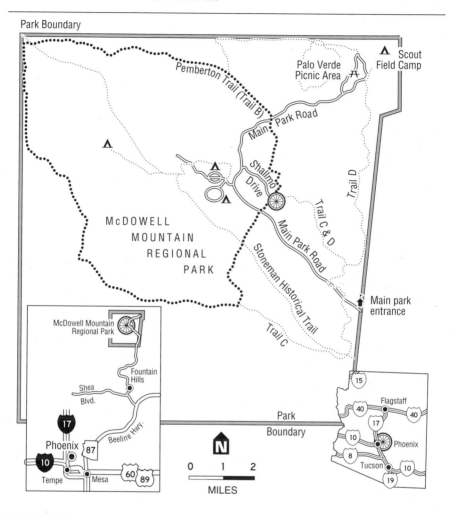

Finding the trail: Access to the park entrance road from Phoenix is found by heading east on any main road and getting on State Highway 87 (also called the Beeline Highway). You will head north until you reach Shea Boulevard, or signs for the town of Fountain Hills. The main road that takes you into Fountain Hills turns into McDowell Mountain Road, which will take you to the park entrance. Once inside the park continue on the main road past the campgrounds to Shallmo Drive and the Horse Staging Area. There is parking here and this is where the trail begins.

A mountain biker delights in the colorful blooms of Sonoran desert cacti that thrive in the hills surrounding Phoenix.

Sources of additional information:

> Maricopa County Parks and Recreation Department
> 3355 West Durango Street
> Phoenix, Arizona 85009
> (602) 272-8871

Notes on the trail: The Pemberton Trail is designated as Trail B and the trail markers are marked with letters A through N. Some parts of these trails are shared and so may be doubly marked as B and C, for example. The Pemberton Trail shares portions of its route with trails C and D. When you look to pick up the trail, ride the circumference of the parking lot. If you are going to head in a clockwise direction you will be looking for the trail marked B and C, heading out from the west side of the parking lot. If you have chosen a counterclockwise direction you will be heading out the north side of the parking lot looking for the trail marked B and D.

Once you have picked up the trail in the direction you choose, you will be cruising at a good pace through desert scrub and cacti. Keep an eye out for trail markers—and have a great ride!

Approximately halfway through this ride, whether you have chosen to ride it in a clockwise or counterclockwise direction, you will be at the farthest northwestern point in your ride. The historical Stoneman Trail intersects the Pemberton Trail at this point. If you take this route option you will bisect your loop by heading in a southeasterly direction back to the parking area where you left your car. This trail is not as well marked and can be difficult to follow. This was the wagon route that took settlers from the safety of Fort McDowell to Fort Whipple near Prescott.

RIDE 4   *GOLDFIELD TRAIL*

The Goldfield Trail, which is marked as Trail C, is an easy eight-mile loop that will take only one to two hours to complete. This trail is a hard-packed single-track trail requiring little or no technical skill and only a moderate level of physical fitness.

On this ride you encircle two of the small mountains, or hillocks, in the park, twice crossing the paved main road into the park as you go. You will also be crossing the historical Stoneman Trail, which follows the wide drainage that intersects the entire park at a diagonal. While this ride is anything but strenuous, it offers some excellent desert cruising.

General location: McDowell Mountain Regional Park, 15 miles northeast of Scottsdale, Arizona.

Elevation change: You begin this ride from the Horse Staging Area at an elevation of 1,850' above sea level. You will be making a gradual descent until you reach the low point of your ride, in the southeast corner of the loop, at an elevation of 1,600'. The return leg of this loop is a gradual climb back to the Horse Staging Area. Total elevation gain is 250'.

Season: Fall through spring months are the best for riding in the Lower Sonoran Desert, with the mid-winter month's temperatures averaging a comfortable 60 degrees. Riding in the summer months is not recommended, except for the later evening and early morning hours.

Services: All services are available in Phoenix. Water is available at the park. Camping is also available at the park for $8 a night, showers included. Closed in summer.

Hazards: All the hazards of exerting yourself in a desert environment exist here. While trails are marked, it is always a good idea to carry a compass and to continue to orient yourself as you go. Watch out for equestrians. There are lots of them out here, and they have the right-of-way.

Rescue index: McDowell Mountain Regional Park is somewhat remote. In the event of an emergency, help should be sought first at the park campground, where a park employee who oversees the campgrounds can often be found. Your next option for help is the town of Fountain Hills just a few miles from the entrance to the park.

RIDE 4 *GOLDFIELD TRAIL*

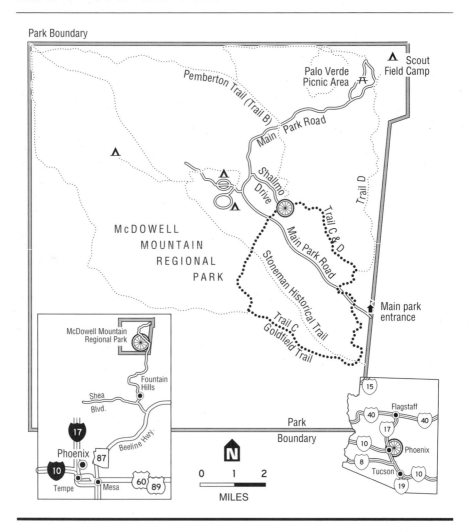

Land status: Maricopa County Regional Park.

Maps: Maps are available from the Maricopa County Parks and Recreation Department. USGS quads are McDowell and McDowell Peak.

Finding the trail: Access to the park entrance road from Phoenix is possible by heading east on any main road and getting on State Highway 87 (also called the Beeline Highway). You will head north until you reach Shea Boulevard, or signs for the town of Fountain Hills. The main road that takes you into Fountain Hills turns into McDowell Mountain Road, which will take you to the park

Sweeping views abound from the Goldfield Trail in McDowell Mountain Regional Park northeast of Phoenix.

entrance. Once inside the park continue on the main road past the campgrounds to Shallmo Drive and the Horse Staging Area. There is parking here and this is where the trail begins.

Sources of additional information:

Maricopa County Parks and Recreation Department
3355 West Durango Street
Phoenix, Arizona 85009
(602) 272-8871

Notes on the trail: The Goldfield Trail is Trail C, with portions shared with trails B and D. Trail C takes off and returns to the Horse Staging Area parking lot from the west and east sides of the parking lot.

Once again you will be cruising at a good speed through desert scrub. Very gradual elevation changes are almost imperceptible. Keep an eye out for trail markers.

Two options exist for this ride. One is to make the ride a little easier by taking the paved main road, where it intersects the trail, back to your parking area instead of the trail. The other is something you would probably want to do if you began this ride in a counterclockwise direction. About a half mile after you have crossed the main park road the second time, there is an intersection with Trail D, listed as the Scenic Trail on the park map. Trails C and D go left about another 2 miles back to the Horse Staging Area. You may continue straight instead, bearing right, following Trail D in a northerly direction, which will intersect the main park road in approximately 3.5 miles. This route takes you around the 2,020′ Lousley Mountain. You will come out near the Scout field camp and the Palo Verde picnic area. You can now ride back 3 miles on the park road to the Horse Staging Area at the end of Shallmo Drive.

RIDE 5   *TRAIL 100*

Trail 100, also known as the Charles M. Christiansen Memorial Trail, is a difficult single-track trail which requires good physical condition and a moderate-to-advanced level of technical skill. This trail, which is a favorite of mountain bikers in the Phoenix area, gives a total distance of just over 21 miles as an out-and-back. Most riders, after negotiating over 10.5 miles of this sometimes loose, rocky, and often steep mountain trail, choose to make a loop out of the ride by pedaling back to their car on pavement.

This is slightly more rugged and hilly country than that of South Mountain or McDowell Mountain Parks. The tightly knit hills and valleys of this mountain preserve harbor healthy stands of saguaro cacti as well as a full spectrum of Sonoran desert vegetation. Trail 100 traverses the whole of Phoenix Mountain Preserve from east to west, providing challenging mountain biking just minutes from downtown Phoenix. This trail is the main artery for an extensive system of trails that runs throughout the preserve.

General location: Phoenix Mountains Preserve (which includes, and is sometimes referred to as, North Mountain Park; adjacent to the Phoenix Mountains Preserve you will also find Squaw Peak City Park). Located in the Phoenix metro area.

Elevation change: If you are starting your ride at the east end of the preserve your elevation is approximately 1,400′ above sea level. If you are starting from the west end of the preserve your elevation is 1,300′. From either direction you will climb gradually to an elevation high of 1,600′. You will maintain this approximate elevation, experiencing several short climbs and descents, until you reach North Canyon where you will descend to 1,400′. At this point you will cross Northern Avenue, climbing back up to 1,600′, eventually descending back to approximately 1,300′. Total elevation gain is 600′. ·

Season: Fall through spring months are best for riding in the Lower Sonoran desert, with temperatures in the mid-winter months averaging a comfortable 60 degrees. Riding in the summer months is not recommended except for the late evening and early morning hours.

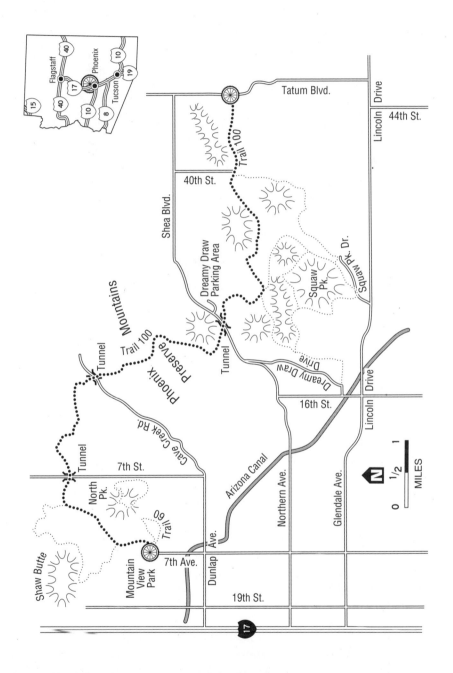

A rider enjoys one of the smoother sections of Trail 100 in the Phoenix Mountains Preserve.

Services: All services are available in Phoenix. Drinking water and restrooms are available at Dreamy Draw parking lot, about halfway into the ride, as well as the trailhead at 7th Avenue at Mountain View park.

Hazards: There is a fair amount of hiker and equestrian traffic at certain times of the day and on weekends in this park. Plan your ride accordingly. All the hazards of exerting yourself in a desert environment exist here. There are certain points in the trail that are very loose and rocky. Use caution and wear your helmet.

Rescue index: The Phoenix Mountains Preserve is surrounded by neighborhoods and other city conveniences. It is also a busy park. Help is not far away on this ride.

Land status: City of Phoenix, Municipal Mountains Preserve.

Maps: Maps are available from the City of Phoenix, Parks and Recreation Department, Northeast District, 17642 North 40th Street, Phoenix, Arizona 85032. The USGS 7.5 minute quads are Sunnyslope and Paradise Valley.

Finding the trail: Phoenix Mountains Preserve lies roughly between 19th Avenue and 45th Street on an east-west axis, and between Glendale Avenue and Thunderbird Road on a north-south axis. Seventh Avenue taken all the way north ends at Mountain View Park, where parking and the trailhead for Trail 100 is located. The trail leaves from the north end of the parking lot. There is another trail that leaves from this parking lot on the east side, Trail 60.

16th Street taken all the way north ends at the intersection with Northern Avenue. Take a right and you will find the Dreamy Draw parking lot. To reach the preserve from the east, take 16th Street to the intersection with Lincoln Drive and go right; head east until you reach Tatum Boulevard. Go left on Tatum until you reach the parking area just across from Tomahawk Drive. Parking here is limited. There is a much larger parking area with access to Trail 100, on 40th Street just south of Shea Boulevard. Continue heading north on Tatum until you reach Shea Boulevard, go left on Shea Boulevard until you reach 40th Street, then go left on 40th to reach this parking area.

Sources of additional information:

Phoenix Parks and Recreation Department
Northeast District
17642 North 40th Street
Phoenix, Arizona 85032

Notes on the trail: From any of these starting points you will begin climbing one of several hills traversed by Trail 100 in North Mountain Park. There are many short, steep, technical ascents and descents along this route with hard, fast stretches of trail that traverse or parallel the valley floor. The figure listed for total elevation gain does not reflect the strenuousness of this ride. The trail is fairly well marked and you should see other mountain bikers along the way. This is challenging terrain, so wear your helmet and use caution.

There are many options available here, too many to list. I would strongly suggest obtaining a map of the preserve if you are interested in further riding opportunities in this area.

The best option for a shorter ride is parking at the Dreamy Draw parking area, which is not quite halfway along Trail 100, and beginning the ride from this point. This makes the prospect of an entirely off-road out-and-back or loop ride somewhat less intimidating.

RIDE 6   *TRAIL 1A (PERL CHARLES MEMORIAL TRAIL)*

Trail 1A, or the Perl Charles Memorial Trail, is another favorite of accomplished local mountain bikers. This is a short, 4.8-mile loop that is strenuous and very difficult. Sections of this trail are extremely loose and rocky. There are several options for combining this route with other trails in the preserve. Advanced and intermediate riders in good physical condition should allow one to two hours to complete this loop.

The topography of this park, with its deep canyons and the small steep mountains of Squaw Peak and the rest of her rocky sisters, is in sharp contrast to the flat desert floor which stretches out in all directions beyond the preserve's

RIDE 6 TRAIL 1A
(PERL CHARLES MEMORIAL TRAIL)

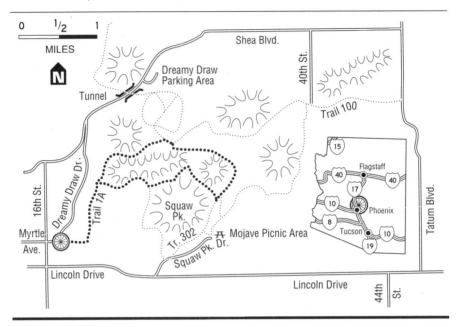

boundaries. Saguaro, some of which are very large, manage to cling to these rocky slopes which are too rough and steep for much else. These mountains are a favorite spot for the desert raptors which hunt rabbits and soar on the rising desert thermals. Excellent views can be seen from the higher peaks and passes along this route.

General location: Phoenix Mountains Preserve, Phoenix metro area.

Elevation change: From the trailhead, at 1,300' above sea level, you begin climbing. You will climb several saddles, traverse a small valley, and negotiate a number of short, steep climbs and descents, formed by Squaw Peak's drainage runoff. Eventually you will reach an elevation of 2,000' at the top of a pass that crosses over and drops steeply into the largest valley in the preserve, which will take you back to the main trail. Elevation gain is about 700'.

Season: This is a hot one, best ridden during the coolest hours of the day. Riding here during the summer months is not recommended.

Services: All services are available in Phoenix. There is no water available at the parking area or trailhead of this ride, so be sure to bring plenty of your own.

Hazards: This ride is extremely technical at points with super-steep descents and climbs on loose or unstable surfaces. Portions may need to be portaged. Be-

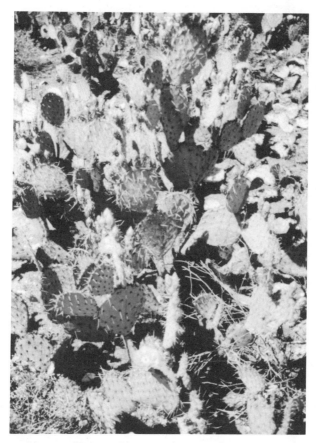

Golden prickly pear blossoms decorate the mountainsides around Phoenix in spring.

ginners should not attempt this ride. This ride should not be ridden without a helmet.

Rescue index: The Phoenix Mountains Preserve is surrounded by neighborhoods and other city conveniences. It is also a busy park. Help is not far away on this ride.

Land status: City of Phoenix, Municipal Mountains Preserve.

Maps: Maps are available from the City of Phoenix, Parks and Recreation Department, Northeast District, 17642 North 40th Street, Phoenix, Arizona 85032. Phone (602) 262-7901 or 262-7797. The USGS 7.5 minute quads are Sunnyslope and Paradise Valley.

Finding the trail: The Perl Charles Trailhead is located on the east side of 16th Street at the Arizona Canal, and is a spur off the Maricopa County Sun Circle Trail (no parking available). The trail follows 16th Street north to Myrtle, then east along Myrtle and through a tunnel at 19th Street (Squaw Peak Parkway). The trail then follows the wash east to 20th Street, to the Perl Charles dedication plaque. Alternate access to the trail at this point is through the horse tunnel at 19th Street and at Pleasant Drive just south of Northern Avenue (limited parking available).

Sources of additional information:

> Phoenix Parks and Recreation Department
> Phoenix, Arizona 85032
> (602) 262-7901 or 262-7797

Notes on the trail: Follow the trail signs past the cookout area and east from that point. This loop trail begins to climb one of several saddles into a quiet valley. After the valley, the trail drops steeply into the largest valley in the preserve system, follows the valley, and then loops back to the trailhead.

Several options are possible here. Trail 302 shares a portion of the trail with Trail 1A and is a circumference trail of Squaw Peak. Instead of climbing the pass that takes you to 2,000' and along the north slope of Squaw Peak, continue heading south on Trail 302 (also marked as 304). This route takes you over a steep little saddle before traversing the west side of the peak where it eventually rejoins Trail 1A.

The bailout option is also available by riding out to the Mojave Picnic area, down the pavement on Squaw Peak Drive to Lincoln Drive, back to 16th Street where you go left, then back to the parking area.

There are many more possibilities for alternative routes. The maps issued by Phoenix Parks will be most helpful here.

RIDE 7   *PASS MOUNTAIN TRAIL*

This seven-mile loop, which will take most bikers two to three hours to ride, is a moderate-to-difficult single-track that is often loose and rocky. This area receives a fair amount of traffic from mountain bikers as well as equestrians. Weekends can be especially busy.

This 3,324-acre recreation area actually lies between the Usery Mountain Range and Pass Mountain, and is considered to be the gateway to the extremely rugged Superstition Mountains. It was among the granite hills of the Usery and Goldfield Mountains of this area that gold was discovered, prompting a flood of settlers into this region in the mid-1800s. The jagged peaks of the Superstition Mountains were created by a series of violent and extremely hot volcanic eruptions. The welded tuff resulting from these formations has been sculpted

RIDE 7 *PASS MOUNTAIN TRAIL*

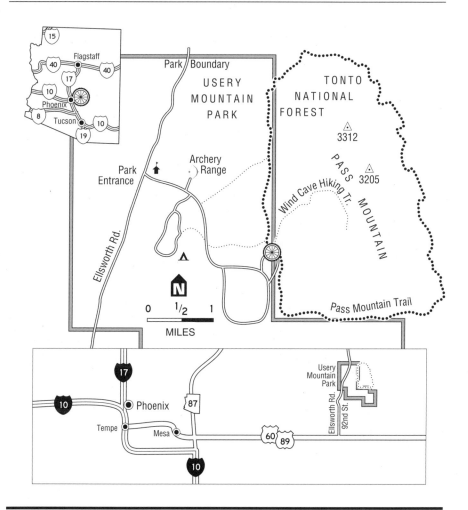

into the Superstition's formidable towers and pinnacles over the eons. There are stories of large veins of gold that have been found deep in these mountains, at their granite core, but those who have tried to find them mysteriously disappear. The Superstition Mountains were a fortress of the Apache of this region, who were able to swoop down upon mining camps and settlers and then return to the maze of canyons with little fear of being followed.

Views are fantastic on this ride. Typical Sonoran desert vegetation graces these rocky slopes, but pockets of ponderosa pine can be seen clinging to the highest reaches of the peaks beyond. This rugged and remote wilderness is a good place to spot wildlife.

General location: Usery Mountain Recreation Area, 12 miles northeast of Mesa, Arizona.

Elevation change: From where this ride begins, at the Horse Staging Area in the park, the elevation is approximately 1,900' above sea level. In either direction you decide to take this loop you will climb, sometimes steeply and on switchbacks, to a high elevation, in the most northern point in your ride, to an elevation of 2,600'. Total elevation gain is 700'.

Season: Late fall through early spring will provide the most comfortable riding temperatures in this area. Try to plan your ride for the cooler hours of the day in the morning and evening, if you are riding during the hotter months.

Services: All services are available in Phoenix. There is camping at the park, with showers available. Closed in summer.

Hazards: This ride covers some rough terrain, and demands a good amount of technical skill. As always wear your helmet, bring plenty of water, and cover up. The sun can be brutal.

In the past there has been some conflict between mountain bikers and other trail users at Usery Mountain Recreation Area. This means that we, as mountain bikers, need to be especially sensitive while riding here. When you approach a horse from behind let the rider know you are there before you get too near. Don't forget to smile and say hello.

Rescue index: Park personnel should be present during most of the day. Other help is just a few miles away in the suburb of Mesa.

Land status: Maricopa County Park.

Maps: Maps are available from the Maricopa County Parks and Recreation Department. The USGS 7.5 minute quad is Apache Junction.

Finding the trail: From downtown Phoenix head east on Apache Boulevard, or US 60/89, until you reach Ellsworth Road or 92nd Street. Go left onto Ellsworth and continue to head north until it turns into Usery Pass Road. Go right onto the Usery Park Road and take that all the way to the end, where you will find the Horse Staging Area. The trailheads to the Pass Trail and other options listed all leave from here.

Sources of additional information:

Maricopa County Parks and Recreation Department
3355 West Durango Street
Phoenix, Arizona 85009

Notes on the trail: Traveling this route in a counterclockwise direction from the Horse Staging Area, you will begin climbing up along the eastern flank of Usery Mountain. At times you will climb steeply up switchbacks which are technically

A rider begins her ascent on the Pass Mountain Trail in Usery Mountain Park east of Phoenix.

demanding. You will be at your highest elevation at the most northern point in this loop. You will then make a gradual descent along the western flank of the mountain back to your car.

There is a short 3.8-mile circuit called the Blevins Trail that also leaves from the Horse Staging Area. This can be ridden as a warm-up loop or added to the Pass Trail ride. A short loop also exists that takes you around the larger of the two small peaks you see on the Blevins Trail; this is called Superstition Loop. These are classic desert cruising routes that require little or no technical skill. This is a good area to ride out and explore.

RIDE 8   *HOHOKAM CANALS (THE SUN CIRCLE TRAIL)*

The Sun Circle Trail is a route put together by Maricopa County's Parks and Recreation Department that encircles the entire Phoenix metro area. The trails are laid out mainly on the canals but also include routes through the city's moun-

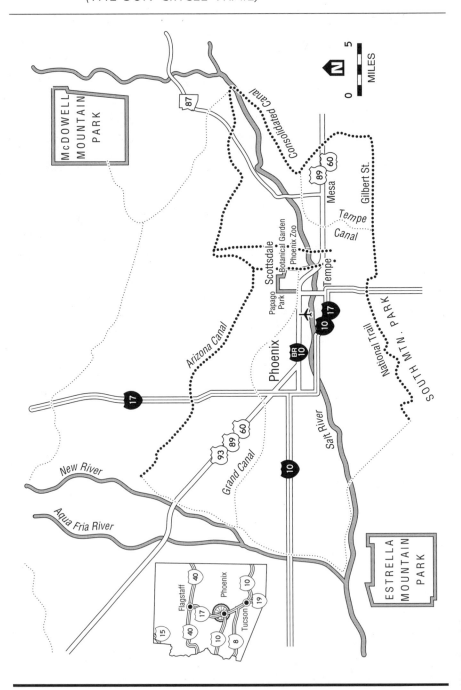

tain parks on the outskirts of town. Many parts of the Sun Circle Trail are under construction, while other parts of the route are still in the proposal stage. By its projected completion date, sometime in the mid-1990s, the Sun Circle Trail will be a well-established route for all types of trail users. Bikers, pedestrians, and equestrians will be able to access points all over the city without the worry of automobile traffic. Eventually the route will form an enormous 110-mile circle around the Valley of the Sun, with many secondary trails reaching points of interest around the city.

The canals are flat dirt roads that traverse the valley floor for over a hundred miles. You can ride for any distance you like; use the canals to get to downtown shops or museums, to get to one of the city's parks, or just get out for a cruise. Of the five main canals that cross the valley, three of them run east to west and two run north to south. There is also a route linking the canals north to south on the west side of the valley along the Agua Fria River.

These canals provide some of the best sightseeing and touring opportunities in a major city anywhere in the country. On your off-road bike you can reach downtown Phoenix, as well as its eight major suburbs. Canal-touring is an excellent way to get around; not only is it free, good exercise, and environmentally sound, but it is also free of vehicular traffic and a lot of fun. Jump off and tour some of the city's ritzy neighborhoods, or visit one of the many malls for a little vacation shopping. Riding the canals downtown to visit any of the city's tourist attractions is easy. Even if you don't set out with a specific destination in mind, these canals provide an excellent chance to get out for a little desert air and a look around.

Ride the Grand Canal downtown to the Heard Museum, the Phoenix Art Museum, or the Public Library. Grand Canal will also take you to Tempe Park where you can find the Desert Botanical Gardens and the Phoenix Zoo. The Western and Highline Canals will take you to South Mountain Park, where you can ride one of the rugged single-tracks listed above. The Arizona Canal will take you to the Phoenix Mountains Preserve, North Mountain Park, and Squaw Peak City Park. The possibilities are endless. Choose your destination, look at almost any Phoenix city map, and you're on your way.

General location: Phoenix, Arizona.

Elevation change: Phoenix lies at an elevation of 1,100' above sea level. There is little or no elevation gain or loss on this ride unless you are riding into the mountain parks scattered about the perimeter of the city.

Season: The canals can be ridden at any time of year and in most weather conditions. Riding in the city during the summer is not recommended, however, due to extremely high temperatures. It is always more pleasant to ride during the cooler hours of the day, and in the cooler seasons.

Services: All services are available in Phoenix.

Hazards: Once again there are a lot of equestrians who use the canals to exercise their animals. There are also a lot of runners and pedestrians on the canals.

The canals that run throughout the city of Phoenix make sight-seeing, running errands, or just getting out for some exercise fast and easy.

The routes are wide enough to accommodate everybody, but we as bikers need to be especially courteous to those with whom we share the trails. Why? Because we're the newcomers, and horses especially aren't yet used to us.

Rescue index: A call to 911 from any pay phone on any corner will bring immediate help in the event of an emergency.

Land status: City of Phoenix, Salt River Valley Water Users' Association.

Maps: Almost any city map will show the city's main canals. Should you want a more detailed map contact the Salt River Valley Water Users' Association. Also, the Maricopa County Parks and Recreation Department has maps illustrating the canals and the Sun Circle Trail.

Finding the trail: It is possible to reach the canals from locations all over the city. No parking is available for those specifically using the canals. You may want to begin your ride from one of the metro area parks where public parking is available. Street parking is the other alternative. Your options for routes are unlimited here.

Sources of additional information:

Salt River Valley Water Users' Association
Maricopa County Parks and Recreation Department
3355 West Durango Street
Phoenix, Arizona 85009

Tucson Area Rides

The city of Tucson and surrounding mountains, while located deep in the heart of the Sonoran Desert, provide riding opportunities in all types of environments and settings. The many ranges of the area boast an enormous variety of climate, temperature, vegetation, and wildlife, all of which make every outing an interesting study in this region's life zones.

The city of Tucson lies in the Tucson Valley at an elevation of 2,400 feet above sea level, and receives just over 11 inches of rain a year. Mt. Lemmon (9,157 feet), which is only 20 miles away from town, is the highest peak in the Santa Catalina Mountains. This mountain receives enough snow in the winter months to entertain skiers at the Mt. Lemmon Ski Valley from December through March. Temperatures around Tucson are slightly cooler than Phoenix, averaging 98 degrees for highs and 70 degrees for lows during the summer. In the winter, 60 degrees for the average high is normal with lows in the 30s. The city of Tucson is unique in that the surrounding area offers excellent desert riding with the added challenges and benefits of riding at high elevation.

There are a number of top-notch bike shops in town that sponsor some tough area racers. They also hold some great races and weekend rides. The University of Arizona, in Tucson, contributes to the young population of mountain bikers who are keeping the sport growing in the area. The city itself is a lively, progressive spot with a love for music (particularly the blues), the arts, and good food. The desert and mountains, as well as a lively, outdoors-oriented population, combine to make Tucson one of the most agreeable cities I found in my travels. Give this town and its surroundings some time and you won't be disappointed.

The ancient Hohokam Indians irrigated and farmed the Tucson Valley some 2,000 years ago. Their crops flourished with water from the once-flowing Santa Cruz River. But it was the Pima and Tohono O'odham (Papago) Indians that the Spanish found when they entered the Tucson Valley in the 1500s. The Spanish went right to work at the task of civilizing and Christianizing the native inhabitants of this desert valley. They achieved considerable success with these sedentary, agricultural tribes.

The Apache, who lived in the mountains that surround this valley, did not appreciate the white intruders and did not make their lives easy. At one point the settlers of this valley were forced to erect an adobe wall, 750 feet long and 12 feet high, around their settlement, to protect themselves as well as weary travelers from persistent Apache raiders. The barricade earned the settlement the name of "Old Pueblo," which has become a traditional nickname that is still used for the city today.

There also survive in the area some of the original Spanish missions and cathedrals, built by the Franciscans and their Pima Indian followers in the 1700s. The San Xavier del Bac Mission, nine miles southwest of Tucson on the San Xavier

Indian Reservation, is one of the oldest churches in the country. The beautiful architecture of this mission has earned it the name of "White Dove of the Desert."

Slowly but surely white settlers established a permanent foothold here, pursuing trade, business, cattle ranching, and all the opportunities that came to a frontier town with the railroad. The legacy of the Spanish fathers and missionaries who established themselves in this valley is an important part of the cultural history of Tucson. A more recent influx of emigrants from Mexico has added to the Hispanic flavor of this area, and today over 20 percent of the population of this valley claims some Spanish or Mexican heritage. The Papago continue to live today on a large reservation west of Tucson. The various cultural accents of this area are well pronounced, adding to the city's color and vitality.

Like the Valley of the Sun, the geology of the Tucson Basin lies hidden beneath thousands of feet of valley fill. Fine sediments carried from the mountains, and through washes by the rivers that once coursed through the valley, did the work that has produced this broad, flat valley floor. The Rincon, Catalina, and Tortolita Mountains, which wrap around the valley like a great wall from the east to the north, are composed of gneiss and granite that have been thrust upward as fault blocks. In many parts of these mountains this granite has become extremely weathered, creating beautifully carved boulders and pillars. In the weathering process the rock has been broken down into sands and clays, leaving large pieces of quartz and silvery mica lying about on the surface. In places, the sands and clays that have weathered out of the rock have bonded together to create a hard-packed riding surface that is sometimes referred to as "desert pavement." In some areas, however, the rocks have weathered into pebble-size pieces which can create a loose and very challenging riding surface.

The Sierrita and Santa Rita Mountains to the south have similar granite cores that are surrounded by a complex overlapping of volcanic and sedimentary rock. These granite domes, as well as the surrounding rock, were uplifted by faulting, which created the landscape throughout the basin and range region. Because of the amount of faulting and intrusion of metamorphic and igneous rock, this region is rich in minerals and holds some of the largest low-grade copper deposits in the world. The Museum of Geology at the University of Arizona has beautiful mineral specimens from all over Arizona, as well as many interesting geological displays. Tucson is the home of the largest gem and mineral show in the world. It is a four-day event held every February and is open to the public. If you happen to be here in February you will find this incredible display of rocks and gems a great way to spend an afternoon.

The variety of plant, animal, and bird life in this region is astounding. Not only do you have all the life that thrives on the Sonoran Desert floor, but all the creatures and plant life that love the cooler, wetter climes of the Transition and Canadian Zones. The Saguaro National Monument (existing in two separate units, one to the east of Tucson and another to the west) harbors some of the largest saguaro forests found anywhere in the Sonoran Desert. Healthy specimens of all types of fantastic cacti can be found in the Monument as well.

In the rocky foothills, dense stands of acacia and mesquite tend to dominate, but must share the slopes with one seed juniper, Mexican pinyon, Gambel oak, and emory oak. In the drainages of these mountains you will find narrowleaf cottonwoods, sycamore, alder, mulberry, box elder, and an occasional maple tree intermixed. The beautiful Arizona cypress is found only in isolated spots on north-facing slopes in the Upper Sonoran Zone of this area. It is easy to identify due to its feathery evergreen branches. Vigorous stands of ponderosa pines grow quite dense and are an easy way to identify the Transition Zone. Forests of Douglas fir, white fir, white pine, and quaking aspen grace the slopes of the Canadian and lower Hudsonian Zones, found in only the highest reaches of the Santa Catalina Mountains. While sliding along in the cool shadows of these giants it is easy to forget that you are still in the Arizona desert!

The rainbow of animal life that lives within this region is no less colorful. Grazers such as white-tailed deer, mule deer, elk, pronghorn antelope, and the occasional bighorn sheep can be spotted ambling about in these hills. The very rare and nocturnal coatimundi, similar to a raccoon in demeanor but with a longer tail and snout, also lives in the highest, most remote parts of these mountains, but is rarely seen. Black bear, bobcat, and cougar have previously held healthy populations in the Santa Catalina and Rincon Mountains, although ranchers continue a deadly campaign against these carnivores in defense of their cattle.

Grazing practices, predator control practices, and the issue of government subsidies to support cattle ranching in this area, have recently become highly controversial topics in Tucson, as they have throughout much of the country. Animal Damage Control (ADC), a division of the Department of Natural Resources, routinely baits, traps, and poisons predators native to these mountains at the request of ranchers who contend they lose too much of their livestock to these magnificent and seldom-seen creatures. Cougars have been especially hard hit, for the deer, which are their natural prey, have been forced out to look for forage elsewhere as grazing cattle have depleted their traditional range. The dry Upper Sonoran region of the foothills, on which the majority of beef cattle are grazed in this area, is fragile, and shows signs of overuse and deterioration in many places.

The dry, rocky foothills of the Catalinas and Rincons are also a favorite hangout for rattlesnakes and other reptiles native to this desert country. Keep an eye out for them in the early morning when they are warming themselves in the sun, often along open places in the trail. As the day progresses it becomes too hot for them and they will retreat to underground burrows well out of your way. The streams in these mountains support several species of turtles and frogs, which are a surprise to find thriving in the arid desert. The bird life that visits the canyons and desert around Tucson has established the city as a destination for bird watchers from all over the world. The exotic trogon, which travels north from Mexico to spend the summer in the spring fed Madera Canyon in the Santa Rita Mountains, is a favorite of avid bird watchers. More than 200 species of birds have been identified in this one canyon alone. Sabino Canyon, in the Santa Catalina Mountains just east of Tucson, is alive with the noise and color of birds from south of the border a good part of the year. A field guide to the birds that visit this area, tucked into your tool pouch or fanny pack, will provide many rewarding moments of discovery in these desert wilds.

All of the wildlife in the Tucson area, as well as the plant and bird life of this region, is well represented at the Arizona–Sonora Desert Museum just west of town. This is a private museum that is more like a zoo and botanical gardens combined. The exhibits are excellent; this is a "don't miss" stop while you are here. Allow yourself at least a couple of hours for your visit.

Once again heat, sun intensity, and aridity are factors that need to be figured into any desert outing. Each of these factors needs to be carefully considered, and constantly evaluated, to avoid sunstroke, dehydration, heatstroke, and heat exhaustion. Any one of these heat-related conditions is serious and can become fatal if immediate action is not taken. Even though you may be riding in cooler temperatures at a higher elevation, dehydration and sunstroke are still real and present dangers.

Riding at higher elevations also throws in the extra challenge of trying to equip yourself for rapid temperature change. Storm buildups are born off the higher, moister slopes of these mountains, and this is where they hit first and hardest. A thunderhead may be growing over the ridge out of sight, and the next thing you know the temperature has dropped 20 degrees and it is starting to hail. If thunderstorms are anywhere in the forecast, do yourself a favor and carry a thin layer of clothing for warmth *and* a weatherproof shell. They may seem unnecessary as you are dripping sweat in 90 degree heat on your way up, but you'll be wearing a big smile if it's cool and rainy on the way down and you've come prepared.

I like a lightweight, long-sleeve polyester underwear top for warmth. Most long-sleeve bike jerseys are a combination of polyester and lycra, and will work fine. Avoid cotton, for it will sop up moisture like a sponge and help to lower your body temperature, especially on the ride down. A long-sleeve cotton shirt is just what you want on the desert floor, but not in the mountains.

The Santa Catalinas and Rincon Mountains receive the majority of recreation traffic in this area, while the Tortolita, Santa Rita, and Sierrita Mountains are further out of the way and are less traveled. Watch out for car traffic on some of the dirt roads, like Reddington Road or the Mt. Lemmon Road from Oracle. All services are available in Tucson. Here are the information and service sources you will need to start planning your biking trip to Tucson:

Tucson Metropolitan Chamber of Commerce
465 West Saint Mary's Road
P.O. Box 991
Tucson, Arizona 85702
(602) 792-1212/792-2250

Metropolitan Tucson Convention and Visitors Bureau
130 South Scott Avenue
Tucson, AZ 85701
(602) 624-1817

Coronado National Forest
300 West Congress
Tucson, AZ 85701
(602) 670-4522

Bicycle West
3801 North Oracle Road
Tucson, AZ 85705
(602) 887-7770

The Bike Shack
940 East University Blvd.
Tucson, AZ 85719
(602) 624-3663

Bob's Bargain Barn
2230 North Country Club
Tucson, AZ 85716
(602) 325-3409
Topographical maps, camping gear, and all types of outdoor equipment are
available here.

RIDE 9 *STARR PASS / TUCSON MOUNTAIN PARK*

This ride is a loop that gives two different total distances, one of 8 miles and one
of 12.5 miles, depending on where you begin. This loop will take riders in good
physical condition with intermediate riding skills two to three hours to complete.
Trail surfaces include hard-packed, single-track sections of fist-sized rocks, and
loose sand and gravel in drainage areas.

Besides being surrounded by gorgeous desert scenery, you'll find the views are
fantastic from here! You will see the city of Tucson stretching out behind you
to the east. Surrounding the city are the high peaks and rolling foothills of the
Santa Catalina and Rincon Mountains. When you reach Starr Pass you'll find
that views to the west fall away into the expansive Avra and Aguirre Valleys. The
sunsets from atop this perch are sensational!

This is beautiful Sonoran desert hill country, where gigantic saguaro cacti are
huddled in close to the sheltering slopes of the mountains of Tucson Mountain

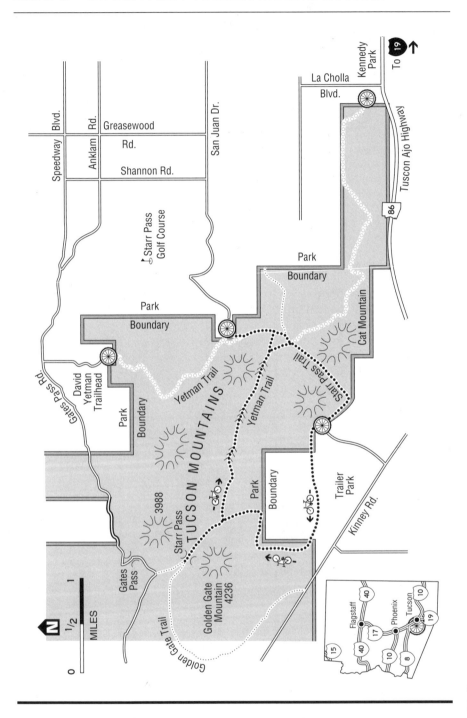

Park. The mountains of this park are close to town, which makes them well suited for shorter outings. All the critters that thrive in this desert environment, including jackrabbits, coyotes, and javelina, can be found here. Keep an eye out during the cooler hours for movement in the brush. This is their activity time, too.

General location: Tucson Mountain Park, just west of the city of Tucson.
Elevation change: From either starting point, your elevation is approximately 2,700' above sea level. You will roll gently along the desert floor until you begin to climb to the pass, which will take you to an elevation of about 3,200'. Total elevation gain is 500'.
Season: Late fall through early spring is comfortable for riding any time of day. During the rest of the year, riding between the hours of 10 A.M. and 3 P.M. is not recommended. Early morning and evening are the best times for enjoyable riding temperatures.
Services: All services are available in Tucson.
Hazards: While it is fairly hard to get lost (you are between the Gates Pass and Kinney Roads, which converge on the west side of Golden Gate Mountain in Old Tucson—an old movie set), there are lots of side trails and confusing intersections in this park. This is where a topographical map and a compass really come in handy, especially if you are interested in any of the ride options. The map that the park had available wasn't of much use.

This ride should be ridden in a clockwise direction, for the Yetman Trail heading east down through a drainage is extremely hard to negotiate going uphill.
Rescue index: While there are no park personnel on duty at Tucson Mountain Park, the park borders a residential area on the east—the busy Gates Pass Road to the north, and Kinney Road to the south. The west side of the park is somewhat remote.
Land status: Pima County Park.
Maps: Maps are available from Pima County Parks and Recreation. The USGS 7.5 minute quads are Cat Mountain, Jaynes, and Avra.
Finding the trail: First you will need to find Speedway Boulevard, which is a main east to west route across town. Travel west on Speedway Boulevard, then take a left when you reach Greasewood Road. You will then go right onto Anklam Road and then left onto Shannon Road. Continue south on Shannon Road until you reach San Juan Drive, where you will want to go right. San Juan Drive dead-ends where a number of trails begin to wind through the park. You will want to park on Shannon Road so as not to crowd the people who live on San Juan Drive.

If you choose to start from Kennedy Park, the fastest way to get there is by taking Ajo Way, or State Highway 86, west until you reach Cholla Boulevard. Kennedy Park will be on your right at the intersection of Cholla Boulevard and Ajo Way.

Sections of loose dirt and gravel make the climb up to Starr Pass a real challenge.

Sources of additional information:

Pima County Parks and Recreation
900 South Randolph Way
Tucson, Arizona 85713
Phone (602) 740-2690

Notes on the trail: From the trailhead at the end of San Juan Drive, you will begin your ride by winding through cacti and other desert vegetation on a fast, hard-packed trail. You will begin to climb when you reach the base of Golden Gate Mountain up a rough, washed-out old jeep trail. After reaching Starr Pass you will go back down the steep, rocky road you came up, bearing left at the bottom of the hill following the drainage. This fork onto the Yetman Trail is approximately 1 mile downhill from Starr Pass. In 2.3 miles you will intersect the Starr Pass Trail again; go left to where you began this ride.

Options include 3 starting points: 1) from the David Yetman Trailhead located at the end of Camino de Oestes Road, 2) from West 22nd Street, or 3) from Kennedy Park at the corner of Ajo Way and Cholla Boulevard. From the top of Starr Pass you may want to ride down around the west side of Golden Gate Mountain on the Golden Gate Trail. There are a number of trails that wind around on the west side of the park, which make for some fun cruising. To return to the Starr Pass trailhead, go south on the Golden Gate Trail until it intersects Kinney Road, then go right onto Kinney Road heading southeast. You will then want to take a left on Sarasota Road, which will dead-end at the Starr Pass Trail. From there you will head east, and then head back to your starting point.

RIDE 10   *CHIVA FALLS / REDDINGTON ROAD*

This ride is an 11.5-mile loop in the mountains east of Tucson, which will take riders in good physical condition with intermediate riding skills three to four hours to complete. This trail follows some very rough four-wheel-drive jeep roads. These roads are mostly hard-packed dirt with sections of loose rock, ruts, and sand. In several spots you will find rock obstacles and ledges that will be a welcome challenge for more advanced riders, but may have to be portaged by inexperienced riders. Many options for alternate routes and further exploring are available on this ride.

This ride is an excellent introduction to the rugged mountain country of this region. As you approach the falls you will be looking at the north and west slopes of the Rincon Mountains. Mica Mountain towers in the background at an elevation of 8,666 feet, with the distinctive rock of Helen's Dome and Spud's Rock protruding just to the west. Beautiful granite boulders, gently shaped by the elements, crop up throughout these foothills and are arranged around the falls themselves like a lovely rock garden. The views returning west on Reddington Road and looking out over the Tucson Valley are also very fine.

The overall scenic quality of this ride is excellent, but arriving at Chiva Falls puts the cherry on the cake. For most of the year, except late summer and fall, the Rincon Mountains feed a beautiful, clear stream that cascades down over a 25-foot drop into a pool of emerald green water. Sycamore and cottonwood trees have grown up through a jumble of boulders to shade many of the deeper pools. This tiny oasis harbors an abundance of aquatic creatures. Small, iridescent frogs can be found clinging to the rocks by the water's edge, or you may be lucky enough to spot a shy mud turtle. A colorful variety of bird life and other wild creatures also frequent these pools. This is an ideal spot to enjoy whatever goodies you brought along. Go ahead, splash your face and enjoy the cool, clear water flowing through the desert. But try not to disturb the creatures who make their home here.

RIDE 10 *CHIVA FALLS / REDDINGTON ROAD*

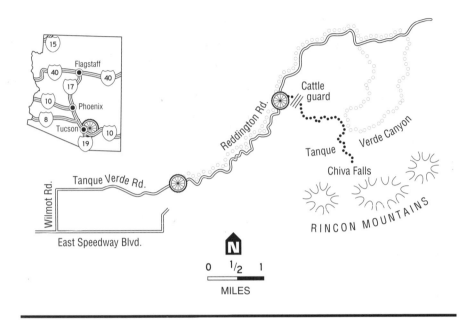

General location: East of Tucson, Arizona, in the Rincon Mountains of the Coronado National Forest.

Elevation change: From the base of Reddington Road where it begins to climb, the point where you may choose to begin your ride, your elevation is approximately 2,600' above sea level. From the cattle guard where you leave Reddington Road to ride to the falls your elevation is 3,800'. You will then proceed over rolling high desert hill country experiencing only modest elevation changes of perhaps 100' to 200' before you reach Chiva Falls at 3,600'. You have many options here; you can either return the way you came or choose one of two other routes. Both of these trails will take you up over a rise at 4,000', and then you'll continue to climb back to Reddington Road, which at approximately 3.5 miles from where you started is at 4,200' above sea level. Many total elevation change figures are therefore possible.

Season: This is desert hill country where all desert riding rules apply. Late fall through early spring is comfortable for riding any time of day. During the rest of the year, riding between the hours of 10 A.M. and 3 P.M. is not recommended. Early morning and evening are the best times for riding, as well as for viewing desert wildlife.

Services: All services are available in Tucson.

Riders working up a sweat on their way to Chiva Falls in the Rincon Mountains just outside Tucson.

Hazards: The car traffic on Reddington Road can sometimes be heavy, especially on weekends. There is often a jeep or two to be found bumping along at a snail's pace on these back roads; give them a holler so they know you're there and then fly by. This is always a moment of supreme satisfaction for fat-tire enthusiasts.

There are a few technical spots, so be prepared and wear your helmet. It is not possible to ride right to the falls because of the boulders. Find a place that is out of sight to stash your bike and then walk up.

This is rugged, very hilly country with a lot of confusing trail intersections. I strongly recommend carrying the 15 minute USGS topo for Bellota Ranch with a compass on this ride. Take a minute about every quarter of an hour to orient yourself as you go. It is also very helpful, before you start riding, to spend a few minutes identifying geographical markers and considering how they will correspond with the direction you will be traveling. With the Rincons to the south, the Catalinas to the north, and Reddington Road running between, it is hard to get too lost. Still, I managed to get pretty turned around on this route.

Rescue index: This area is somewhat remote but receives a substantial amount of recreational traffic from Tucson. It should not be hard to flag down help, especially once you reach Reddington Road. Other help and a phone can be found at the base of Reddington Road in the Tanque Verde residential area, or at the convenience store 2 miles from the beginning of Reddington Road.

Land status: Coronado National Forest.

Maps: Coronado National Forest, Safford and Santa Catalina Ranger Districts. The USGS 15 minute quad is Bellota Ranch.

Finding the trail: Reddington Road can be reached by taking Speedway Boulevard east until it intersects Wilmot Road. Go left onto Wilmot Road and then right onto Tanque Verde Road. Tanque Verde Road becomes Reddington Road where it turns into dirt. Park there if you are going to ride Reddington Road. If you are going to drive it, continue up the dirt road for 4.7 miles to where a cattle guard crosses a road heading off to the right. There is a watering trough and a group of trees where you may see cows congregated in the shade. You will want to leave your car here, off the main road.

Sources of additional information: The Coronado National Forest address is listed in the Tucson introduction.

Notes on the trail: You will ride over a small hill and be looking west over another series of rolling hills and the Rincon Mountains as you set out on this ride. Follow this jeep trail as it rolls along, gently descending through some sand and gravel sections and across rock slabs and ledges. You will remain on this main road, which continues to roll up and down but allows for easy progress. At a point approximately 1 mile from the falls you will reach a "T" intersection. Go right to reach the falls. You will not be able to ride your bike to the falls. Stash your bike and hike through the boulders for 25 yards or so to reach your final destination.

The first option that you may consider is whether or not you want to make the 4.7-mile, 1,200' climb from the base of Reddington Road to where you take the jeep road to the falls. It is a good warm-up going up, and the views are great going down, but it can be washboarded and very busy with car traffic. Reddington Road continues rolling through these desert foothills until it drops into the San Pedro River Valley and ends at the town of Reddington, some 23 miles later. If you're a real adventurer, you may want to give this a try.

As I briefly outlined in the elevation section, there is a choice of routes to take back to Reddington Road from the falls. It is somewhat tricky to identify the 2 routes that head back in a north to northeast direction from the falls. To find either of these routes, start to head back the way you came, and when the road bends sharply to the right (that was the way you came), go straight. If you come to Chiva Tank, you missed it, so go back and try again. The last trail heads off from a circumference road of the falls area heading almost due east. Eventually it turns north and climbs, leading you back to Reddington Road. Both alternate routes have substantial climbs to negotiate, but also get you to a higher, more fantastic vantage point from which you can view your surroundings. Once back to Reddington Road take a left and head back to your car—and your cooler.

RIDE 11 *CHAROLEAU GAP*

This ride follows a steep and rocky jeep road up to the pass called Charoleau Gap (pronounced "*Shar*-loo"). Total distance for this ride is 10 miles out and back with an option that will give a distance of 16 miles round-trip. Riders in good-to-excellent physical condition with intermediate riding skills will find this ride only moderately difficult and should allow three hour's riding time. The long, consistent climb will be a challenge for those unused to steep terrain and elevation.

The views of the Santa Catalinas from the gap are worth the grunt it takes to get up here. The Catalinas rise in a jumble of ridges, peaks, and canyons to the east once you have reached Samanlego Ridge. Canada del Oro Creek runs out the valley to the north below you. A trail parallels this creek and will take you all the way to Oracle, Arizona, for those who feel adventurous. Canada del Oro Creek runs from late fall through spring and can be a real treat halfway through this ride. Mount Lemmon distinguishes the skyline as you look to the south. Spend a few minutes taking it all in, for this is some of Arizona's most spectacular country.

General location: North of Tucson in the Santa Catalina Mountains, Coronado National Forest.

Elevation change: The point at which you begin this ride is just over 3,200' above sea level. From there you will begin to climb, slowly at first and then more steeply toward the top, to an elevation of 5,100'. With the option, you may drop another 250' over 3 miles. Elevation gain is 1,900'.

Season: This is one you want to ride on a cool day. Watch out for thunderstorms building in the fall or anytime they are forecast. Early mornings are strongly recommended for this ride, as it is a very exposed west-facing slope.

Services: All services are available in Tucson.

Hazards: This is a long, steep climb that requires, at a minimum, a moderate level of physical fitness. The potential for dangerous heat-related conditions is therefore greatly increased. This is an exposed west-facing slope with no shade; an afternoon attempt of this ride will therefore be especially brutal. Try to plan this one for an early morning.

Stretches of this jeep road are very loose and rocky, which can make descents a hair-raising experience. Unless you are a motocross rider, you're going to want to keep your speed down when you're heading downhill. Don't forget your helmet! Vehicular traffic on this road is rare and it is almost impossible to get lost.

Rescue index: There are several ranches out this way but otherwise the area is fairly remote.

Land status: Coronado National Forest, Santa Catalina Ranger District.

RIDE 11 *CHAROLEAU GAP*

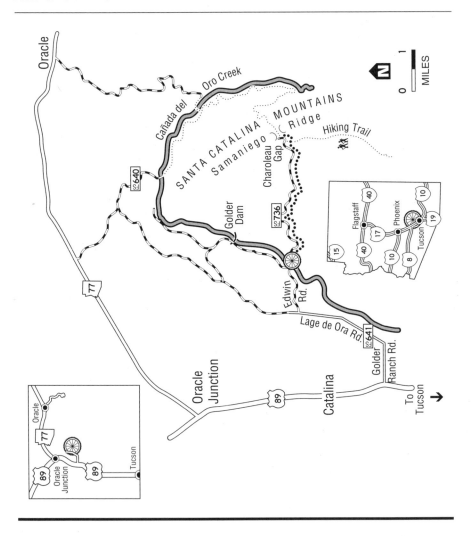

Maps: Coronado National Forest map, Safford and Santa Catalina Ranger Districts. The USGS 15 minute quads are Oracle and Mount Lemmon.

Finding the trail: To get to this ride head north on Oracle Road, or State Highway 89, past Catalina State Park, and take a right onto Golder Ranch Road just before the town of Catalina. This is Forest Service Road 641. This turnoff is also 5 miles before Oracle Junction. Continue for 1.5 miles on Golder Ranch Road (FS 641), past where the road angles off to the left. After the road makes this turn it is called Loge de Ora Road, which is still FS 641. After approximately

White granite boulders and desert scrub make for beautiful scenery on the way up to Charoleau Gap in the Santa Catalina Mountains north of Tucson.

2 more miles on Loge de Ora Road you will take a right onto Edwin Road, a dirt road. You will stay on Edwin Road until it forks. Park at this fork. The ride begins on the road that takes off to the right about 100 yards from the fork. This is FS 736.

Sources of additional information: The Coronado National Forest address is listed in the introduction to this section.

Notes on the trail: The first mile of FS 736 begins to climb, then rolls over some rocky terrain before starting to climb steeply and steadily up hard-packed dirt switchbacks. The trail climbs more gently for the next 2 miles and then becomes quite steep for the last 1.5 miles. Some of the pitches of the last switchbacks are impossibly steep. This is a long, hot, demanding climb. Go back the way you came. Be sure to check your speed around hikers and other riders. Have fun!

The main option, which comes highly recommended, begins once you have reached the gap, or pass, the highest point of the ride. From here you will continue down the other side of the pass for another 3 miles, only a 250' drop, to Canada del Oro Creek. Here you can soak those tired bones, splash around a little, and get refreshed for the ride back to the ridge and down the other side.

Another possible option, if your group is big enough and if you have extra cars, is to shuttle a car up to the town of Oracle and ride the trail that follows

Canada del Oro Creek out to town, buy an ice-cream cone, and wait for the designated driver to bring the car back. This is an adventurous option that will take you down an often brushy, rocky single-track, which crosses the stream many times.

RIDE 12 *PEPPERSAUCE LOOP*

This ride is a 12-mile loop that follows a rough, rocky, and sometimes very loosely surfaced jeep road, giving you a total distance of just about 20 miles. This is a ride that has earned epic status among local riders, and will be a challenge for even the most experienced mountain bikers. Riders of advanced-to-intermediate riding ability should allow four hour's riding time to complete the loop. With the drive from Tucson, which is just about an hour each way, this is a full-day adventure.

Although your elevation is fairly high on this ride you are still in the desert, and it can get pretty hot, so take the proper precautions. But as you ride the loop, bent over your handlebars and blinking the sweat out of your eyes, don't forget to look up every now and then and take in the scenery.

General location: Northeast of Tucson, southeast of the town of Oracle, in the Santa Catalina Mountains of the Coronado National Forest.
Elevation change: At the Peppersauce campground, where you will park your vehicle and begin the ride, your elevation is 4,650' above sea level. From either direction you will begin to climb to a high of about 5,800'. Total elevation gain is 1,150'.
Season: The Peppersauce Loop is a great ride to do year-round.
Scenery: This is one of the most scenic rides in the area. Apache Peak and Oracle Ridge rise in front of you to the west, while a compact maze of drainages runs out helter-skelter below you to the east. Mount Lemmon looms large to the south, beckoning riders to its summit.
Services: Food, gas, and essentials are available in Oracle. Any bike shop needs will have to be addressed in Tucson. Drinking water is available at the Peppersauce campground.
Hazards: This ride is not for sissies. Many portions of this trail are steep, rutted, and rocky. Some spots are very loose with fist-sized rocks that can send you over the handlebars in a flash. If you didn't bring your helmet and you plan on riding, you should have your head checked.

There are a number of side roads that branch off the main loop road, but most climb steeply in the direction you don't want to go and aren't a big temptation. Check hubs and brakes before your descent.
Rescue index: This area is fairly remote, although the Mount Lemmon Road

RIDE 12   *PEPPERSAUCE LOOP*

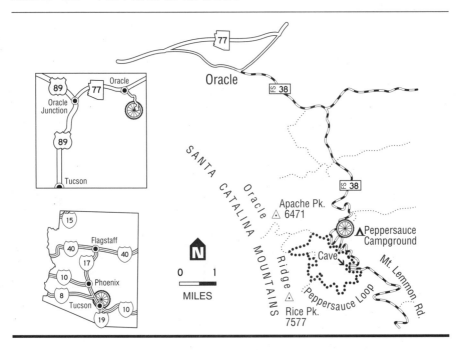

receives quite a bit of car traffic. The Peppersauce Loop also gets a lot of use from mountain bikers. More help and a phone can be found at the start of this ride at the Salvation Army Camp, or 5 miles back toward the town of Oracle.

Land status: Coronado National Forest.

Maps: Coronado National Forest map, Safford and Santa Catalina Ranger Districts. The USGS 7.5 minute and 15 minute quads are Campo Bonito, Bellota Ranch, and Mount Lemmon.

Finding the trail: From Tucson you want to head north on Oracle Road, or State Highway 89, all the way to Oracle Junction. Bear right onto AZ 77, continuing for another 10 miles until you exit right for the town of Oracle. You will pass through the town of Oracle looking for signs to the Mount Lemmon Road on the right. Drive for about 5 miles on the Mount Lemmon Road (also Forest Service Road 38), until you reach the Peppersauce campground.

Sources of additional information: The Coronado National Forest address is listed in the introduction to this section.

Notes on the trail: To begin this ride in a counterclockwise direction, find the trail across the road from the campground parking area. You will start out by heading west up Peppersauce Canyon. You will climb on a pretty good surface

Big grins mean the end of a great ride!—heading back to camp after riding the Peppersauce Loop in the Santa Catalina Mountains.

for the first mile, having to negotiate large, loose rocks in the trail. From here the trail gets steeper and the condition of the trail worsens. Loose dirt, small boulders, and repeated stream crossings make this section of the ride a real challenge. Most riders will be walking long stretches of this section. You will continue climbing, reaching the first hairpin turn at about the 2-mile mark. In another mile you will encounter an intersection. Either direction will eventually hook back up to the main trail. To the left you will see the trail descend steeply and then begin to climb. To the right the trail is smooth and level. Go right for .8 miles before going left. You have missed the turn if you begin climbing steeply. You will then go another short distance before encountering another fork, where you should go right. Now you'll begin descending, sometimes over very rough, rocky, eroded terrain. Next is another 400′ climb and final descent through treacherously loose, fist-sized rocks before you reach the Mount Lemmon Road. It is 3 miles downhill over a fast, even dirt surface back to Peppersauce campground. Congratulations, you made it!

Peppersauce Loop can be ridden in either direction; neither way is easy. Riding clockwise gets more of the climbing done sooner and provides somewhat better surfaces for the uphill sections. But if you're up for the greatest challenge, follow my directions to pedal it in reverse. You'll love it—if you live.

RIDE 13 *MOUNT LEMMON*

This is a 20-mile *up*-and-back ride designed for those who love to punish themselves. Riders in good-to-excellent physical condition with intermediate riding skills can expect to complete this route in about 6 hours. While this road sees a fair amount of vehicle traffic and is for the most part hard-packed dirt, there are sections which are quite steep and also sections that are washboarded. It is in the steep sections that you can also expect to find some loose and rocky surfaces.

The views to the north, caught momentarily through the trees on your way up, are fantastic. Tall ponderosa pines provide welcome shade for this climb. Once you get to the top have a look around. You can check out Mt. Lemmon Ski Resort, ride up to the observatory, and stop in at the grocery store in Summerhaven for a few goodies to fortify you for the long ride down.

General location: Northeast of Tucson, southeast of Oracle, in the Santa Catalina Mountains of the Coronado National Forest.

Elevation change: From the Peppersauce campground to the town of Summerhaven, atop Mount Lemmon, is a 3,850′ climb. The highest point you can reach on Mount Lemmon is 9,157′.

Season: This is a great ride to do spring through fall. Because it gets you to a high elevation you can expect cooler temperatures throughout the year. The elevation of this ride also means you will need to stay alert to local weather forecasts and bring appropriate weather gear if thunderstorms are predicted. In winter and early spring, the road is impassable due to mud and snow.

Services: Food, gas, and essentials are available in Oracle. Any bike shop needs will have to be addressed in Tucson. Drinking water is available at the Peppersauce campground.

Hazards: This road receives a fair amount of car traffic during certain times of the year; a brightly colored piece of clothing or helmet cover will help signal your presence. If you are riding early or late in the season be prepared for mud, snow, or ice. Hidden patches of ice can be treacherous on your descent. You will probably want to check your brakes and hubs before you head down, for this is a long, bone-jarring descent.

Rescue index: This area is fairly remote, although the Mount Lemmon Road receives a good amount of vehicular traffic. The Peppersauce Loop also gets a lot of use from mountain bikers. More help and a phone can be found at the start of this ride at the Salvation Army Camp, or 5 miles back toward the town of Oracle.

Land status: Coronado National Forest.

Maps: Coronado National Forest map, Safford and Santa Catalina Ranger Districts. The USGS 7.5 minute and 15 minute quads are Campo Bonito, Bellota Ranch, and Mount Lemmon.

RIDE 13   *MOUNT LEMMON*

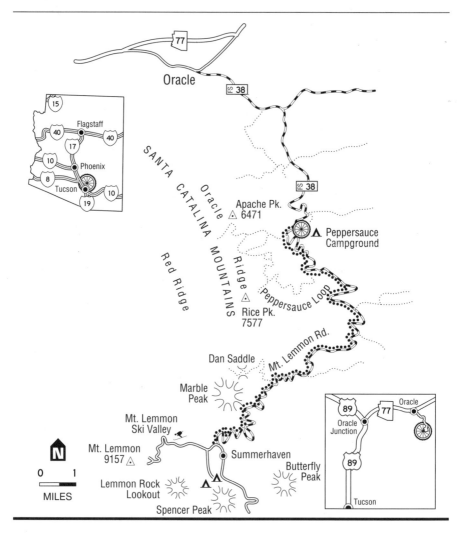

Finding the trail: From Tucson you want to head north on Oracle Road, or State Highway 89, all the way to Oracle Junction. Bear right onto Arizona 77, continuing for another ten miles until you exit right for the town of Oracle. Pass through the town of Oracle looking for signs to the Mount Lemmon Road on the right. Drive for about 5 miles on the Mount Lemmon Road, also Forest Service Road 38, until you reach the Peppersauce campground. Park here.

Riding on Mount Lemmon in May; spring storms can still mean snow when you're at 9,000 feet!

Sources of additional information: The Coronado National Forest address is listed in the introduction to this section.

Notes on the trail: From here you will get on your bike and get back out onto FS 38, which will take you all the way to the top of Mount Lemmon. The road surface is hard-packed and smooth for the first 11 miles of the ride with some sections washboarded. You will roll along through hilly country for the first 5 miles, dropping about 500′ over the next few miles, before starting the main climb. About halfway through the ride you will fork left. This is where the road condition begins to worsen with sections that become loose and rocky. The road climbs steadily and steeply for the rest of the way. The last 5 miles are a grueling climb that tests the endurance of all who come this way. The views from this road are amazing, and the big trees provide welcome shelter from the sun's fierce rays.

After this comes a long, tiring descent that will shake your screws loose. You may want to stop and rest to save some energy for the last 700′ or so of climbing you'll have to do to get back to your car. You may also want to camp at Pepper-sauce campground when doing this ride. If you decide to stay a few days at the campground, you might be interested in the maze of roads that runs out toward the San Pedro River. They're great for exploring. Topographical maps are a must if you are planning to go adventuring in this area.

This is an out, up, and back affair. Because of the distance and the climb involved, options weren't really explored for this ride, but I'm sure they exist. You could begin your ride by taking the Peppersauce Loop route for the first 8 miles or so to where it comes out onto the Mount Lemmon Road, and then begin your assault on the peak from there. You may also want to shorten the length of this ride by driving up FS 38. If you choose to do this be sure to park your vehicle well off the road.

RIDE 14   GREATERVILLE / T.V. REPEATERS

This is an out-and-back ride that gives a distance of 18 miles round-trip from where you start just off State Highway 83. Several options are possible. You can adjust the length of this ride by driving farther up the road where you turn off to begin this ride. This route, for riders with intermediate riding skills and who are in good physical condition, will require three to four hours to complete. It rolls along on hard-packed dirt jeep roads with only a few steep and rocky sections.

These mountains have an entirely different flavor and feel than the Rincon and Santa Catalina Mountains. The Santa Rita, Whetstone, Huachuca, Patagonia, and all the mountains of the Sonoita region and Cochise County rise off of plains grasslands. While this is classified as Upper Sonoran desert, the yellow grasses that stretch out across these broad valleys are reminiscent of the steppe grasslands of the Patagonia in southern Argentina. The foothills of these mountains support beautiful oak woodlands which give way to large piñon and juniper forests. Some of these trees are quite big by desert standards, and are very old. Ponderosa pines and other mixed conifers can be found as you move up in elevation. The soils of these hills are red, mixed with rounded grayish gravels.

The peaks of Mount Wrightson rise to the south of you once you reach the T.V. Repeaters, but are mainly out of sight. The area surrounding Mount Wrightson is a wilderness area and is off-limits to mountain bikes. In the group of peaks flanking Mount Wrightson you will find Florida Peak and McCleary Peak, which rise to elevations close to 8,000 feet. Mount Wrightson itself is still further to the south and rises to an elevation of 9,453 feet.

There is not much left of the formerly bustling little mining town of Greaterville, just a few old weathered shacks. This area is honeycombed with the efforts of miners who brought lead, zinc, silver, and gold out of these mountains for

RIDE 14 *GREATERVILLE / T.V. REPEATERS*

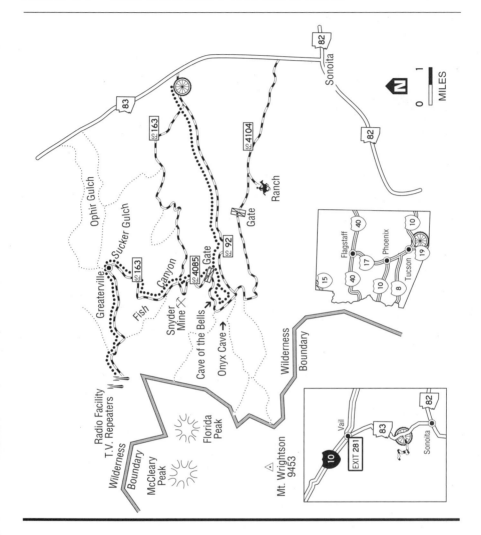

almost 150 years. Stone ruins and mine shafts can be found throughout these hills, and there are many claims being worked by individuals and small outfits today.

And in case you're wondering, the "Repeaters" relay television signals.

General location: Thirty-five miles southeast of Tucson. Santa Rita Mountains of the Coronado National Forest.

Elevation change: At the point where Box Canyon Road (also Forest Service

Starting down from high in the Santa Rita Mountains of south-central Arizona.

Road 62) leaves AZ 83, your elevation is approximately 5,000′. You will climb gradually to the abandoned mining town of Greaterville, which is at an elevation of 5,400′ and will eventually reach the T.V. Repeaters at an elevation of 5,896′. Total possible elevation gain is 900′.

Season: This is desert hill country where all desert riding rules apply. Late fall through early spring is comfortable for riding any time of day. During the rest of the year, riding between the hours of 10 A.M. and 3 P.M. is not recommended. Early mornings and evenings are the best bets for finding enjoyable temperatures for riding.

Services: All services are available in Tucson. Food, gas, phone and more are available in Sonoita, another 8 miles south on AZ 83.

Hazards: Many of the stone ruins and abandoned mine shafts that were left behind by the old-timers are fun and interesting places to poke around, but they are also dangerous. Never enter an abandoned mine shaft, for they can easily collapse and are usually filled with asphyxiating gases escaping from the earth.

While it is hard to get very lost, there are many jeep roads that take off in all directions and are very tempting. If you feel like doing a little exploring, be sure to equip yourself with topographical maps and a compass.

The car traffic on the Box Canyon Road can become moderately heavy, but is usually not a problem.

Rescue index: The Santa Rita Mountains are a lot more remote and receive a lot less traffic than the Rincon or Santa Catalina Mountains surrounding Tucson.

There are a fair number of campers, however, on the weekends. In the event of an emergency, the closest help and phone you will find will be at the ranch you passed at the beginning of the Box Canyon Road.

Land status: Coronado National Forest.

Maps: Coronado National Forest, Nogales and Sierra Vista Ranger Districts. The USGS 7.5 minute quads are Empire Ranch, Helvitia, Mount Wrightson, and Sonoita.

Finding the trail: To reach the east side of the Santa Rita Mountains from Tucson take I-10 east to Exit 281 where you will take AZ 83 south. You will continue heading south for approximately 16 miles at which point you will be turning right onto FS 92 which is also the Gardner Canyon Road. You can park anywhere along the right side of this road for the first 2 miles or so, but much of the land on the left is private property. There is a ranch with private holdings on both sides of the road at about the 2-mile mark and you may have to go through a gate. Be sure to close all gates that you open. After a quarter mile it is all National Forest. Park as far up the road as you like.

Sources of additional information: The Coronado National Forest address is listed in the introduction to this section.

Notes on the trail: You will begin this ride by heading up the Gardner Canyon Road or FS 92. When you get to the intersection of FS 92 and 4085, you will want to go right, heading up Sawmill Canyon on FS 4085. You will continue up this canyon, in this direction, for about 1 mile. You may see on your left, about .5 miles from your turn onto this road, a trail heading up through the scrub; it goes to Onyx Cave. At the 1-mile mark from the beginning of FS 4085 you will go right, rolling gently downhill through piñon and juniper and then out onto open, grassy hillsides. You will be traversing the eastern slope of the Santa Rita Mountains as you go for the next 5 miles. Depending on what the ranchers in the area are doing, you may encounter several fenced gates along this part of the ride. If you find them open, leave them open. If they are closed make sure you close them behind you. A mile from your last right-hand turn look for another trail, really a rough jeep road, that heads off to the left. It leads to Cave of the Bells. Another 2.5 miles along this route you will encounter the remains of the Snyder Mine. Old camp buildings and a dilapidated shaft are all that's left. Not quite a mile past the Snyder Mine you will encounter an intersection; go left onto FS 163, which heads up Fish Canyon. You will begin climbing gently up Fish Canyon from this point, bearing right following the road, and then will climb a little more steeply and descend into the ghost town of Greaterville. From Greaterville you will follow the jeep road to the left, up Ophir Gulch, which will climb until you reach the group of towers that are the T.V. Repeaters. Return the way you came.

There are many jeep trails that follow the canyons of this range. One possible option is to follow the jeep trail up Enzenberg Canyon, one canyon to the north of Ophir Gulch Road. Both of these roads lead up to the T.V. Repeaters.

Another possible option is from the top of the T.V. Repeater station. On your way back down look for a road leading off to your right. This is Fish Canyon Road (Forest Service Road 163), which will take you all the way out to AZ 83 where you can ride 4 miles back to FS 92 on pavement. Two miles before you reach AZ 83, about 6 miles from where you left Ophir Gulch Road, look for a road taking off to the left. This is a 3-mile jaunt that is somewhat hard to find, but it will take you up over the ridge and down into Posos and then Empire Gulch where you left your car. I strongly suggest either a National Forest map or a topo if you are going to try these options.

You can vary the length of this ride by parking your vehicle any distance up Gardner Canyon Road.

RIDE 15 GARDNER CANYON / CAVE CREEK CANYON LOOP

This ride is a 20-mile loop which follows hard-packed dirt jeep roads with some slightly rocky sections and several water crossings. This ride will be moderate to easy for riders of intermediate riding ability, and will take four to five hours for most to complete.

The scenery along this route is gorgeous. The forests of piñon and juniper are beautiful and perfume the air. The woodlands of these mountains give a feeling that is worlds away from the Sonoran Desert and giant saguaro cacti that dominate the landscape just 30 miles distant. Vegetation in these canyons provides precious shade on the way up. This trail offers some excitement for those who like to splash around a little bit. There is a fair amount of water in these canyons from fall through spring, which offers welcome refreshment when flying downhill. From where the jeep road ends (at the wilderness area boundary) in Gardner Canyon, the 3.4-mile hiking trail to Mount Wrightson begins. Those who choose to make the hike will be richly rewarded with fantastic views from the highest peak in the range.

General location: Thirty-eight miles southeast of Tucson, in the Santa Rita Mountains of the Coronado National Forest.
Elevation change: From where this ride begins, your elevation is approximately 4,900' above sea level. From this elevation you will begin to climb, gradually at first and then more steeply, to an elevation of 6,600'. Total possible elevation gain is 3,200'.
Season: This is desert hill country where all desert riding rules apply. Late fall through early spring is comfortable for riding any time of day. During the rest of the year, riding between the hours of 10 A.M. and 3 P.M. is not recommended. Early morning and evening are the best times to find enjoyable temperatures for riding.

RIDE 15 *GARDNER CANYON / CAVE CREEK CANYON LOOP*

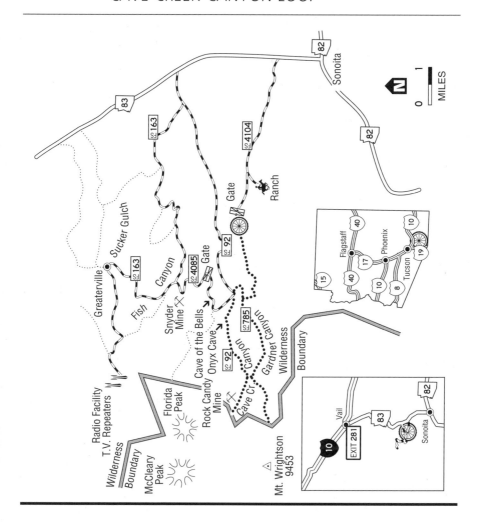

Services: All services are available in Tucson. Food, gas, phone and more are available in Sonoita, another few miles south on AZ 83.

Hazards: Once again there are a number of abandoned mine shafts and buildings along this route. Never enter an abandoned mine shaft, for they can easily collapse and are usually filled with poisonous gases. Many of the timbers and stone walls of these ruins are unstable and should not be climbed on or leaned against.

Rescue index: The Santa Rita Mountains are a lot more remote and receive a lot

Puddles provide a refreshing splash on the way down Gardner
Canyon in the Santa Rita Mountains.

less traffic than the Rincon or Santa Catalina Mountains surrounding Tucson.
There are a fair number of campers, however, on the weekends. In the event of
an emergency, the closest help and phone you will find will be at the ranch you
passed at the beginning of Box Canyon Road.

Land status: Coronado National Forest.

Maps: Coronado National Forest, Nogales and Sierra Vista Ranger Districts.
The USGS 7.5 minute quads are Mount Wrightson and Sonoita.

Finding the trail: To reach the east side of the Santa Rita Mountains from Tucson
take I-10 east to Exit 281, where you will take AZ 83 south. Continue on AZ 83
for approximately 20 miles. At this point you will need to take a right onto Forest Service 92 (Cave Creek Canyon) and drive the distance to which you want to
adjust the length of your ride. To get to Gardner Canyon, continue down AZ 83
for another 2.5 to 3 miles and go right onto FS 4104. You will need to continue
on this road for almost 4 miles, for the land surrounding the road is a private
horse ranch. Park off the road and you're there.

Either road you decide to take, FS 92 or 4104, will reach the same area. You can easily cross over between Cave Creek and Gardner Canyon on FS 785, about halfway along on the ride.

Sources of additional information: The Coronado National Forest address is listed in the introduction to this section.

Notes on the trail: From either starting point you will begin riding by following the road uphill. Both routes climb and roll gently through large piñons and junipers. Although it depends upon where you begin this ride, you will encounter a main intersection on both routes that connects Cave Creek and Gardner Canyons. At this point the Gardner Canyon Road, or FS 4104, becomes FS 785. FS 4104 actually meets FS 785 in a "T" intersection. If you go right you will climb over into Cave Creek Canyon; if you go left you will be continuing up Gardner Canyon. Ride back down the way you came.

There are two ways to reach this ride: from FS 92, 4 miles north of Sonoita, and FS 4104, which is just 2 miles further south along AZ 83. FS 4104 turns into FS 785, which is Gardner Canyon Road. FS 92 is Cave Creek Canyon, which closely parallels Gardner Canyon. Both of these canyons (as well as Sawmill and Fish Canyons) are connected by FS 4085, which run perpendicular to all these canyons. This combination of roads makes for some good adventuring, but I would suggest equipping yourself with a topo or Forest Service map before you start exploring side roads. If you begin this ride from FS 92 you will need to cross over or head south on FS 4085 to get to Gardner Canyon, or you may simply want to ride Cave Creek Canyon to its end at the boundary of the wilderness area.

RIDE 16 *KITT PEAK*

This ride is another long, brutal climb designed for those seeking to test their strength, willpower, and endurance. At just under 20 miles this loop takes you to the top of Kitt Peak and the Kitt Peak National Observatory. The route follows the paved road to the observatory for a few miles before taking off on the old abandoned road to the top. Much of this road is in pretty rough shape and maintaining traction along certain sections is a real trick. Erosion has left the surface of this road very loose and gouged with ruts from water runoff. Some sections are being reclaimed by desert flora, which tend to snag in your spokes and pedals and leave burrs in your socks. This ride is for experienced riders with excellent riding skills in top physical condition. It will take most of five hours to complete the loop.

The Kitt Peak National Observatory is on Papago Indian Reservation land; please be respectful of their domain. The views on the way up and from atop

RIDE 16 *KITT PEAK*

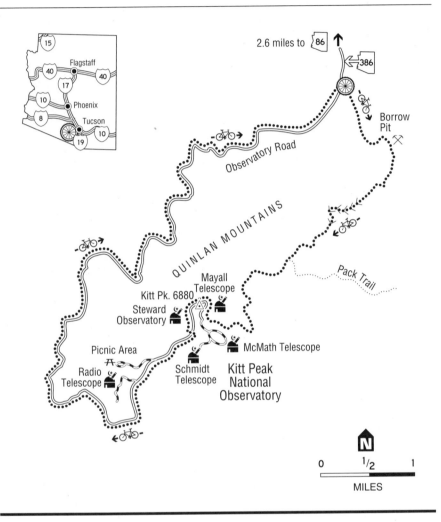

6,875-foot Kitt Peak are fabulous. To the east are the Baboquivari Mountains, which run to the south. The jagged tooth of Baboquivari Peak rises to the south at an elevation of 7,730 feet, a sacred site for the Papago people. To the north and east the Santa Catalina and Rincon Mountains look quite massive. You are surrounded by the Papago Indian Reservation.

General location: Just over 35 miles west-southwest of Tucson, within the boundaries of the Papago Indian Reservation.

Elevation change: From where you begin this ride, just after the turnoff of AZ 386, your elevation is approximately 3,675′. From here you will climb almost 3,200′ to reach an elevation high, at the top of Kitt Peak, of 6,875′.

Season: This ride is deep in the heart of the Sonoran Desert, and despite the elevation that is gained it should not be attempted during summer months. The winter months are best for trying this ride, for it is very exposed and offers no shelter from sun on the way up.

Services: All services are available in Tucson. Water and snacks can be obtained at the top of Kitt Peak, at the observatory's Visitor Center.

Hazards: Exposure to heat and sun on this ride means that the threat of heat exhaustion, sunstroke, and dehydration are constant. Stay covered up and drink lots of water, more than you think you need. You may want to carry a pair of tweezers for removing cactus thorns from tires on this ride. Watch out for cars on your way down. The peak is officially closed before 10 A.M. and after 4 P.M., so plan your ride accordingly.

Rescue index: Except for the traffic you will find using the paved road up to the observatory, this is pretty remote country. Your best option for finding help is at the Visitor Center or out on the road.

Land status: Papago Indian Reservation.

Maps: USGS 7.5 minute quad for Kitt Peak, or the 15 minute quad for Baboquivari Peak.

Finding the trail: From Tucson you will need to find Ajo Way, in the south part of town, and head west. Continue west on Ajo Way as it turns into AZ 86. After about 35 miles you will turn south onto AZ 386. Park immediately off to the right-hand side of the road in the dirt turnout area.

Sources of additional information: Kitt Peak Observatory. Call (602) 555-1212 for the current phone number.

Notes on the trail: You will begin riding by following the paved road up to the observatory. Follow this road until it makes a right-hand turn, about 2.5 miles from where you started. A dirt road continues straight ahead toward the peak; this is the road you want. You will climb gradually at first and will soon reach an open pit area which you need to cross to arrive at a chained gate, beyond which the road continues. You'll start climbing more steeply and will soon encounter sections of loose gravel, which make it a challenge to keep your traction. After crossing over to the far side of the ridge you've been climbing, the road levels out somewhat. You will soon discover the observatory's dump. The road from there is better maintained and is probably paved by now. It is about a mile from the dump to the top.

From the top you will most likely want to take the paved road down. You can go back down the way you came up if you are ready for a wild descent. The loose surfaces, ruts, rocks, and weeds make staying on your bike the whole way down a gamble. Return to your car where you left it at the beginning of AZ 386.

RIDE 17 *BAJADA LOOP*

No matter what your riding ability, or level of physical fitness, this ride is an easy one. The Bajada Loop takes you for 6.3 miles, on a graded gravel road, for an incredibly scenic tour of the western unit of Saguaro National Monument. This is a "don't miss" stop while you are in the Tucson area.

This desertscape, containing more than 50 kinds of cactus, can sometimes seem like another planet. Besides the dominant saguaro there are hedgehog, fish-hook and barrel cacti, as well as ocotillo, prickly pear, teddybear cholla, and mesquite trees. As it is intended, the enormous members of the healthy saguaro community steal the show. Some of these individuals are over 150 years old, reach as high as 50 feet in the air, and weigh up to eight tons! These are the largest cacti that grow in this country, and their unique growth patterns and many arms give them distinct personalities. Visit the Red Hills Visitor Center to learn more about these fascinating plants and all the animals that make this desert their home.

General location: Saguaro National Monument West.
Elevation change: From the picnic area where this loop begins, your elevation is approximately 2,100' above sea level. From there the road dips and then climbs slightly to an elevation of 2,350'. Total elevation change is a modest 500'.
Season: This is the Lower Sonoran desert hill country and it can get hot, *really hot*, down here. The best time of year to find comfortable temperatures for mountain biking is fall through spring. Early morning is going to be the coolest time of day, and it's a good time to see and hear the chorus of the songbirds that live in this desert.

To see this desert in early April when it is a kaleidoscope of brilliant blossoms is an experience that everyone should have at least once in a lifetime. The saguaro's blossoms are beautiful, glossy, white, saucer-sized flowers that open in the cool of the evening and are wilted by the next afternoon. They bloom throughout the month of June, producing a fruit with sweet red meat that is about the size of kiwi fruit. The saguaro can produce as many as one hundred fruits each, which have long been a food staple for the native Indian inhabitants of this area. The fruit is knocked from the top of the cactus, then gathered and made into wine, jams, and many other types of foods by the Pima and Tohono O'odham peoples. The many birds that visit and live in the Sonoran Desert celebrate the blossoming and fruiting of the saguaro cactus with feasting and song. Javelina, coyote, and a wide variety of desert rodents are also able to feast on the fruit that drops to the ground. The saguaro makes springtime in this desert a time of plenty for all.
Services: All services are available in Tucson. Drinking water is available at the Red Hills Visitor Center.

RIDE 17 *BAJADA LOOP*

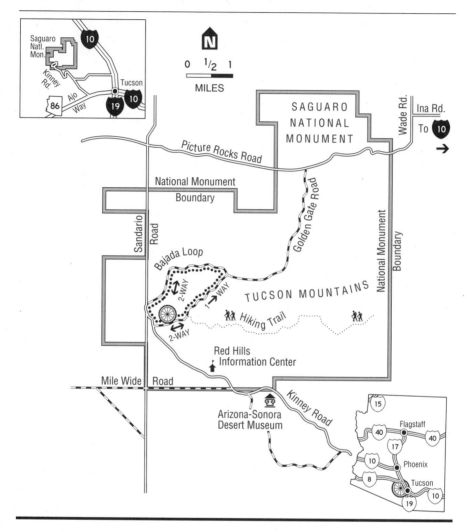

Hazards: Watch out for car traffic on this road. Drivers in campers can be rubbernecking at the scenery with little awareness of what is going on around them. But then so can mountain bikers.

If you want to cruise without a helmet, letting the wind blow through your hair, this is the place to do it.

Rescue index: There is plenty of traffic on this road in case of emergency. The Red Hills Visitor Center is the place to go for help and a phone.

Land status: Saguaro National Monument.

The creamy, saucer-sized blooms of the majestic saguaro cactus later turn into juicy red fruit—a favorite food source of the Sonoran Desert's native peoples and wild creatures.

Maps: Saguaro National Monument map, from the Visitor Center.

Finding the trail: From Tucson take Speedway Boulevard west. Speedway Boulevard will turn into the Gates Pass Road, which crosses through Tucson Mountain Park. Continue on the Gates Pass Road, past the Arizona-Sonora Desert Museum, and you will come to the Red Hills Visitor Center inside the Monument in another 2 miles. The beginning of the Bajada Loop begins another mile past the Visitor Center on the right. Drive in and park at the picnic area.

Sources of additional information:

Saguaro National Monument
3693 South Old Spanish Trail
Tucson, Arizona 85730-5699
(602) 296-8576

Notes on the trail: This is a one-way road which is graded and well maintained. It is well marked and heavily traveled. No further explanation of this route is needed.

Mountain bikes are allowed only on the road. Do *not* ride the trails out across the desert floor.

Southern Arizona Rides

In this section I'll cover six rides sprinkled throughout the extremely varied countryside to the south of Arizona's Phoenix-Tucson population centers. From west to east I go first to a remote part of the Sonoran Desert famed for the organ pipe cactus, another gigantic spiny cactus that grows only in the hills of the National Monument that bears its name. Heading east and south from there, but gaining in elevation, are the Patagonia Mountains. Here, among the grassy rolling hills and big trees that characterize this region, you'll find the remnants of what were once bustling mining communities. Continuing east, after a brief stop in the historic town of Tombstone (kind of a tourist trap but worth a visit), I came to one of Arizona's most beautiful and best kept secrets, the Chiricahua Mountains (pronounced "chee-ree-*kah*-wah"). While none of the rides in this section are listed as difficult, they traverse some of Arizona's wildest and most scenic country and make for some great adventuring.

ORGAN PIPE CACTUS NATIONAL MONUMENT

One hundred twenty miles west of Tucson, and about five miles south of Why, Arizona, you will find yourself inside the boundaries of Organ Pipe National Monument. This landscape, at first glance, appears empty and lifeless, but in fact supports a surprising abundance of plant and animal life well adapted to this desert's harsh environment. Organ Pipe National Monument is sandwiched between the Papago Indian Reservation to the east, and the road-less Cabeza Prieta National Wildlife Refuge to the west. To the north the Barry M. Goldwater Air Force Range stretches from 60 miles east of Gila Bend all the way to Yuma, Arizona. While this area is quite remote, a visit is well worth the trouble.

The monument was established to protect the giant cactus that bears its name, as well as the entire undisturbed ecosystem in which it thrives. While the organ pipe cactus grows only in a small region of the United States, it is quite common along the Baja Peninsula and throughout Sonora, Mexico. The organ pipe cactus blooms later than most of its spiny comrades, producing small purplish-white blossoms in May, June, and July. The delicate flowers of this cactus don't open until the cool of the evening and close again with the heat of day. The organ pipe favors the hottest, driest, south-facing slopes to grow, where its roots are well drained and where it can keep warm during the winter.

The Puerto Blanco, Bates, Cipriano, and Ajo Mountains inside the monument boundaries are all fault block ranges, typical of basin and range country. These mountains are made up of rugged, deeply eroded volcanic rocks, which include layers of lava and tuff that have been tilted and thrust upward. The central por-

75

tion of the Puerto Blanco Mountains are rounded hills of granite, and rougher hills of metamorphic gneiss and schist, which extend to the south. The sands and gravels have eroded off of these mountains over the eons and their deposition has created long, gently sloping grades that fan away from these small ranges. These sediments have compacted to create what is referred to as "desert pavement," which over time becomes almost entirely erosion resistant. This is a geological feature common to the Sonoran Desert, and creates the beautiful, sweeping valleys between ranges.

The Papago, or Tohono O'odham Indians, were the original inhabitants of this country. They ranged over a substantial area gathering the fruits, saguaro ribs, and other materials the cacti of these hills offered. Quitobaquito Springs is a beautiful oasis within the monument and is visited by a variety of waterfowl and other rare bird life. The spring, which is located in the southwestern corner of the monument off Puerto Blanco Drive, was formerly a sacred site for the Tohono O'odham people, but their shrines and huts were removed when the government acquired the property for the monument. The spring has a long history as a watering stop for missionaries, gold seekers, and settlers traveling north into the new country, along the almost waterless Camino del Diablo ("Devil's Highway") between Sonoita, Mexico, and the Colorado River.

This is a true wilderness adventure of a very different kind, one that is unique to this part of the country. There is a campground at the Visitor Center and permit camping at the Alamo Canyon Primitive Campground 14 miles away. There's drinking water available at the main campground, but no showers.

PATAGONIA GHOST TOWN REGION

One hundred seventy miles to the east, as the crow flies, is a far different world of hilly grasslands called the Patagonia Mountains. This place often looks more like parts of Northern California than it does Arizona. Small mountain ranges and their foothills rise off the grassy uplands that are unique to this narrow corridor of south-central Arizona. Large cottonwoods, sycamores, and oaks grace the canyons of this region, many of which are spring fed. Broad meadows rimmed with wildflowers can be found where canyon bottoms widen out. The abundance of grass has made this area famous as horse and cattle country. A number of well-known horse ranches make their homes in this part of the state; the Straddling Museum of the Horse is also here.

You'll need to keep an eye on those big bulls when you meet up with herds while riding the open range around here. I would encourage you also to take note of the grazing practices in this region, especially around delicate springs and riparian areas, and to contact the Coronado National Forest with your own observations and assessments of the ways in which extensive cattle grazing has impacted this landscape. There are routes well suited to mountain biking in this area that I chose not to include because of the damaged and polluted condition of the landscape. Proper grazing benefits all; overgrazing accomplishes the opposite.

These rolling hills are mainly made up of granite and limestone. Granitic intrusions form the spine of the Patagonia range which helped to create the precious ores that brought settlers to the region. These hills are riddled with the pockmarks of mining efforts long since ceased. There remain, however, many adobe ruins, artifacts, and graveyards of the people who toiled here hoping to make their fortune. The towns of Harshaw, Mowry, Washington Camp, Duquesne, and Sunnyside all sprang up in the last half of the nineteenth century. But most were abandoned by the 1920s, as the ore that fueled them was exhausted.

The setting of these old ghost towns is lovely and makes for an interesting tour of this area. While the riding is not of a technical variety, the Forest Service roads and old mining roads offer some great scenic cruising. There are many options for alternative routes and longer tours on these roads. You may want to consider a support trip with riders taking turns at the wheel. You can cover more ground this way, pile in when you've had enough, and stop to camp along the way.

THE CHIRICAHUA MOUNTAINS

The extraordinary rock formations found in Chiricahua National Monument, at the north end of the Chiricahua range are without a doubt the main attraction. Purplish pillars of volcanic tuff, saucers and discs of sculpted rock balanced atop one another in precarious piles, and intricate passageways that wind among them, are some of the unique formations that can be found here.

The Chiricahua Mountains, which extend to the south, beyond the monument's boundaries, are quite stunning in their own right. Deep shadowy canyons hide sparkling streams, while ridge lines rise to elevations of 9,000 feet. Mountainsides bristle with shadowy forests of spruce, pine, and aspen, some of which are quite old and grand. A healthy assortment of bird and animal life thrives in these quiet mountains in surprising numbers. The Chiricahua Mountains run for about 60 miles north to south, and lie in the extreme southeastern corner of Arizona. Almost the entire range falls within, and is managed by, the Coronado National Forest. While mountain bikes are not permitted on any of the trails within the monument or in the wilderness area (which, unfortunately for us, comprise the majority of high peaks and ridge lines in the range), there are a couple of good days of riding in these mountains. This is spectacular country that is deserving of a visit if you are traveling through the southern extremes of Arizona.

The Chiricahua Mountains are named after a band of Apache Indians who lived here and believed these mountains to be their place of origin and their eternal home. Among the most famous of the Chiricahua Apache was a medicine man named Geronimo. These people were among the very last tribes in the United States to be removed from their native range and relocated on reservations. The Chiricahua Apache fought fiercely for their land during the days of white settlement, and at times had more than a third of the United States cavalry engaged in their pursuit. From the safety of the pinnacles and canyons of these rugged mountains they would send out raiding parties to attack weary travelers as they struggled across the open desert.

The springs, clear streams, and abundant wildlife of these mountains, which sustained the Chiricahua Apache for centuries, made their land especially attractive to newcomers. Waves of white settlers moving through the area grew in size and number, and as they became permanent in the area the demand for protection from the Apache grew louder. The Chiricahua's struggle for their land ended in 1886 with the final surrender of Geronimo, one of history's most famous Indian personalities. Although Geronimo was not a Chiricahua chief he was revered by his tribe for his ability to escape his captors. Broken promises and deception by his white captors resulted in the removal of the Chiricahua people from this country. They were not immediately given a reservation, but were loaded onto railway cars and shipped to Florida, where many died from disease and starvation. After several years they were moved to a second reservation, this time to Oklahoma—where remnants of their tribe remain to this day. While relaxing on a grassy bank next to Turkey Creek, watching a deer graze along the edge of an open meadow, it is not hard to understand why the Chiricahua loved their home and fought for it.

These mountains are almost entirely volcanic. In a few places in the range siltstones and sandstones, deposited in lake beds which were then uplifted, have been revealed in distinct banding. The strange figures and formations at the north end of the range, the centerpiece of Chiricahua National Monument, were created by a series of enormous, and extremely violent, volcanic events, which sent gases, ash, and molten pellets of pumice shooting down the slopes of these mountains with hurricane force. These avalanching ash flows quickly welded into tuff as they came to a stop. Eight different layers of tuff, representing as many eruptions, have been identified inside the monument, totaling almost 2,000 feet of deposition. The persistent efforts of rain, wind, and ice have since done their work in sculpting the magnificent towers and spires of purple rock, which are showcased within the monument. Wind, water, and temperature fluctuation pound away at the soft tuff by weakening the rocks' cracks and joints. In the creek bottoms further south in the range, you can find a collage of soft colors in the rocks. These are pieces of different types of volcanic rock, eroded out of the conglomeration that is prevalent here.

The Chiricahuas are home to all types of animals, big and small. Among them are the black bear, the deer, the mountain lion, and the coatimundi. If you are camping in these mountains you will need to store food and garbage well out of reach, or you may be awakened in the middle of the night to the sounds of a curious coati peeking in your dinner pots, or a bear sorting through your leftovers. Carrying a few extra stuff sacks and a length of rope to suspend them from a branch is a good way to keep edibles out of reach of these opportunistic creatures. The Chiricahua Mountains are a "sky island," an ecosystem isolated by the desert that surrounds it. These desert "islands" occur throughout the Southwest and usually have developed plant and animal species specific to their particular mountain range. In the Chiricahuas the Apache fox squirrel is one of these isolated species.

By Forest Service estimates, almost three-quarters of the annual visitors to the Chiricahuas are bird watchers. They come to identify a mind-boggling number of species that migrate through these mountains every year. The 15 different species of hummingbirds that visit these mountains are the main attraction for bird enthusiasts, but the exotic coppery-tailed trogon draws a lot of attention as well. The wild turkey, which can often be seen scratching around in the shadows, is no doubt the namesake of Turkey Creek, one of the main drainages in this range. While resting on the mountainside it is not uncommon to see one of several types of raptors floating beyond the treetops, soaring on the swirling thermals which rise off these mountains in the afternoon. Turkey vultures are a constant in the Arizona sky, and can usually be spotted soaring overhead as soon as the day begins to warm. While they won't win a beauty contest, turkey vultures are some of the strongest and most graceful fliers you'll find in the Arizona skies.

Although the riding here is not extremely technical, there is some substantial climbing to be done. A good level of physical fitness is recommended to meet the challenge of long climbs and riding at high elevation. A day hike in the monument is a good way to acclimate to your surroundings, familiarize yourself with the area, and view some amazing rock formations. There is an excellent selection of field guides and other books at the Visitor Center, as well as some interesting exhibits. The American Museum of Natural History has its Southwest Research Station located in Cave Creek Canyon just outside Portal. Here scientists and students study the habitats and behaviors of many types of insects, reptiles, and amphibians. Stop by for a visit. These folks will be happy to answer any questions you might have about the creatures you see in southern Arizona.

Here are a few information sources to get you going:

Superintendent
Organ Pipe Cactus National Monument
Route 1, Box 100
Ajo, Arizona 85321
(602) 387-6849

Coronado National Forest
300 West Congress
Tucson, Arizona 85701
(602) 670-4522

RIDE 18   *AJO MOUNTAIN DRIVE*

This ride is a 21-mile loop on a bladed dirt road, and is one of the main sight-seeing routes within the monument. Little or no technical riding skills are required, but the length of the ride does call for a moderate level of physical fitness. Allow at least three hours' riding time to complete this loop.

This is a stark but beautiful part of the Lower Sonoran Desert. Small, rugged mountains rise from the desert floor, throwing purple and blue shadows late in the day. The Ajo Range forms the jagged eastern skyline of the monument. Diaz Spire pokes at the sky from among the Ajo Mountains to an elevation of 3,892 feet. Behind it Diaz Peak rises to 4,024 feet, but is out of sight from the road. Mount Ajo is the highest peak in the range, rising to an elevation of 4,808 feet above sea level. Tillotson Peak rises from among the Diablo Mountains in front of you as you turn west. As you ride out along the valley flats in a south-westerly direction you will be looking into the Sonoyta Valley and across to the jagged Cubabi Mountains in Mexico. These views give a feeling of enormous expanse and emptiness, and one shudders to think of the early Franciscan fathers, missionaries, and gold hunters who traipsed across this desert with only their canteens and leaky goat skin bags!

Be sure to stop at the Visitor Center before your ride, for you can pick up a pamphlet with numbered points of interest that correspond to numbered posts along the trail. This is a big help in identifying specific cacti and shrubs, as well as landmarks.

The organ pipe cactus, the namesake of the monument that protects it, is a truly wonderful thing to behold. Its long spiny arms reach high and wide into the blue desert sky. It is easy to see how this cactus earned its name. To see the tips of these arms covered in lavender blooms during spring is a spectacular sight. The organ pipe cactus and its kin, the saguaro, along with the strange expansiveness of the surrounding wilderness of this desert, combine to create a feeling of other-worldliness that you won't soon forget.

General location: Organ Pipe Cactus National Monument, 5 miles south of Why, Arizona, close to the Mexican border.
Elevation change: From where this ride begins, directly across from the Visitor Center, your elevation is 1,670' above sea level. You will ride out across gently downhill sloping flats until you begin the one-way loop, at which point you begin to climb gradually, up and around the Diablo Mountains. At the north end of the loop, at the Arch Canyon Picnic Area, you will reach an elevation high of 2,600'. Total elevation gain is 930'.
Season: Late fall through spring is the best time to visit this low-lying part of the Sonoran Desert. The winter months are especially fine down here as the days are

RIDE 18   *AJO MOUNTAIN DRIVE*

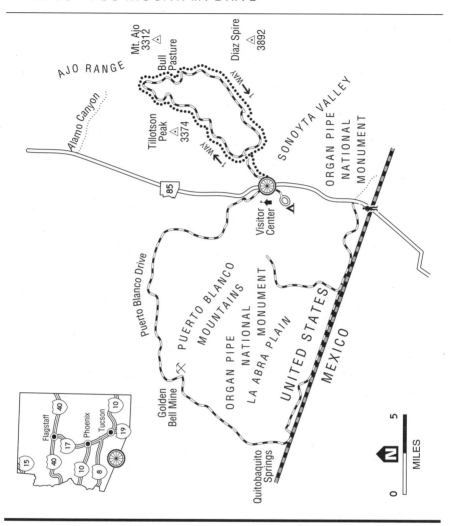

warm and the nights are clear and not too cold. Of course the very best time of year in the Sonoran Desert is when all the cacti are in bloom. Most cactus varieties found within this monument bloom in late March or early April and last for three weeks to a month. The organ pipe cactus continues to blossom through June. If you are visiting during the warmer months of the year it is strongly recommended that you restrict your activity to the hours before 10 A.M. and after 5 P.M.

The enormous organ pipe cactus. In May, June, and July its spiny arms are covered by tiny lavender flowers that open at night.

Services: Groceries and gas can be obtained in Why, about 20 miles north of the Visitor Center, or in Ajo, 10 miles beyond Why. Drinking water is available at the Visitor Center. Restaurants, gas, groceries, motels and more can also be found in the small Mexican town of Sonoita just 2 miles southwest of the border. Traveler's auto insurance can be purchased on either side of the border and is strongly recommended if you plan to head this way.

Hazards: This is low-lying desert country and it can get *very* hot. If you are here in the warmer months of the year, every precaution should be taken to prevent any of the dangerous heat-related conditions from developing. Even if you are here in the cooler winter months, dehydration is still a constant threat; always take more water than you think you'll need and don't allow thirst to regulate your intake of fluids. Wear a hat and long sleeves to avoid being scorched by the intensity of the sun's rays.

Automobile traffic can periodically become heavy, but it is not usually a problem. The road can at times be made impassable due to flooding. If there have
been heavy rains in the area, or if heavy thunderstorms are predicted, check in
with the ranger at the Visitor Center to find out about road conditions.

Rescue index: This harsh environment is very remote country. Take special care
in planning your ride in this area. There is a fair amount of traffic on any of these
roads, and help can be found at the Visitor Center.

Land status: Arizona National Monument, National Park Service, Department
of the Interior.

Maps: Maps can be obtained from the Visitor Center or by contacting the
Superintendent, Organ Pipe Cactus National Monument, Route 1, Box 100, Ajo,
Arizona 85321 or by calling (602) 387-6849. The USGS 7.5 minute quads are
Lukeville, Diaz Peak, Mount Ajo, and Kino Peak.

Finding the trail: Drive to Organ Pipe Cactus National Monument from Tucson
via AZ 86 heading west. Head south on AZ 85 and proceed 20 miles to the
monument's Visitor Center. Ajo Mountain Drive leaves directly across the main
road from the Visitor Center.

Sources of additional information:

Superintendent
Organ Pipe Cactus National Monument
Route 1, Box 100
Ajo, Arizona 85321
(602) 387-6849

Notes on the trail: You will begin this ride by heading down a very gentle grade
across the valley floor toward the Diablo Mountains. You'll begin climbing as
you start the one-way loop, and will continue rolling along but gaining in elevation until you reach the north end of the loop. From there it is downhill until
you reach the road you came out on, which will be a gentle climb back to the
Visitor Center.

All off-road travel other than hiking is strictly forbidden.

If you are feeling strong and are up for a long day, you may want to try riding
the 53-mile-long Puerto Blanco Drive. This can be a long, hot, dusty tour, and
extra water should be carried in panniers or a fanny pack. You may also want to
ride this route with the support of a vehicle. This is an all-day affair.

RIDE 19 *PATAGONIA GHOST TOWNS LOOP*

The length of this ride is approximately 25 miles, but the many options that are
available will give you varying distances. The route follows both well-maintained
bladed dirt roads and unmaintained four-wheel-drive jeep roads. It will only

RIDE 19 *PATAGONIA GHOST TOWNS LOOP*

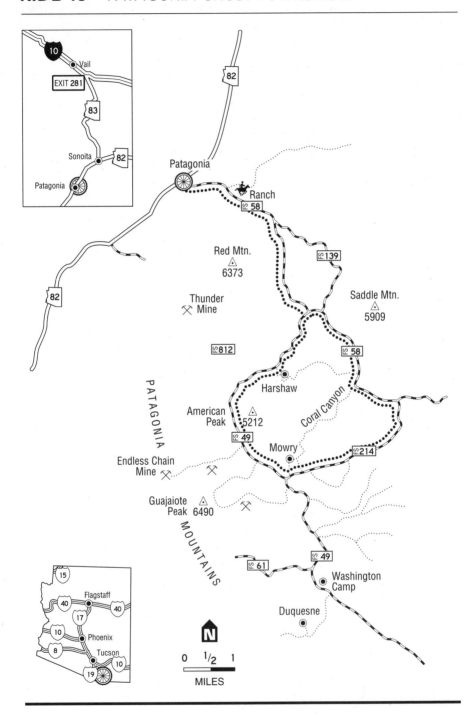

take three to four hours' riding time to complete the loop itself, but with time spent poking around in these old towns and exploring side trails you can plan on a full day's adventure. For riders of intermediate skills and fitness, this route will be easy to moderate.

These small, hilly mountains are grass-covered and thickly vegetated with big, beautiful trees growing in the canyons. Enormous sycamores branch out with crooked white limbs, their light bark making them seem like ghostly guardians of the abandoned landscape. This region is classified as Upper Sonoran Woodlands, and you will find the thick, healthy stands of oak, juniper, and piñon to support this characterization. The area is also referred to as the Eastern Plains of Arizona. Whatever you choose to call it, the countryside of this region is gorgeous and not what you'd expect to find in a southern Arizona desert.

The spine of the Patagonia mountains runs north to south just to the west of this loop. You will be riding toward its soft ridge lines and canyons as you begin. You'll then turn south and east, following some of the drainages that lead away to the east and the Santa Cruz River bottom. If you decide to explore some of the steeper roads leading up to the old Thunder or Endless Chain Mines, you'll be approaching some of the higher points in the range at elevations of 6,000 feet.

The remains of the old towns of Harshaw and Mowry, and those of Sunnyside, Washington Camp, and Duquesne nearby, are some of the most famous ghost towns in the Southwest. Their histories, their peaceful settings, and the beautiful buildings all combine to make this ride a really fun and interesting tour of the past.

The town of Harshaw was named after a successful miner and cattleman named David Tecumseh Harshaw. The town's economy was supported by the Hermosa Mine, a lead and silver mine which began operations in 1877. At one time the town's population swelled to over 2,000, and Main Street stretched for over one-half mile. On what was once Main Street stand two old cabins, beautifully constructed out of wood and brick with a sloping roof and handsome wood columns that support a wraparound porch. Be sure to find the old cemetery located to the west of the main road that brought you here. There is some elegantly wrought ironwork to be seen, and weathered gravestones dating from the 1880s. The lives of these early miners were not easy. They often ended violently, long before old age.

The town of Mowry has a colorful history. Its adobe ruins all now stand roofless. Sylvester Mowry is the namesake of this ghost town, which was originally supported by a lead and silver mine called The Patagonia. Mowry owned and worked the mine from 1859 until 1862, when he was abruptly arrested and charged with aiding the Confederates by supplying them with lead bullets. The crime led to his incarceration in the infamous Yuma Territorial Prison and resulted in the seizure of his property. He was eventually released for lack of evidence, at which point he fled to England, ostensibly to secure funds to reclaim The Patagonia and begin operations again. Unfortunately, he met with an untimely death at the young age of thirty-nine while he was still in England. Under

A mud-brick cabin, typical of those built by miners and ranchers who came to the Patagonia region to find their fortunes in the late 1800s.

new owners the mine prospered for the next fifty years. In 1913 the post office closed for the last time.

The towns of Washington Camp and Duquesne both sprang up in the early part of the 1890s. The Duquesne Mining and Reduction Company created the town of Duquesne where the mine, the mining headquarters, and residences for mine officials are located. Washington Camp included the general store, school house, and miners' bunkhouses. The post office was kept in one town and then another until it finally closed in 1920.

General location: Patagonia Mountains, Coronado National Forest.
Elevation change: From where you begin this loop, in the town of Patagonia, your elevation is 4,078' above sea level. From there you will begin to climb gradually. At the intersection of Forest Service Roads 58 and 139 your elevation is 4,228'. Where FS 58 joins FS 49, thus creating the loop, your elevation is 4,600'. As you proceed in a counterclockwise direction you will continue to climb gradually. The town of Harshaw is at 4,816', and the town of Mowry (5,400') is the high point in the ride. Total elevation gain is 1,320'.
Season: Fall through spring riding will be very comfortable any time of the day. The late spring, summer, and early fall seasons can be hot, but the large trees and vegetation that cloak these hills help by providing some shade. August and September become quite green with moisture that comes from the monsoonal

storms during this time of year. The wildflowers will start to bloom again, too. Winter is wonderful in this part of the country, as is the spring, so it's pretty hard to go wrong any time of the year.

Services: Basic services are available in Patagonia. Any bike-related needs will have to be taken care of in Tucson or Sonoita.

Hazards: Keep an eye and an ear out for car traffic. It isn't usually a problem, but cars can sneak up on you around some of these turns.

You will be a guest of private land along certain stretches of this ride. Be sure to leave gates behind you as you find them, and be careful not to disturb any livestock. Also, many of these ruins exist on private land. Treat them with respect.

The ruins and old mine shafts that dot these hills are unstable structures and should not be climbed in, or on top of, as they can collapse. Old mine shafts are especially dangerous, for the timbers are usually in some stage of decay, and the gases escaping from the earth are noxious and can quickly overwhelm the unexpecting.

While the main road is bladed and is not hard to recognize, there are many tempting and worthwhile side roads to explore. I strongly suggest supplementary maps for this area. Choose either a Coronado National Forest map or a topo.

Rescue index: This is remote country. At certain times of year, however, these roads get a fair amount of tourist traffic. Help should be sought at the town of Patagonia.

Land status: Coronado National Forest.

Maps: Coronado National Forest, Nogales and Sierra Vista Districts map, USGS 7.5 minute quads of Mount Hughes, Harshaw, Duquesne, and Cumero Canyon.

Finding the trail: From Tucson take I-10 heading east to Exit 281, where you should then head south on AZ 83 to Sonoita. Turn right at the intersection of highways 82 and 83. Continue heading south on AZ 82 to the town of Patagonia. When you reach Patagonia you can park on Main Street.

Sources of additional information: The Coronado National Forest address is listed in the introduction to this section.

Notes on the trail: Once you're on your bike you'll need to cruise Main Street and find the old train depot. Turn left in front of the old depot, and then left again at the first street you come to. Take this paved road heading uphill and out of town past the church. This road turns into Forest Service Road 58. Bear right at the intersection of FS 58 and 139. From this intersection you will continue for another 3 miles on FS 58 before it intersects FS 49. Bear right onto FS 49 and continue heading south for another 2 miles to the town of Harshaw. You will then continue on FS 49 for almost another 5 miles to the intersection with FS 214. At this point you may want to continue heading south on FS 49 to the ghost towns of Washington Camp and Duquesne, which is 4 miles from the intersection with FS 214, or bear left onto FS 214 to the town of Mowry. Once you are on FS 214 heading east, look for a left within the next .25 mile. This road will take you to the town site of Mowry. More ruins exist on the south side of FS 214. From Mowry find the road heading northeast down Corral Canyon (this road is not numbered on the Forest Service maps). The road is a shortcut that eventually hooks back up with FS 58, which will take you back to Patagonia. There are 2 roads which take off north from the Mowry town site. One turns northwest toward American Peak (6,212'); you do not want this one, so go back and find the other road heading northeast. You can take FS 139 for a change of scenery. It is a little longer but will hook up with FS 58, which takes you back into town.

There are many options here, but you will need supplementary maps to make the best of them. There are several old mines located just west of the main road, FS 49, heading south. These are mostly short, steep climbs that will take you up the eastern slope of the Patagonia Mountains and then down the other side to AZ 82, if you continue. The old Thunder Mine can be found by taking FS 812, which takes off heading northwest, across the main road from Harshaw. If you continue on this road you will follow Alum Canyon out to AZ 82. Another 2.5 miles south along FS 49, a road takes off heading west which will take you to the Endless Chain Mine and then up to Soldier Basin at the crest of this ridge. Continuing down the other side on this road you will follow Canada de la Paloma out to AZ 82. Another mile past that right you will see another right-hand turn that will take you in a loop to the old Morning Glory Mine. This road turns back to join FS 49, where you will need to take a left to get to the intersection with FS 214 and the town of Mowry.

To reach the towns of Washington Camp and Duquesne continue heading south, past the intersection with FS 214, for another 4 miles. This leg adds another 8 miles to your total distance of 20 miles, but the roads are good, the riding is easy, and it is well worth the effort.

RIDE 20 *PINERY CANYON LOOP*

This ride is a 15- to 20-mile loop, depending on where you decide to leave your vehicle and start pedaling. It is a moderately difficult route for riders of intermediate riding ability and fitness, and should take three to four hours to complete. The riding surface consists of hard-packed and bladed dirt roads, as well as sections of unmaintained four-wheel-drive roads with one steep, rocky section.

The mouth of this canyon is broad and grassy with healthy stands of piñon and juniper trees flanking the hillsides. As you move further up into the canyon you will find large oaks, sycamores, and cottonwoods, characteristic of riparian areas of the Upper Sonoran Woodlands Zone. As you begin to climb you will start to see these deciduous trees mixed with, and then replaced by, forests of

RIDE 20 *PINERY CANYON LOOP*

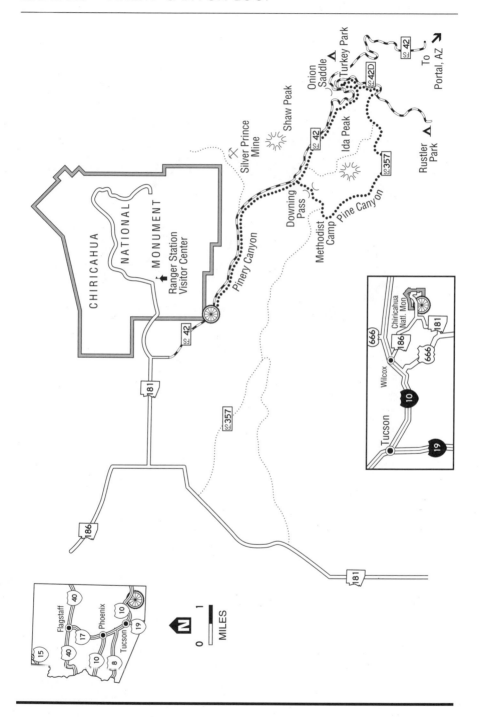

Atop Onion Saddle in the Chiricahua Mountains, one of Arizona's most beautiful ranges.

ponderosa Chihuahua, and yellow pine. You're in the Transition Zone. The pines grow larger and are mixed with spruce and Douglas fir as you continue to climb up to Onion Saddle toward Rustler Park. The big trees and dense vegetation along this route provide cool shade for the climb up. And this is southeastern Arizona!

The grassy canyons and their big trees (some of which are 500 years old) give way to old growth pine forests. This little range is a spectacular study of changing life zones.

The views out into the desert grassland valleys (Spring Valley to the west, Simon Valley in New Mexico to the east) are superb. One can imagine Apache scouts keeping a close eye on the progress of wagons moving across the open stretches below.

Time spent in these mountains will be richly rewarding.

General location: Chiricahua Mountains, extreme southeastern Arizona, Coronado National Forest.

Elevation change: The elevation at the mouth of Pinery Canyon is approximately 5,300' above sea level. At the intersection of the Pinery Canyon Road and the Downing Pass Road (the road where you will come out), your elevation is 6,000'. When you reach Onion Saddle you will have climbed to 7,600'. You will continue climbing while following Forest Service Road 42D, and the signs to Rustler Park, to the intersection with FS 357. Here you will have reached your highest elevation—8,400'. From here you will ride a rapid descent, eventually rejoining the Pinery Canyon Road via Downing Pass Road. Elevation gain is 3,100'.

Season: You can expect snow and colder temperatures at these altitudes in winter, and fairly hot temperatures in summer. Generally, riding in these mountains is delightful year-round. The road to Portal is sometimes closed, due to snow from December through March.

Services: All services are available in Wilcox, Arizona, 27 miles northwest of the Chiricahua National Monument headquarters. Biking needs will have to be satisfied in Tucson.

Hazards: Vehicular traffic can be heavy at times. Weather can change rapidly at these elevations and thunderstorms can be violent. If thunderstorms are forecast or if dark clouds are threatening, it would be wise to retreat to lower elevations. It is a good idea to carry a weatherproof shell anytime you are riding in the mountains.

This is a long climb, and a good level of physical fitness and aerobic fitness will make this a much more enjoyable adventure. The descent down Pine Canyon is steep and rocky, so be careful and wear your helmet.

Rescue index: This is remote country. In the event you need help you should try flagging down a vehicle, or contact the Park Service headquarters at Chiricahua National Monument.

Land status: Coronado National Forest.

Maps: The Chiricahua, Peloncillo and Dragoon Mountain Ranges map of the Coronado National Forest. The USGS 7.5 minute quads are Fife Peak, Rustler Park, and Chiricahua Peak.

Finding the trail: To reach the Chiricahua Mountains from Tucson take I-10 heading east until you reach Exit 340 at Wilcox, Arizona. Head southeast on AZ 186, and follow signs for Chiricahua National Monument. One mile before you reach the monument entrance there will be a road heading due south; this is FS 42. Take this road and follow it as far as you like. Park at one of the many campsites along this road and begin your ride. You may want to leave your car at the parking lot at the monument entrance, or at the Visitor Center, although this will make your ride a little longer.

Sources of additional information: The Coronado National Forest address is listed in the introduction to this section.

Notes on the trail: You will follow FS 42 all the way, about 7 miles up Pinery Canyon, until you reach Onion Saddle. At this point you will follow signs to Turkey Park and Rustler Park via FS 42D. About 1.2 miles past Onion Saddle you will take FS 357, which heads downhill and west. Buena Vista Peak will be in front of you. Continue downhill, past the Methodist Camp, and take FS 42C up over Downing Pass and back to the Pinery Canyon Road where you began. This descent is great! Have fun!

If you've made arrangements to be picked up you can cross the Chiricahua range and end up in Portal, Arizona, by continuing on FS 42 (which heads downhill and east for another 10 miles).

Or, instead of turning onto FS 42C (which takes you back to FS 42 and Pinery Canyon), you can continue down FS 357 all the way to AZ 181. Once you reach AZ 181 you will need to ride the pavement for 6 miles back to the entrance of the monument, or up Pinery Canyon to the point where you left your car.

RIDE 21 *WHITETAIL CREEK*

This is a 16-mile out-and-back ride with several options available. It follows hard-packed dirt and four-wheel-drive jeep roads that get steep and rocky in a few sections. This route will be moderately difficult for cyclists who possess intermediate riding ability and are in fairly good physical condition. Allow three hours' riding time.

In this lower northeastern side of the Chiricahua range there's a more open feeling, as grassy slopes roll into oak, piñon and juniper forests that give way to numerous ponderosa pines. This road approaches the monument from the back side, so you will begin to see the rock formations particular to this monument, and near the top you'll be looking across at Masai Point.

This is a favorite birding spot for many, and is well known by bird watchers throughout the Southwest.

Don't miss the ghost town of Hilltop five miles up the Whitetail Canyon Road. Hilltop actually has existed at two different sites. The original location was on the northwest slope of Shaw Peak (7,730'), on the far side of the peak that rises to your left as you are riding up the road. In 1917 a one-mile tunnel was excavated through the mountain, which enabled the town to be moved to its present site. This location was more convenient for ore transportation and mine opera-

RIDE 21 *WHITETAIL CREEK*

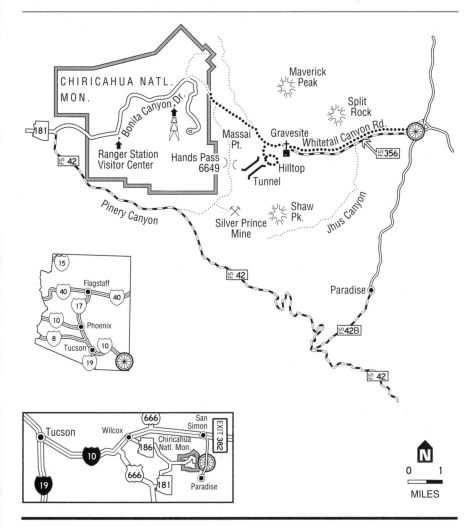

tions. At the tunnel site on the side of the mountain existed a machine building, a bunkhouse, the superintendent's house, and several other buildings, all of which were dismantled and taken through the tunnel in pieces! Below in the canyon was the residential section of Hilltop, where some buildings are still in use. The finest building at the lower site was formerly the mine superintendent's home, moved down from the mountainside in three parts.

A sunny spring morning ride in Whitetail Creek Canyon on the eastern flank of the Chiricahua Mountains.

General location: Chiricahua Mountains, extreme southeastern Arizona, Coronado National Forest.

Elevation change: The Whitetail Creek Road, or Forest Service Road 356, begins at an elevation of approximately 4,694' above sea level. The short spur road, which takes you to the ghost town of Hilltop (elevation 5,600'), leaves to the left at an elevation of 5,250'. The jeep road is shown on topographical maps dated 1964 and reaches an altitude of 5,400'. More modern maps show the road continuing up to an elevation high of 6,083'. Elevation gain is 1,389'.

Season: Good weather for riding persists almost year-round in these mountains. Summers can be hot, in the mid-90s, so desert-riding precautions should be taken. Winters can be cold enough to warrant a pair of fingered gloves and a warm pair of tights. Snow can close this road at higher elevations from December through March.

Services: Accommodations and water are available in Portal, but that's about it. Accommodations, gas, and groceries are available 26 miles southeast in Sunizona, at the junction of AZ 181 and US 666. All biking needs will have to be addressed in Tucson before you come this way.

Hazards: All the hazards of riding in a desert wilderness setting are present.

Rescue index: This is remote country. In the event you need help you should try flagging down a vehicle, or contact the Park Service headquarters at Chiricahua National Monument.

Land status: Coronado National Forest.

Maps: The Chiricahua, Peloncillo and Dragoon Mountain Ranges map of the Coronado National Forest. The USGS 7.5 minute quads are Chiricahua Peak, Cochise Head, Portal, and Blue Mountain.

Finding the trail: To get to the main road that reaches the east side of the range, and the towns of Paradise and Portal, take I-10 heading east from Tucson. About 3 miles past the town of San Simon you will take Exit 382 heading due south. You will continue on this road for approximately 17 miles, at which point you should look for signs to Whitetail Canyon and a road heading off to your right. This is FS 356. Park at this intersection and begin your ride.

Sources of additional information: The Coronado National Forest address is listed in the introduction to this section.

Notes on the trail: The road climbs gradually, gaining a little less than a thousand feet in 7 miles. Where FS 356 heads south, however, it gets quite steep and is difficult riding. Portions of this steep section may have to be pushed. Return the way you came.

The Whitetail Canyon Road is shown as a four-wheel-drive road until it meets the monument boundary, at which point it turns into a single-track trail. In less than a mile this trail meets the Bonita Canyon scenic drive inside the monument, which takes you down to the Visitor Center. Please remember that bikes are not permitted to ride off the main road in the monument.

This next option takes you from the east side of the range to the west, and you'll need to arrange for a shuttle or have a car meet you on the other side. Less than one-half mile before Whitetail Canyon Road meets the monument boundary, FS 356 takes a sharp turn left and heads due south. This is a steep, very rocky jeep trail that takes you up over Hands Pass, to an elevation of 6,650'. This is the old road to the town of Hilltop; only 2 small rickety shacks remain but rubble and foundations abound. As you begin to descend you will also pass the old Silver Prince Mine, and then will drop into Pinery Canyon onto FS 42. Ride out on this road to meet your shuttle.

RIDE 22 *SILVER PEAK LOOP*

This loop is about 15 miles long and should take riders of beginning-to-intermediate skill and fitness levels some three to four hours to complete. The route consists of almost 11 miles of well-maintained bladed dirt roads and a little over four miles of paved surfaces.

While this ride is somewhat civilized, the scenery is terrific. Tours of the small

RIDE 22 *SILVER PEAK LOOP*

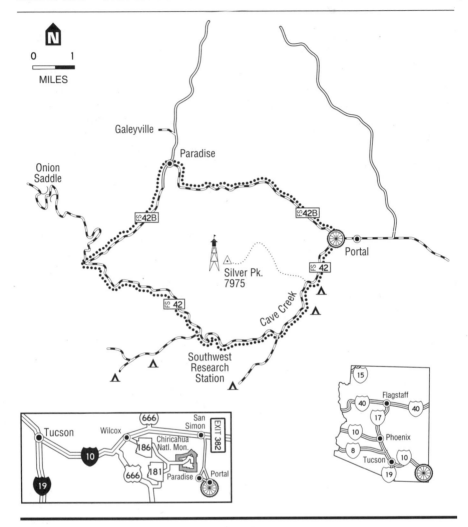

semi-ghost towns of Paradise and Portal are included, as well as the beautiful Cave Creek Canyon. And you'll be riding around Silver Peak Mountain (elevation 7,975 feet). You will also have the opportunity to stop in at the American Museum of Natural History's Southwestern Research Station, just across the road from where FS 42 turns to dirt and starts heading uphill in a northwesterly direction. These folks are friendly and will be happy to field any questions and observations you have gathered concerning the animal life in the area.

Cave Creek Canyon is a deep, shadowy canyon that exhibits many fantastic rock formations, which characterize this range. It's fun too, to tour these little towns that have been able to eke out an existence here for so long. This is a good ride, so enjoy!

General location: East slope of the Chiricahua Mountains, in extreme southeastern Arizona, Coronado National Forest.

Elevation change: Your elevation at the town of Portal is 4,800' above sea level. At the Southwestern Research Station your elevation will be 5,400'. At the intersection with FS 42B your elevation will be 6,400'. You will then descend to the town of Paradise at 5,500', returning back to Portal at 4,800'. Elevation gain for this ride is 1,600'.

Season: Good weather for riding persists almost year-round. Summers can be hot, in the mid-90s, so desert riding precautions should be taken. Winters can be cold enough to warrant a pair of fingered gloves and a warm pair of tights. Snow can close the roads at higher elevations from December through March.

Services: Limited services—water and accommodations only—are available in Portal and Paradise. Gas is available in San Simon on I-10. Accommodations, gas, and groceries are available 26 miles southeast in Sunizona, at the junction of AZ 181 and US 666. Bike services are far away in Tucson, so come prepared.

Hazards: Car traffic is something to be aware of here, especially on the paved portion of this route through Cave Creek Canyon. All the precautions of riding in a desert environment need to be taken.

Rescue index: Help and a phone can be found not too far away at either Portal, Paradise, or the Southwest Research Station.

Land status: Coronado National Forest.

Maps: The Chiricahua, Peloncillo and Dragoon Mountain Ranges map of the Coronado National Forest. The USGS 7.5 minute quads are Portal and Rustler Park.

Finding the trail: To get to the main road that reaches the east side of the range, and the towns of Paradise and Portal, take I-10 heading east from Tucson. About 3 miles past the town of San Simon you will take Exit 382 heading due south. Continue heading south for 17 miles, at which point you will come to an intersection. Bear left to the town of Portal, where you can park on Main Street and begin your ride.

Sources of additional information: The Coronado National Forest address is listed in the introduction to this section.

Notes on the trail: From Portal take the main road heading southwest up Cave Creek Canyon, directly across from the Southwestern Research Station. This is FS 42 which heads northwest. Continue heading uphill for 4 miles until you reach FS 42B, which turns downhill heading northeast and will take you to the town of Paradise. At the end of the town of Paradise, as you are heading north, FS 42B takes a sharp turn to the right. Follow that turn and you will arrive back in the town of Portal in 5 miles.

There are a couple of short options that only add a few miles to your total distance and are worth checking out. You may want to continue up the paved section of this ride, depending on which direction you are riding this loop, or take a right at the bottom of FS 42. This will take you another mile and a half up to the John Hands and Herb Martyr Campgrounds, and allow you to take in more of this beautiful canyon.

You are probably going to want to check out the ghost town of Galeyville, less than a mile north of the town of Paradise on the left side of the road. While there is not much left but foundations at this site, it has a wild history. The Texas Mine and Smelter was opened up in Galeyville in 1881, but was only in operation for 2 years when it was dismantled and taken to be used at a site in Benson over 90 miles away. The buildings that remained became the refuge for outlaws in the area. Curly Bill Brocius and Johnny Ringo ran a cattle rustling operation in the area for many years. Later, to prevent further habitation by the wrong sort, the remaining buildings were removed to Paradise.

Prescott Area Rides

The town of Prescott is just over one hundred miles north, and slightly west, of Arizona's capital city of Phoenix. Snuggled in amongst the Bradshaw Mountains, at an elevation of 5,347 feet, this area is high enough to enjoy a full spectrum of seasons. The small, quiet town of Prescott and surrounding mountains have long been a favorite summer getaway for those seeking to escape the heat of the Sonoran Desert to the south. Almost pure ponderosa pine forests thrive in these dry, sandy hills, scenting the air and providing precious shade for sun-weary summer vacationers.

The Arizona Territory's very first governor, John Goodwin, arrived in 1863 in what would become the town of Prescott, to set up the affairs of the territory. The site was chosen because it was in the most timber- and mineral-rich region of the country. The ponderosa pines covering these hills provided the materials for frame buildings and log cabins, unlike the adobe houses that settlers had to adapt to in the south. But water from the Salt River, the coming of the railroad, and the resultant rapid growth soon gave Phoenix the political and economic might to wrest capital city status from Prescott. Phoenix was established as the territory's capital in 1889, 23 years before Arizona became a state.

Prescott was firmly established by this time, however, and with the discovery of gold nearby the town grew rapidly in the years before the turn of the century. The Yavapai and Tonto Apache Indians did not make it easy for these new settlers and fortune seekers, but the lure of gold for some, and a new home for others, made the whites persistent. The gold rush in these hills was huge, and permanently established the region, though there is little mining activity here today. These hardy miners left behind an extensive network of roads, numerous ghost towns, and hills honeycombed with shafts and tunnels. The Sharlot Hall Museum in Prescott is made up of several original buildings from this period, and has some interesting displays which give excellent insight into the history of this area.

This mountainous mid-section of Arizona is commonly referred to, in geologic terms, as the central highlands of the state. The geologic events that created the rich deposits of minerals in the mountains surrounding Prescott were a series of granitic intrusions. Minerals were sorted in response to pressure and heat at the margins of these intrusions, and along the dikes and veins that entered already solid rock, forcing them to cool at a rapid rate. Some greyish basalt lava overlies the granite core of these mountains in many places, but for the most part the core of the Bradshaws is granite. Throughout these hills it is common to find boulders that have weathered out of the granite, due to vertical jointing, which now exist as sculpted blocks and strange pillar formations. A product of this weathering process is an extremely coarse variety of grey, sandy soil, which is indigenous to the Bradshaw Mountains. While it can compact to create a nice, hard riding surface, it tends to remain loose and erodes easily on steeper slopes.

The Prescott area has a number of nearby creeks and lakes that provide recreation and drinking water for the town's inhabitants. The streams and dense ponderosa forests surrounding the town also support populations of white-tailed deer, desert mule deer, pronghorn antelope, and in the more remote parts of the Bradshaws, black bear and mountain lion. This is a favorite climate for rattlesnakes, which like to come out to warm themselves in the morning sun, but will retreat to burrows once the day warms up. Gambel oak can be found in abundance in these hills, and is often accompanied by a thick underbrush of almost impenetrable chapparal and manzanita.

This is a charming town in a beautiful location full of friendly, outdoorsy folks. Prescott is home to several colleges which help support two full-service bike shops complete with knowledgeable people to help you out. Prescott College, a four-year liberal arts college with an emphasis on outdoor leadership, also makes its home here. Following are a few information sources you might want before you hit the trail.

The Prescott Chamber of Commerce
Box 1147
Prescott, Arizona 86302
(602) 445-2000

Prescott National Forest
Supervisor's Office
344 South Cortez Street
Prescott, Arizona 86303
(602) 445-1762

Prescott National Forest
Bradshaw Ranger District
2230 East Highway 69
Prescott, Arizona 86301
(602) 445-7253

Bikesmith
320 East Sheldon Street
Prescott, Arizona 86301
(602) 445-0280

High Gear Bike Shop
1060 Iron Springs Road
Prescott, Arizona 86301
(602) 445-0636

RIDE 23   *THUMB BUTTE LOOP*

This loop is an easy ride for bikers of beginning-to-intermediate riding and fitness levels, and should take only two to three hours to complete. The route gives a total distance of ten miles, and follows both paved and bladed dirt roads.

The mountains you'll be pedaling are small and compact, and are thickly forested with ponderosa pine. Short steep climbs and descents on sandy dirt roads characterize a lot of the riding in this area. Brief views of distant peaks and ridges come occasionally through the trees at high points, before you dive into the shade of tight, winding canyons. This ride is a good introduction to the area. Thumb Butte is one of the most distinct landmarks around, and can be seen from town. This ride also takes you to one of the best views of the surrounding Bradshaw and Sierra Prieta Mountains. The valley below you, as you look west, is known as the Copper Basin.

General location: Just west of Prescott, Arizona.

Elevation change: Your starting point for this ride, in the town of Prescott, is 5,347'. From there you will climb gradually at first, and then more steeply. You will reach a high elevation of 6,900' at the Sierra Prieta Overlook. Elevation gain is 2,353'.

Season: Prescott has an ideal climate for riding year-round. Average daytime highs in July reach 90 degrees, while January's average highs are in the low 50s. At this elevation you are probably not going to run into any great snow accumulations, but you will more than likely run into some pretty hot temperatures during summer months. You are still riding in the desert and all desert riding precautions should be taken.

Services: All services are available in Prescott.

Hazards: You'll need to watch the car traffic on this road, as this is a favored route for sightseers and they won't be watching for you.

It can be really dry, hot, and dusty back in these hills, so be prepared. Carry lots of water, drink more than you think you need, and don't let thirst regulate your liquid intake. Be ready for quickly changing weather and temperatures if thunderstorms are forecast.

A century of mining and logging in this area has left a maze of roads. I strongly recommend equipping yourself with Forest Service or topo maps (or both) for riding in these hills. Supplemental maps will provide information about the area, and will prevent time-consuming mistakes.

Rescue index: You are close to town on this ride, and this route gets a fair amount of car traffic. You won't be far from help on this one.

Land status: Prescott National Forest.

Maps: Prescott National Forest map. The USGS 15 minute and 7.5 minute quad is Iron Springs.

RIDE 23 *THUMB BUTTE LOOP*

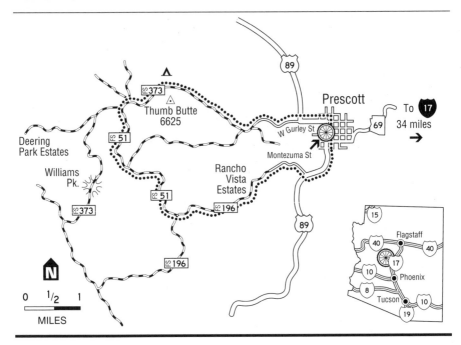

Finding the trail: You will want to leave your car close to the intersection of Gurley and Montezuma Streets for this ride. You'll begin this ride by heading west on West Gurley Street, which will take you out of town and eventually turn into Thumb Butte Road. This road will change to dirt at Thumb Butte Park, and become Forest Service Road 373.

Sources of additional information: The Prescott National Forest address is listed in the introduction to this section.

Notes on the trail: Just over a mile onto this dirt road there will be an intersection; go left, heading south. This is FS 51. The main road continues straight and will take you to a housing development called Deering Park Estates. If you get to this point you have missed your turn. Continue heading south until you reach FS 196, on which you will need to take another left. This road heads back downhill, past the Rancho Vista Estates, and will turn into Copper Basin Road. This road then turns into White Spar Road as you enter town. White Spar Road becomes Montezuma Street, which intersects Gurley Street at the point where you left your car.

There are literally thousands of options here. Many, many roads in all directions can make any ride longer, shorter, steeper. . . . You will need to supplement this information with extra maps if you are interested in doing any exploring.

RIDE 24 *GROOM CREEK / SPRUCE MOUNTAIN LOOP*

This loop ride has two options for a starting point. You can begin from town, which will give you a distance of 17 miles, or you can start at the community of Groom Creek, which will shorten the mileage to nine miles. This is a moderate-to-difficult ride for bikers at an intermediate fitness and skill level. Allow three hours' riding time if you are starting from Groom Creek, more if you are starting from town. This route covers a little bit of every kind of trail surface, including pavement, hard-packed dirt roads, and single-track. Sections of this ride can get pretty steep and rocky.

Good views of these rolling, pine-covered hills abound from Spruce Mountain. To the north you can see the town of Prescott and the Chino Valley. To the south stretches the spine of the Bradshaw Mountains. The 360-degree views from atop Spruce Mountain are well worth the effort it takes to get there.

The single-track descent on this ride can be kind of wild, but is a lot of fun. Don't forget your helmet—and have a blast!

General location: Four miles south of Prescott, Arizona.

Elevation change: From where this ride begins, at the settlement of Groom Creek, your elevation is 6,300' above sea level. From there you will begin to climb steadily, and at a substantial grade, to reach a high elevation (in just over 3 miles) of 7,600'. Elevation gain is 1,300'. You will add almost exactly another 1,000' of elevation if you are starting this ride from the town of Prescott.

Season: Prescott has an almost ideal climate for mountain biking year-round. At the top of Spruce Mountain you might find snow in the winter, but in the summer you will be coping with some pretty hot temperatures. You are still riding in the desert and all desert-riding precautions should be taken.

Services: All services are available in Prescott.

Hazards: You do not want to be on the top of Spruce Mountain in the late afternoon if thunderstorms are predicted, so plan accordingly. Weather can change fast up here; carry a shell on this ride. Some of this downhill single-track gets pretty hairy, so check your speed and tighten the chin strap on your helmet!

There are a number of camps in the area that use these trails for horseback rides. Keep an eye out for equestrians and give them a wide berth if you come upon them, especially if they're children.

Rescue index: This route does not take you too far from help. Find the ranger at the Groom Creek Ranger Station in the event of an emergency, or get out to the main road.

RIDE 24 *GROOM CREEK / SPRUCE MOUNTAIN LOOP*

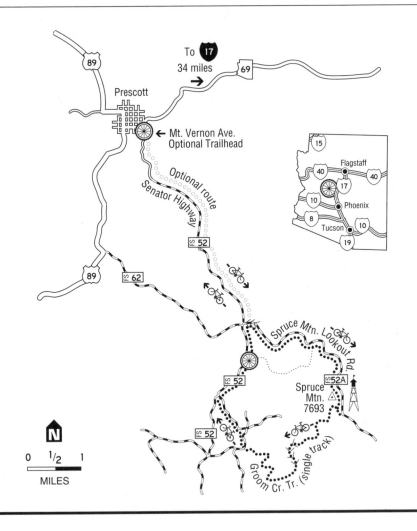

Land status: Prescott National Forest.

Maps: Prescott National Forest, and the USGS 7.5 minute quad for Groom Creek.

Finding the trail: From downtown Prescott take Mt. Vernon Avenue heading south. This road turns into what is known as Senator Highway. Continue heading south on Senator Highway (Forest Service Road 52), for approximately 5

Riding through dense stands of ponderosa pine just outside Prescott, Arizona.

miles, until you reach the community of Groom Creek. Park off the road and out of the way near the ranger station.

Sources of additional information: The Prescott National Forest address is listed in the introduction to this section.

Notes on the trail: Ride north approximately .6 miles to where FS 52A takes off on the right side of the road. This road leaves from the intersection with FS 62. This is Spruce Mountain Lookout Road. You will follow this road to the top of Spruce Mountain, unless you have chosen to ride up the single-track. At the top of Spruce Mountain you will find the Groom Creek Trail coming up the west side of the mountain, and going down the ridge heading south. This trail is marked by the Forest Service as Trail #307. Take either route back down; the trail heading south is longer and more fun heading downhill. When you reach the main road, go right back to Groom Creek and your car.

Once again there are many, many options here, too many to include. This ride can be ridden from town, which will increase your elevation gain substantially.

RIDE 25 *WOLF CREEK LOOP*

This ride is a 12-mile loop that covers 4 miles of pavement and 8 miles of bladed dirt roads. This is an easy-to-moderate ride for beginning-to-intermediate bikers in good physical condition. For most cyclists this ride will take about 2 hours to complete.

This is classic, rolling, central highlands country. Coarse, grayish, sandy soils nurture deep woods of ponderosa pine, whose needles carpet the forest floor and send their sweet scent into the air. Glimpses through the branches reveal shadowy-blue mountain silhouettes outlined in the distance. This is another great ride close to town. These roads take some fun rolls and turns through tight canyons and big trees. Keep up your speed and watch for cars.

General location: South of Prescott 1.2 miles, in the Prescott National Forest.
Elevation change: From where you start this ride, in downtown Prescott, your elevation is 5,347' above sea level. From there you will climb, riding this loop in a counterclockwise direction, reaching a high elevation of approximately 6,300' at the intersection of Wolf Creek Road and Senator Highway. Elevation gain is 953'.
Season: Great temperatures for riding persist almost year-round. Summers can be hot. All desert riding precautions should be taken.
Services: All services are available in Prescott.
Hazards: Watch for cars and activity along these roads. You'll be riding by the summer community of Ponderosa Park, and there will be a lot of folks camping who came up to escape the heat. Be especially careful when riding the pavement out of town on AZ 89.

There will also at times be a fair amount of equestrian traffic along this route. While they do most of their riding on the trails in the area, they occasionally can be found in groups crossing or making their way on the roads. Be polite and let them know you're there well ahead of time. Take extra care if they are children.
Rescue index: You are close to town on this ride, and this route gets a fair amount of car traffic. You won't be far from help.
Land status: Prescott National Forest.
Maps: Prescott National Forest map, and the USGS 7.5 minute quads for Groom Creek and Wilhoit.
Finding the trail: To begin this ride you will want to leave your car in town; somewhere on Gurley near Montezuma Street is best. On your bike you will

RIDE 25 *WOLF CREEK LOOP*

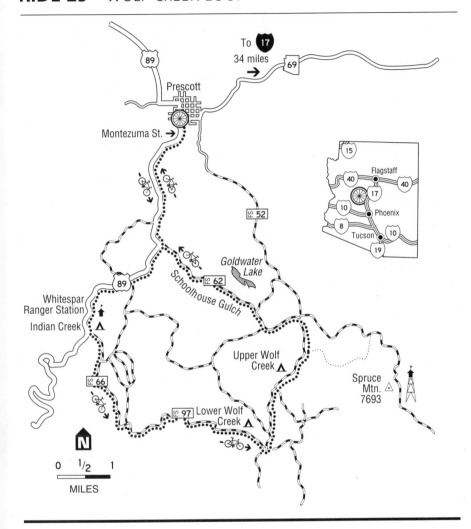

head south out of town on Montezuma Street, which turns into White Spar Road (AZ 89).

Sources of additional information: The Prescott National Forest address is listed in the introduction to this section.

Notes on the trail: You will proceed uphill on AZ 89 for approximately 4.2 miles, until you reach signs for Ponderosa Park and Indian Creek Campground.

Time out to enjoy late afternoon sunlight—on the trail in the Bradshaw Mountains of central Arizona.

There will also be signs for Forest Service Road 97; take this road. The FS Road designations are confusing here. FS 97 takes you into Ponderosa Park, but you want instead to take FS 66 that simply bypasses it. Continue on FS 97 when it joins the road again, following signs for Lower Wolf Creek and Upper Wolf Creek Campgrounds. You are heading almost due east at this point and will eventually intersect Senator Highway. You will then take Senator Highway for just over 2 miles to FS 62, which takes off from the left side of the road. This road will take you through some of the cabins of the Groom Creek community. Continue in a northwest direction through an area known as School House Gulch. This road will end at the White Spar Campground on AZ 89, which will take you back into town to your car.

There are many, many options for riding in this area. Supplementary Forest Service and topographical maps are a must if you plan to do any exploring.

RIDE 26 *MOUNT UNION / YANKEE DOODLE TRAIL*

This ride is a 15.5-mile loop that will be moderate to difficult for experienced and intermediate riders in good physical condition. For most, this ride will take four hours to complete. Surfaces you will encounter on this ride include bladed, hard-packed, and four-wheel-drive dirt roads. There is also a great section of single-track on this ride.

And the scenery is fantastic! The views are wonderful from Mount Union, one of the highest peaks in the area (7,979 feet). Mount Tritle rises to the west at 7,782 feet, and Moscow Peak rises to the south at 7,721 feet. Yankee Doodle Peak stands behind it.

The Yankee Doodle Trail is sure to provide some excitement for those who love a technical downhill single-track.

Don't miss the old Palace Station House about a mile after you meet the Senator Highway at the Orofino Mine. This beautiful hand-hewn cabin was built in 1874 as a homestead and rest stop for travelers taking the stagecoach between Phoenix and Prescott. It was in service until 1910, and is used and maintained today by Forest Service employees.

General location: South of Prescott, Arizona.

Elevation change: You begin this ride at the intersection of Forest Service Road 97 (the Wolf Creek Road) and Senator Highway (FS 52), where Senator Highway turns to dirt. Your elevation at this point is approximately 6,300' above sea level. From there you will begin to climb. At the intersection of Senator Highway and Mount Union Lookout Road you will have reached an elevation of 7,200'. To the top of Mount Union it is another 780', where you will reach the elevation of 7,979'. You will then descend to an elevation of 5,856' at the point of the Palace Station House on Senator Highway. You will climb back to an elevation of 7,200' to the spot where Mount Union Road left Senator Highway. From here it is downhill to your starting elevation. Total elevation gain is 3,010'.

Season: Almost any time is good riding weather in this part of the country. Summers can be quite hot and you may find snow on Mount Union in the winter. Plan accordingly.

Services: All services are available in Prescott.

Hazards: This ride involves some serious climbing that will have even experienced riders who are in good shape huffing and puffing. The Yankee Doodle Trail single-track is extremely technical in spots; don't try this without a helmet.

Watch for vehicular traffic on the Senator Highway. You may also run into horse traffic on this trail.

You need to be careful not to end up on the top of Mount Union in the afternoon if thunderstorms are predicted. Get an early start if there is any chance at all for lightning storms.

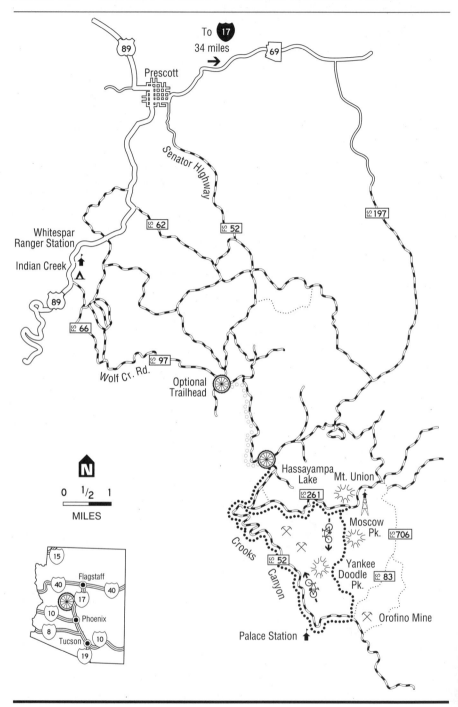

To 🛡17
34 miles
→

89

69

FS 197

Prescott

Senator Highway

FS 62

FS 52

Whitespar
Ranger Station

Indian Creek

89

FS 66

Wolf Cr. Rd.

FS 97

Optional
Trailhead

N

0   1/2   1
MILES

Hassayampa
Lake   Mt. Union

FS 261

Moscow
Pk.   FS 706

Crooks Canyon

FS 52

Yankee
Doodle   FS 83
Pk.

Palace Station

Orofino Mine

15

Flagstaff

40

40

40

17

10

Phoenix

8

Tucson

10

19

Made it to the top! Friendly riders who met on the trail pose for a photo.

Rescue index: This ride is slightly more remote than others listed in this section. Your best bet for finding immediate help is on Senator Highway or at the ranger station at Palace Station.

Land status: Prescott National Forest.

Maps: The Prescott National Forest map, and the USGS 7.5 minute quad for Groom Creek.

Finding the trail: From the town of Prescott, drive south on Mt. Vernon Road. This road eventually turns into Senator Highway (FS 52). Continue heading south on Senator Highway until you reach the intersection with Wolf Creek Road, listed as FS 97. This is the point at which Senator Highway turns to dirt, and is an optional starting point for this ride. Continue another 3 miles south on Senator Highway to the intersection with FS 197 at Hassayampa Lake, to begin from a closer starting point. Park here, off the road.

Sources of additional information: The Prescott National Forest address is listed in the introduction to this section.

Notes on the trail: Once on your bike you will continue heading south for approximately 1.5 miles to FS 261, which is also the Mount Union Lookout Road. Go left onto Mount Union Lookout Road and start climbing. To get to the lookout you will need to take a spur road that is well marked. When you come back down from the lookout go left onto the road you came up on. This road traverses the southern side of Mount Union. At the point that this road begins to drop down, look for the Yankee Doodle Trail which will leave from the right side of the road; it will be marked. You will follow this single-track down until you reach the Orofino Mine. Go right, back onto Senator Highway, and begin climbing up Crooks Canyon, back to the point where you left Mount Union Road. Continue riding north, heading downhill, to the point where you left your car.

You definitely want to ride this route in a clockwise direction. Riding up the Yankee Doodle Trail is not recommended. You may want to drive down Senator Highway to the intersection with Mount Union Road to shorten this ride.

RIDE 27 *CROWN KING GHOST TOWNS RIDE*

This is a ride that goes from the town of Prescott to the settlement at Crown King, for a total one-way distance of 53 miles. Riding the whole thing in a single day is not really an option for most, but the route is offered instead as an opportunity to do an overnight trip with panniers, or a shuttle, or to do it as a supported ride. A one-way trip along this route will take bikers of intermediate riding ability in good physical condition at least six hours to complete. This ride can be made easy for those doing a vehicular support trip. The surfaces you will encounter include maintained hardpack and four-wheel-drive dirt roads with several rough and rocky sections. Some sections of this route may also be washboarded.

Many options are possible here. You may want to ride Senator Highway out one way and then continue your trip elsewhere. You may want to ride out to the highway and drive back to Prescott, or make a loop up to Mayer and work your way back to Prescott through the mountains on Forest Service roads. Senator Highway is maintained but can be pretty brutal on passenger cars. A four-wheel-drive, high-clearance vehicle is best for exploring in these mountains.

This rough-and-tumble country is easy to view and to access by Senator Highway, a historic route that was traveled for almost a century by anyone moving between Phoenix and Prescott. Senator Highway, which is the route that this ride follows, parallels the spine of the Bradshaw Mountains. The road follows canyons and drainages as it takes you south, and then ascends over several ridges before turning east and heading out to highway AZ 69. These tightly knit mountains and canyons are heavily wooded with ponderosa, which give way intermittently to piñon and juniper stands. You will see deciduous trees lining the drainages, their long roots reaching down to find whatever scant water is available. The lower foothills of these mountains are covered by yucca, chaparral, and desert scrub, which give the landscape a drier, more foreboding face.

The historical significance of the route itself, as well as the ghost towns scattered along the way, make this ride a unique journey into the past. You can imagine travelers on the stagecoach, and settlers hauling mountains of belong-

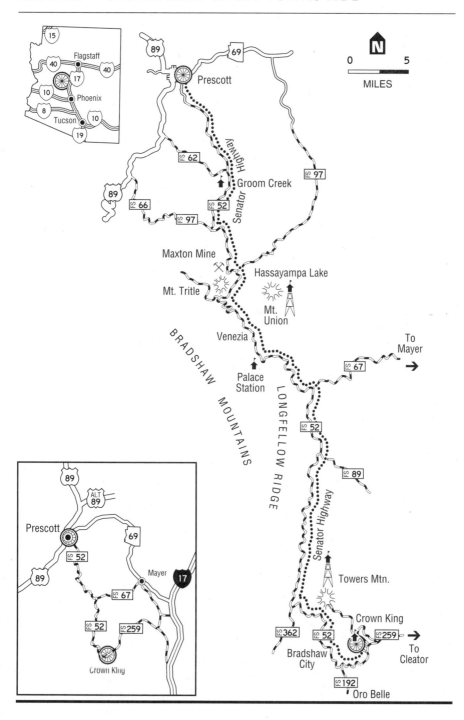

ings up and down the many switchbacks of this route. Through shimmering heat they toiled, hot and dusty, on their way to bustling frontier towns.

Along this route you will find the ruins of the Maxton Mine and the town of Venezia, the beautiful old Palace Station rest stop, and the ghost towns of Bradshaw City, Crown King, and Cleator. Crown King actually survives as a small vacation community. Bradshaw City is marked by only a sign, and the interesting town of Oro Belle lies just five miles southwest of Crown King. The town of Mayer still supports a seasonal population, but is still an interesting ghost town. Several buildings, including the White House Hotel, the Mayer Hotel, and a brothel dating from the 1880s, remain to remind us of this area's colorful past.

Across the drainage from Senator Highway you can see the mine entrance and remnants of mining activity at the Maxton Mine, 4.5 miles south of Groom Creek. The stairs and foundation of the general store and post office, which serviced the miners of this area, can be seen another half mile south of here. Not much remains of the town of Venezia, but the old Palace Station still stands as it did when it serviced travelers on the stagecoach between Prescott and Phoenix. The old building has survived due to the efforts of the Forest Service, which also maintains the small cemetery nearby.

In Crown King, the general store and saloon, which have been in business for almost a century, are the principal attraction. The old schoolhouse is also a favorite of sightseers. The mine that fueled this community was originally thought to house one of the biggest and richest strikes found in these hills during the frenzy of ore discovery in the Bradshaws. The mine was established in 1870, and eventually produced over $1.5 million worth of gold. Five hundred buildings once existed in the town of Crown King, which survived long enough to see electricity and phone service. But by the turn of the century profits from mining were on the decline, and the town became the semideserted seasonal community it is today.

The ghost town of Cleator, which came to life as Turkey Creek Station in 1864, remains as one of the oldest settlements in this area. The road between Cleator and Crown King was originally a railroad bed built by Chinese laborers, as were the connecting roads to Mayer and Prescott. All were completed near the turn of the century.

This is a top-notch mountain bike adventure not to be missed by those who are willing to go a little out of their way.

General location: South of Prescott, in the Bradshaw Mountains of Prescott National Forest.
Elevation change: At the town of Prescott, your elevation is 5,347' above sea level. From there you will be climbing for a while, then rolling up and down through pretty, hilly country. At the vacation settlement of Groom Creek the elevation is 6,300'. At the intersection with Wolf Creek Road, at Hassayampa Lake, the elevation is 6,700'. You will then climb over a pass to 7,000', before descending to 6,100' at Palace Station. This pass will be your highest point on

the ride. You'll then drop to a low of 5,400' at Barrel Spring. Hooper Saddle is 5,977', Bradshaw City is 6,400', the town of Crown King is 5,800', Juniper Ridge is 6,868', and Whiskey Spring, toward the very end of this ride, is 6,600'. Elevation gain over the entire 53 miles is close to 5,000'.

Season: Excellent conditions persist almost year-round for riding in these mountains, although you may find Senator Highway closed at certain times due to snow or flooding. Be sure to check with the Prescott National Forest people before heading out on this ride.

Services: All services are available in Prescott. Food, gas, and water are available in the town of Mayer.

Hazards: This is wilderness where water and food are not available for substantial distances. *Be prepared!* Make sure that you and your vehicle have more than enough fuel to run on, and that both are in good working condition.

While this road is maintained by the Forest Service, it is quite rough and rocky in places. This road is not recommended for passenger cars. Four-wheel-drive, high-clearance vehicles will fare the best.

The vehicular traffic on Senator Highway is something to be wary of; a bright piece of clothing will help alert motorists to your presence.

And remember, this is still the desert and it can get extremely hot in the summer months. Take all the necessary precautions.

Rescue index: While you are in pretty rugged country along this route, it is well traveled. Help can be found at any of the summer cabins along the way, or at the Groom Creek or Palace Station ranger stations.

Land status: Prescott National Forest.

Maps: Prescott National Forest map, and the USGS 7.5 minute quads for Prescott, Groom Creek, Battleship Butte, Battle Flat, Minnehaha, Crown King, and Poland Junction.

Finding the trail: From the town of Prescott take Mt. Vernon Road south. This turns into Senator Highway, or Forest Service Road 52.

Sources of additional information: The Prescott National Forest address is listed in the introduction to this section.

Notes on the trail: You will follow the Senator Highway road south for approximately 53 miles, to the intersection with FS 259. Take FS 259 to the settlement at Crown King. Give yourself some time here, for there are quite a few back streets to explore. Don't forget the mine and the cemetery. From Crown King you will continue on FS 259 up to Cleator. Just past Cleator, about one-half mile, you'll find FS 93 leaving on the left side of the road heading north. This road follows Mineral Creek, and will take you all the way to the town of Mayer. You may want to follow the alternate routes to Mayer and AZ 69.

There are several options here. Because of the distance from Prescott and the length of the route, a shuttle (where you are picked up in Crown King), or a supported ride (where you are followed by a vehicle), or an overnight trip (where you carry all the necessary camping equipment with you in panniers), is suggested.

The two main route options are a straight out-and-back to Crown King from Prescott along Senator Highway, or from Prescott to Crown King via FS 259, followed by a ride out to Mayer (on AZ 69), and finally back to Prescott. There are two ways to get to Mayer: you can take FS 93, which follows Mineral Creek and will take you all the way to Mayer, or you can continue on FS 259, which will take you to the old ghost town of Cordes, where an abandoned gas station is all that remains. From Cordes you can follow FS 259, which is the dirt road, back to Mayer, or take the improved gravel road 3 miles out to AZ 69.

There is excellent camping 6 miles southeast of Crown King in the Horse Thief Basin area, which is surrounded by the Castle Creek Wilderness.

Sedona Area Rides

The town of Sedona and the surrounding area is today one of Arizona's most unique and celebrated tourist destinations. Sedona is located just 116 miles north of Phoenix, and 28 miles south of Flagstaff. Set in beautiful Oak Creek Canyon, and surrounded by towering red rock walls and buttes, the remarkable natural beauty of this area first received national attention when it was discovered by Hollywood in the 1920s. Many early Western films were shot against the dramatic landscape of the Sedona area. The town of Sedona has since gained fame as a thriving artists' community and vacation spot. More recently, New Age spiritualists say they have identified several locations near town as the origin of mysterious energy vortexes. The town now draws a significant number of people seeking spiritual cleansing, enlightenment, and other types of health benefits supposedly made possible by the energy generated by these vortexes. It has not yet been determined if these vortexes make it easier when pedaling uphill.

Sedona is at the very comfortable elevation of 4,240 feet, where inhabitants are able to enjoy a full spectrum of seasons. Oak Creek is the crowning jewel of this breathtakingly beautiful area. This gurgling stream runs year-round, and has many deep, shady pools which offer welcome refreshment to dusty bikers after a hot ride. Any tour of Arizona would be incomplete without a few days spent exploring in and around the somewhat eccentric community of Sedona.

The area that is now Sedona was first visited by prehistoric hunting and gathering nomads. The Sinagua, an ancient tribe that flourished during the same time as the Hohokam and Anasazi civilizations, later moved into the area. They built cliff dwellings, made pottery, and decorated the canyon walls with intriguing figures and designs. As these people evolved into a more complex agricultural society, evidence suggests that they began to merge with the Hohokam. They began building similarly sophisticated pueblos along Oak Creek and the Verde River, where they farmed the soil for squash, corn, and beans. The ruins at Tuzigoot National Monument and at Verde Valley are all that remain of this culture, which reached its zenith somewhere around 1300 A.D. to 1400 A.D. Then, like their counterparts, the Anasazi in the north and the Hohokam in the south, they mysteriously disappeared. About this same time the Yavapai and Tonto Apache Indians migrated into the area and began to establish themselves through seasonal hunting and gathering practices. They were decimated by disease and army attacks until 1873, when they were finally driven out of the region by General George Crook and his troops.

The first white settlers did not arrive in the Sedona area until 1878. Fields were immediately plowed and planted with vegetables and fruit trees. Crops were nurtured, and they thrived with water from the dependable Oak Creek. Theodore Schnebly established a post office here in 1902, and named the town after his wife Sedona. That same year he built a road up to Mogollon Rim that would enable farmers to transport and sell their goods in Flagstaff, and thereby made timber from the plateau more accessible for building. This dirt road exists today much as it did then, and is called the Schnebly Hill Road.

Sedona remained an agricultural community until about 40 years ago, when the area began to gain a reputation for its fantastic natural beauty. Sedona's scenery soon began to draw both artists and tourists seeking to escape life in the big city. The New Age movement has flourished in Sedona since seven vortexes (psychic energy points) were supposedly discovered here in the early 1980s. The town now hosts a New Age center for learning, as well as several bookstores where more information can be found on the vortexes.

The Sedona area is also host to some incredible geology. The town lies at the base of the southern boundary of the Colorado Plateau, which in Arizona is called the Mogollon Rim (pronounced *Muggy*-own). The "rim" extends for some 200 miles across Arizona's midsection. It is very well defined in this area due to the hard basalt layer that caps the plateau, and once flowed as syrupy lava from extinct volcanoes near Flagstaff. This hard layer of basalt protects the softer sandstones below, and is what has allowed the deep and dramatic canyons, such as Oak Creek and Sycamore Canyon, to form here along the rim.

Faulting, uplifting, and wind and water erosion have all worked together to reveal the story in the rocks and the formations around Sedona. Layer upon layer of sandstone tell of epochs when shallow seas and river deltas washed over this land. The catalogue of rock reveals when these seas were interrupted by swirling sand dunes, which reclaimed the land only to be covered by encroaching seas once again. Below the basalt cap (600 feet thick in places) is the Moenkopi formation, then the Kaibab Limestone. The Kaibab Limestone was deposited by a shallow sea, and contains the fossilized skeletons of millions of prehistoric sea creatures. Below the Kaibab Limestone is the Coconino Sandstone, which is an aeolian or wind-deposited sandstone. The crosshatched pattern of this light blond stone is the key to its type of deposition. Below the Coconino Sandstone is the Schnebly Hill Formation, bisected by the Fort Apache Limestone, Hermit Shale, the Supai Group, and the Redwall Formation. All these layers are visible in Oak Creek Canyon and the Sedona area. The red color of the rock comes from a high amount of iron in the deposition material, which then bleeds downward to color the rock below.

Oak Creek is a green ribbon of life through this red desert country. The water that runs through Oak Creek Canyon year-round supports an enormous list of broad-leafed trees and shrubs, birds, mammals, reptiles and at least ten species of fish. The rim, some 2,000 feet above the elevation of Sedona, is thickly carpeted with forests of ponderosa pine. Ponderosa pine dominates the northern half of Arizona's Transition Zones. On the dry, higher slopes, a mixture of vegetation comprising what is commonly referred to as desert scrub can be found, including agave, yucca, cat-claw acacia, manzanita, mountain mahogany, and many types of cactus. In the lower rolling hills that surround Sedona, piñon and juniper dot the landscape. Some nine kinds of oak trees make their home in Oak Creek Canyon, as well as Arizona sycamore, black walnut, alder, narrow leaf, and Fremont cottonwoods.

The amount of bird life that frequents this area is astounding, as it is throughout southern Arizona. If you are a bird watcher, and even if you're not, this is a fantastic opportunity to do a little nature observation in a beautiful setting. The larger mammals that make their home in and around the canyon include white-tailed deer, mule deer, bighorn sheep, and mountain lion. The elk prefer the pine forests and cooler temperatures atop the rim. Black and even grizzly bear once lived in these canyons, but were eventually killed off by settlers. Black bear still roam the woodlands in the more remote parts of the San Francisco Peaks. Stewart Atchinson's *A Guide to Exploring Oak Creek and the Sedona Area* is an informative and interesting book that details the life, geology, and history of this area, and is well worth picking up while you are visiting.

Sedona is a great vacation spot and offers some high-quality mountain biking opportunities. There are a couple of bike shops in town that can address all your biking needs, and a healthy population of outdoors enthusiasts who are knowledgeable about their surroundings. Tourist traffic is heaviest in the spring and fall, but there are always plenty of places to escape the rush. If you are planning to stay in Sedona and would like accommodations in town, be sure to call well in advance of your visit. Hotels are usually booked up way ahead of time. Here are some addresses to help you plan your trip.

Sedona Chamber of Commerce
P.O. Box 478
Sedona, Arizona 86336
(602) 282-7722

Coconino National Forest
2323 East Greenlaw Lane
Flagstaff, Arizona 86004
(602) 527-3600

Coconino National Forest
Sedona Ranger District
P.O. Box 300
Sedona, Arizona 86336
(602) 282-4119

Loose Spoke Bike Shop
2885 West Highway 89A
Sedona, Arizona 86331
(602) 774-7428

RIDE 28 *SCHNEBLY HILL*

This ride is a moderately difficult out-and-back 23-mile adventure. It will take riders with beginning-to-intermediate riding skills, in good physical condition, about four hours to complete. This route follows the old Schnebly Hill Road, a hard-packed dirt road that can become rutted and washboarded in sections due to car traffic and water runoff.

Heading east out of Sedona up Bear Wallow Canyon, you will be surrounded by the spectacular colors and red rock formations that have made this area so popular. The Munds Mountain Wilderness Area boundary follows the Schnebly Hill Road to the south. To the north you will be looking at Mitten Ridge, which includes, from west to east, Thumb Butte, Teapot Rock, Technicolor Corner, and the Cow Pies. The scenery is fantastic; be sure to carry your camera along on this ride. Piñon, juniper, yucca, and prickly pear cacti dominate at the lower elevations, but eventually give way to ponderosa forests once you reach the rim.

The scenery is the highlight on this ride, and the views from Schnebly Hill Lookout let you take it all in. The views into Casner Canyon, Mitten Ridge, Damfino Canyon, the Crimson Cliffs, and Munds Mountain are breathtaking. This ride provides a good introduction to this area, for it gives you a bird's-eye view of Sedona and the surrounding area.

Also, don't miss the attractive ruins of the old resort, just beyond Foxboro Lake. The old carriage house is on the left side of the road, while the main building and swimming pool lie at the meadow's edge to the right. The open meadows and marshes of Clay Park are beautifully rimmed with deep, dark pine forests, and are worlds away from the red rock formations you left only a few miles behind you.

General location: West, just out of the town of Sedona.
Elevation change: At the mouth of Bear Wallow Canyon, which is the beginning of the Schnebly Hill Road, your elevation is approximately 4,280'. From here you will start climbing. At the Schnebly Hill Lookout Point you will have reached an elevation of 5,960'. Continuing west on Schnebly Hill Road you will reach a high elevation of 6,530' just before Foxboro Lake. You will drop only slightly (50 feet) at the point where Schnebly Hill Road meets I-17. Elevation gain is 2,250'.
Season: Within the 2,000 feet of elevation change between the town of Sedona and the Mogollon Rim there are several seasons and environments to be experienced. Summers are hot! In Sedona the temperatures regularly reach 100 degrees, and higher, from June through September. Temperatures atop the rim, however, are anywhere from 10 to 20 degrees cooler. In winter, the town of Sedona can occasionally get a dusting of snow. The rim gets more substantial amounts of

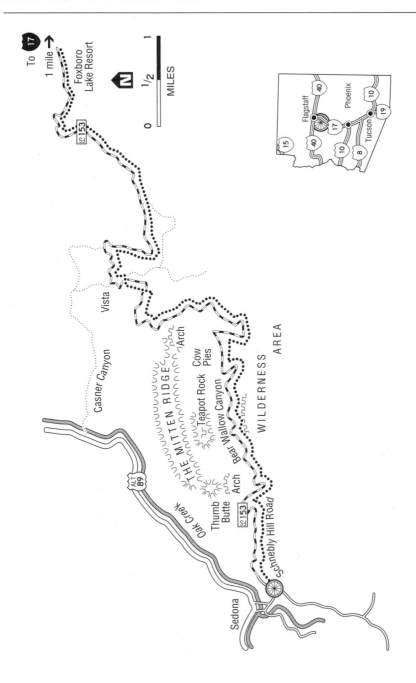

To 17

1 mile

Foxboro
Lake Resort

N

MILES

1

½

0

FR 153

Flagstaff

40

40

15

17

40

10

8

Phoenix

10

Tucson

19

Vista

Casner Canyon

THE MITTEN RIDGE

Arch

Teapot Rock

Cow
Pies

Bear Wallow Canyon

WILDERNESS   AREA

Thumb
Butte

Arch

FR 153

Schnebly Hill Road

ALT
89

Oak Creek

Sedona

The fabulous red rock formations of Mitten Ridge from the Schnebly Hill Road just outside Sedona, Arizona.

snowfall, which tend to stick around a lot longer. Snow can periodically make this road a mud bog. It is often closed to car traffic in winter. Be sure to check with the Coconino National Forest folks on the status of this road if you plan to ride up to the rim during the winter months.

Services: All services are available in Sedona.

Hazards: Vehicular traffic can be heavy on this road, so stay alert. A piece of bright clothing helps to make you more visible to motorists.

All desert riding precautions need to be taken here. Be aware of the mud in winter. It is sticky stuff and is not easy to clean from your bike parts.

Lightning is another hazard that should be considered, as you are quite exposed once you reach the rim.

Rescue index: This is a busy road and you are close to town. Help is not far away on this ride.

Land status: Coconino National Forest.

Maps: Coconino National Forest map. Also, the *Experience Sedona* map, published by Thorne Enterprises (this map can be found in most Sedona area bookstores or at the Sedona Chamber of Commerce). The USGS 7.5 minute quad is Munds Park.

Finding the trail: You will probably want to park in Sedona, or leave your car along the beginning of Schnebly Hill Road where it turns to dirt. Schnebly Hill

Road begins one-half mile after the "Y," heading south off AZ 179, on the left side of the road.

Sources of additional information: The Coconino National Forest address is listed in the introduction to this section.

Notes on the trail: You will ride Schnebly Hill Road, which climbs up the canyon and through several switchbacks, for about 4.5 miles to the lookout point. From here you will climb only slightly to your high elevation, while cruising through forests of ponderosa pines until you emerge into the open meadow of Clay Park, at the ruins of the old Foxboro Lake Resort. You will probably want to turn around here, or you can ride the extra 3 miles out to I-17. Return the way you came.

   Although I did not get a chance to try this option myself, several bikers I ran into mentioned that a loop can be made from the Schnebly Hill Lookout, then across and down Casner Canyon (the canyon draining to the west just below you from the lookout). This is a single-track that takes you out to US 89, the main road coming down Oak Creek Canyon from Flagstaff. The Casner Canyon Trail can actually be reached from two places: the first is a hiking trail that leaves directly from the lookout, the second a telephone line maintenance road that leaves the Schnebly Hill Road on the left side of the road in another one-half mile. The Casner Canyon Trail also follows the telephone line. Once you reach the bottom you will have to cross Oak Creek and then ride the 2.5 miles on the pavement back to Sedona. Bikers also mentioned that the Casner Canyon trail frequently is overgrown with spiny vegetation, so watch out.

RIDE 29   *JACK'S POINT*

This ride is a 12-mile loop that will take mountain bikers of intermediate ability and fitness about 3 hours to complete. This route follows hard-packed dirt road surfaces which are washboarded and rutted in sections. Part of this ride is also on rough and rocky four-wheel-drive jeep roads.

   You will be pedaling through widely spaced piñon and juniper in Bear Wallow Canyon, which begins to mix with ponderosa pine once you reach the rim. You'll then be traveling through the pines, across broken, rocky hills and grass-covered slopes atop the plateau. As you are climbing Schnebly Hill you'll be looking into the Munds Canyon Wilderness. Horse Mesa runs out to the south below Jacks Point, with Jacks Canyon and Woods Canyon flanking it on either side. The views are spectacular from up here! Look for the short spur trails out to Merry-go-round and Committee Lookout Points. Enjoy!

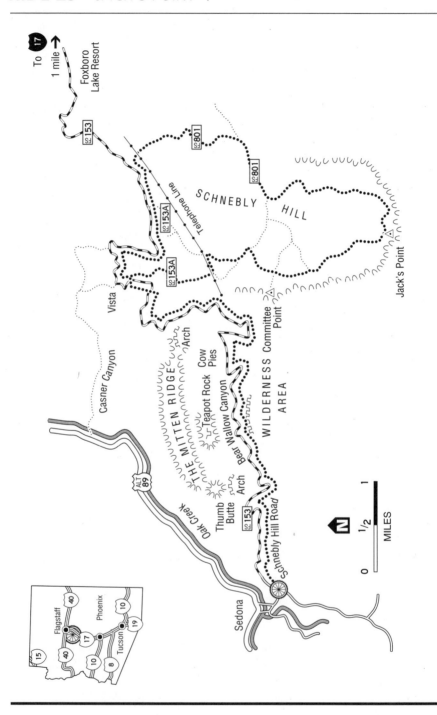

General location: East and south of Sedona.

Elevation change: At the mouth of Bear Wallow Canyon, at the beginning of Schnebly Hill Road, your elevation is approximately 4,280' above sea level. From there you will start climbing. At Schnebly Hill Lookout Point you'll have reached an elevation of 5,960'. You will then head south on Forest Service Road 153A, climbing steadily. Jacks Point Lookout is at an elevation of 6,400', but you will not reach your elevation high of approximately 6,600' until just before you drop back down to Schnebly Hill Road. Elevation gain is 2,320'.

Season: Spring and fall are best for riding in this area; summer can be hot and winter months can be muddy. The Schnebly Hill Road is closed to vehicular traffic in winter.

Services: All services are available in Sedona.

Hazards: Watch out for traffic on Schnebly Hill Road. Also, you are very exposed up here, so start early if thunder and lightning storms are forecasted. Be careful when close to the edge of the rim, for it is a precipitous drop-off. Dismount your bike well back from the edge of the cliffs. And if you must peer over, use caution!

Rescue index: Schnebly Hill is a busy road and you are close to town. Help is not far away on this ride.

Land status: Coconino National Forest.

Maps: Coconino National Forest map. Also, the *Experience Sedona* map, published by Thorne Enterprises (this map can be found in most Sedona area bookstores or at the Sedona Chamber of Commerce). The USGS 7.5 minute quads are Munds Park and Munds Mountain.

Finding the trail: You will probably want to park in Sedona, or leave your car along the beginning of the Schnebly Hill Road where it turns to dirt. The Schnebly Hill Road begins one-half mile after the "Y," heading south off AZ 179 on the left side of the road.

Sources of additional information: The Coconino National Forest address is listed in the introduction to this section.

Notes on the trail: Ride the Schnebly Hill Road, which climbs up the canyon and through several switchbacks for about 4.5 miles, to the lookout. Directly across Schnebly Hill Road from the lookout you will see a rocky road heading up over a hill; this is FS 153A. Take this road heading south; it will follow the edge of the rim, providing excellent views and offering short spurs out to lookouts along the way. Several of these spur roads turn into trails that head steeply downhill into a wilderness area; these are of course off-limits to mountain bikes. You will reach Jacks Point at the farthest point south. The road, which has really become an overgrown double-track, then turns around and heads north as FS 801. Follow FS 801 bearing right at the first fork, then left at the second, to climb up a small hill and descend back onto Schnebly Hill Road. Once again on the Schnebly Hill Road you will go left and back downhill, to where you left your car.

You may want to drive up to the Schnebly Hill Lookout and ride from there, if you are looking to cut out the climb and make it a shorter, easier ride.

RIDE 30 *TWIN BUTTES LOOP*

This short loop ride is a route designed more to get you out to play on the rocks than to cover a lot of distance. The route itself is about five miles long, and will take riders of an intermediate-to-advanced skill level, in good physical condition, two to three hours to complete. You will encounter all types of surfaces on this ride, including pavement, rough and rocky jeep roads, single-track, and slickrock.

Piñon, juniper and yucca dot the red sands around the bases of the fantastic formations of this ride. Riding up Morgan Road you will have Battlement Mesa on your right, and will be following part of the western boundary of the Munds Mountain Wilderness Area. The tight cluster of deep red spires you'll pass to your right is called the Devil's Kitchen. Farther ahead you will find yourself atop Submarine Rock. As you continue heading south, reaching the eastern end of Twin Buttes, you will be looking up at the Church Spires—Madonna and the Nuns.

This ride offers the unique opportunity of trying out your riding skills on slickrock. The rock's surface gives your tires excellent traction, which leaves you to test your strength, balance, and nerve. I encourage everyone to enjoy the red rocks of this incredible natural playground.

Take a minute to visit the Chapel of the Holy Cross. This is a striking monument to faith perched atop a sandstone ridge at the end of this ride.

General location: South of Sedona, Arizona.

Elevation change: At the point where Morgan Road leaves AZ 179 your elevation is approximately 4,200' above sea level. From there you will make a series of short climbs and descents, reaching a high point behind the Church Spires of 4,450'. Elevation gain is a modest 300'.

Season: Summers are hot at this elevation. But the rest of the year temperatures and conditions for riding are almost ideal.

Services: All services are available in Sedona.

Hazards: Watch out for the pink jeeps of Sedona Jeep Tours, for this is one of their favorite short trips. You will see them bouncing along, full of tourists, in many areas close to Sedona.

Slickrock can be tricky. It requires technical skill, strength, and steadiness. Start out slow and wear your helmet.

Rescue index: This route is close to town and is well traveled by Sedona Jeep

RIDE 30   *TWIN BUTTES LOOP*   97, Apr 6.

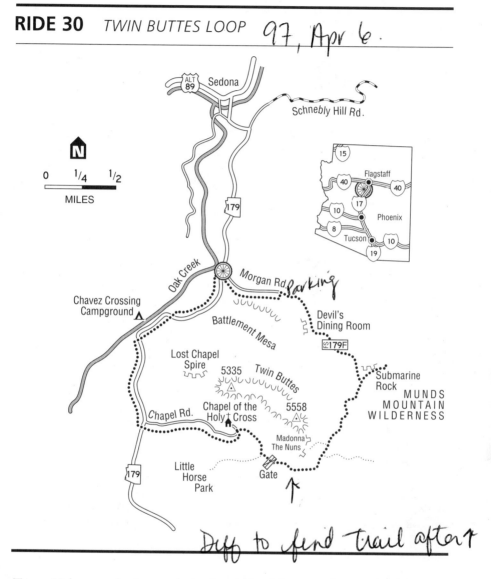

Diff to find trail at start

Tours. Help may also be sought in the residential area at the mouth of Morgan Canyon.

Land status: Coconino National Forest.

Maps: The *Experience Sedona* map, published by Thorne Enterprises (this map can be found in most Sedona area bookstores or at the Sedona Chamber of Commerce). The USGS 7.5 minute quads are Sedona and Munds Mountain.

Finding the trail: From Sedona take AZ 179 south from the "Y," which is the

The sculpted sandstone formations of the Sedona area make for some fantastic scenery, as well as challenging slickrock riding.

intersection of AZ 179 and US 89A. Continue south for just under a mile, where you'll find Morgan Road on the left. You can park along the road here, or proceed to where Morgan Road turns into dirt and park there.

Sources of additional information: The Coconino National Forest address is listed in the introduction to this section.

Notes on the trail: Begin riding by following the dirt jeep trail which leaves from Morgan Road in a southeasterly direction. Take the spur out to Submarine Rock, then continue heading south toward Twin Buttes. As you come around the southern slope of Twin Buttes there will be a hiking trail that takes off to the left on the far side of the drainage; don't follow it. Instead, stay on the right side of the drainage, following the southern slope of the buttes. You will come to a fence before dropping down around to Chapel Road. Go through it and shut it behind you. You will then need to follow the Chapel Road down to AZ 179, where you will go right and head back to Morgan Road where you left your car.

RIDE 31 *LOY BUTTE / RED CANYON RUINS RIDE*

This ride is an out-and-back with a spur, which gives a total distance of 20 miles. This route will take beginning-to-intermediate riders in good physical shape about three hours to pedal. The surfaces are hard-packed dirt roads that are washboarded and sometimes sandy in sections. The best way to get through those tough sandy stretches is to shift down, keep pedaling at a constant rate, and lighten up on your handlebars so your front tire won't dig in.

Instead of peering down on the desert below you, as you have on previous rides in this section, you will be lifting your eyes up to the beautiful textures and hues of the sandstone walls which rise overhead. This is one of the most well-defined sections of the Mogollon Rim. Rolling along through widely spaced piñon and juniper trees, you will be looking at the colorful buttes and spires of the Red Rock Secret Mountain Wilderness Area on your right.

The Indian ruins found at the back of the cavern in Red Canyon, and at the base of Loy Butte, are in fairly good condition. These stone houses were abandoned by the Sinagua people 500 to 700 years ago. Corn cobs, potsherds, and other artifacts can be seen lying in and about these ruins. It is important that we leave what clues to the past we find there for the next person to appreciate. Do not climb in, around, or on top of these ruins, as the walls are fragile and may collapse. The piles of rubble that surround these ruins are the debris left behind by marauding pot hunters.

Look high on the walls above the ruins at both sites, to see the symbols and figures with which these ancient peoples expressed themselves and perhaps signaled visitors. You will be a guest on private property when visiting both these ruins. Please be polite, leave your bike by the roadside, walk on the trails quietly, and do not disturb livestock.

General location: North and west of Sedona, Arizona.
Elevation change: At the point where the Dry Creek Road becomes the Boyton Pass Road, or Forest Service Road 152C, your elevation is approximately 4,450'. Where it turns to dirt your elevation is 4,500'. You will reach a high elevation crossing over Boyton Pass at an elevation of 4,650'. This ride rolls on from here with very slight changes in elevation. Elevation gain is 150'.
Season: Spring and fall are best for riding in this country, for it's hot out here in the summer. If it is dry, riding in the winter is fine, but if the ground is saturated the fine clays in the soil turn into a greasy mess. When mixed with water they turn practically to cement when dry. Trying to struggle through this type of mud, and then trying to clean it from your bike, is an exercise in frustration that will leave you cursing.
Services: All services are available in Sedona.

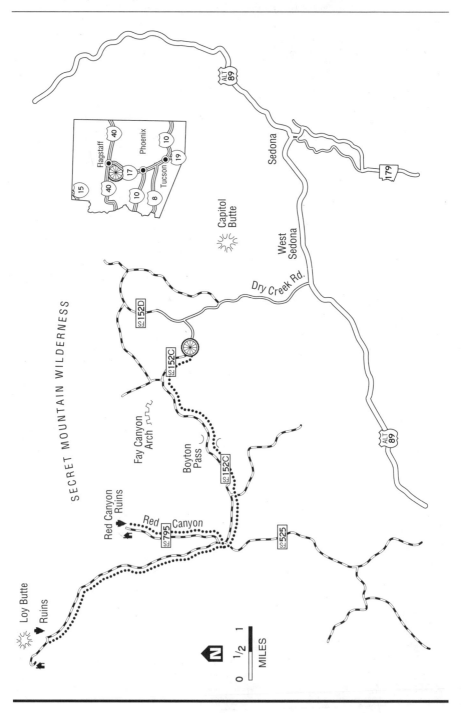

Wind and rain have created alcoves and overhangs in red rock walls around Sedona, hiding and protecting ruins like those found at Loy Butte and Red Canyon.

Hazards: Car traffic can be hazardous; be alert. It can be very hot and dry on this ride, so be sure to carry plenty of water and do not let thirst regulate your liquid intake.

Rescue index: The dirt roads of this ride are well traveled and there are private homes at the end. Help is never far away in this area.

Land status: Coconino National Forest.

Maps: Coconino National Forest map. The USGS 7.5 minute quads are Sedona and Loy Butte.

Finding the trail: From Sedona head west on US 89A to the Dry Creek Road, about 3 miles from the "Y." Go right onto Dry Creek Road and travel for approximately 2.8 miles until you come to a "T" intersection. Go left onto Boyton Pass Road or FS 152C; take it until the road turns to dirt. Park here.

Sources of additional information: The Coconino National Forest address is listed in the introduction to this section.

Notes on the trail: Start riding by following FS 152C to its conclusion at the intersection with FS 525. Go right on FS 525. In a quarter mile there will be a fork in the road. Bear right on FS 795 to reach Red Canyon. You will need to backtrack to this fork and then go left, back onto FS 525, to get out to Loy Butte. You will then reverse your direction, and go back the way you came to get back to your car.

RIDE 32 *COCKSCOMB LOOP*

This ride is a ten-mile loop that will be easy to moderate for riders of both begin-ning and intermediate riding ability and fitness. It will take most bikers two to three hours to complete this route. The ride follows hard-packed dirt jeep roads that are deeply rutted in spots. These deep ruts can be a real hazard. Check your speed and use caution.

Only a few widely spaced piñon and juniper trees live out on these desert flats. Beautiful clump grasses, yucca, and prickly pear cactus thrive, however, in the red desert sand. A wall of brightly colored spires and buttes stretches out to the north. The Cockscomb Spires are set out in the desert like the Emerald City; it is your destination, pedal onward. Fantastic views can be had from amongst the towers of this formation for those willing to scramble up their steep sides.

General location: North and west of Sedona.
Elevation change: At the point where the Dry Creek Road becomes the Boyton Pass Road, or FS 152C, your elevation is approximately 4,450′ above sea level. Where it turns to dirt your elevation is 4,500′. You will reach the highest eleva-tion (4,650′) when crossing over Boyton Pass. This ride rolls on from here with very slight changes in elevation. Elevation gain is only 150′.
Season: Spring and fall are best for riding around Sedona; summers can get ex-tremely hot. If it is dry, riding in the winter is not a problem. But when it's wet the fine clays in the soil around here turn into a greasy mess, and turn practically to cement when dry. Note the ruts made by vehicles that traveled this way when it was wet.
Services: All services are available in Sedona.
Hazards: All desert riding hazards exist. Watch out for those ruts, for they can be hard to negotiate when deep.
Rescue index: Once again, this route is fairly well traveled by bikers, sightseers, and the ranchers who live out this way. Help will not be hard to find.
Land status: Coconino National Forest.
Maps: Coconino National Forest Map. Also, the *Experience Sedona* map (avail-able in most Sedona area bookstores or at the Sedona Chamber of Commerce), published by Thorne Enterprises, is very helpful for this ride. The Coconino National Forest Map shows only a small portion of this route. The USGS quads are Wilson Mountain and Loy Butte.
Finding the trail: From Sedona head west on US 89A to the Dry Creek Road, about 3 miles from the "Y." Go right onto Dry Creek Road for approximately 2.8 miles, until you come to a "T" intersection. Then go left onto Boyton Pass Road (FS 152C); take it until the road turns to dirt. Park here.

RIDE 32 *COCKSCOMB LOOP*

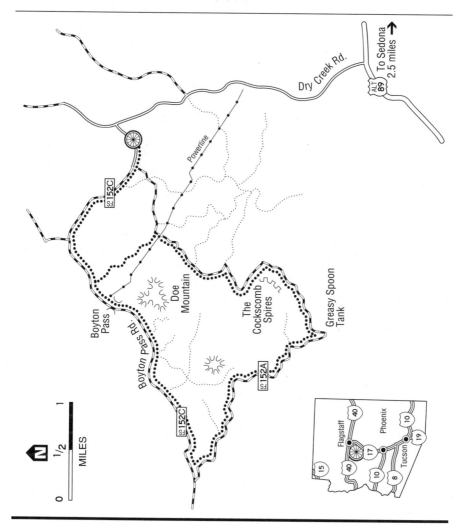

Sources of additional information: The Coconino National Forest address is listed in the introduction to this section.

Notes on the trail: You will ride out heading west on FS 152C for approximately 3 miles, looking for a road that cuts back and out into the flats, heading in a southeasterly direction. This is FS 152A, which you will take out to the Cockscomb. You'll encounter a fork in this road with a route heading almost due

The Cockscomb Spires rise out of the red sands, sage, and juniper trees of the Arizona desert.

east, which will appear to be a more direct route to the Cockscomb. It is not; it's a dead-end road. Bear right at this fork and continue heading south. This road will take you far to the south and west of Cockscomb, to Greasy Spoon Tank, before swinging back around to a northeasterly direction heading toward the Cockscomb. Once you are at the Cockscomb you will pick up the road that wraps around the formation heading in a northwesterly direction. This road will make an abrupt zag and head northeast to where it intersects another road. Go left. In three-quarters of a mile you will encounter another intersection; go left again. In another three-quarters mile you will intersect the Boyton Pass Road, or FS 152C, on which you will take a right turn which will take you back to your car. Possible mistakes you might make will be to go right at the first intersection, which will take you down a dead-end road, or perhaps going right at the second intersection which will take you out to the pavement of Boyton Pass Road. If you did this you would need to go left and ride back an extra mile to your car.

You may wish to combine this ride with the Loy Butte/Red Canyon Ruins Ride, since they share a good portion of the same trail. This would lengthen that already fairly long ride by about 4 miles. Instead of doubling straight back on FS 152C you would bear right onto FS 152A a mile after turning east onto FS 152C. FS 152A was unmarked when I was there.

RIDE 33 *STERLING CANYON*

This ride is a nine-mile out-and-back excursion along hard-packed dirt roads which, unfortunately, have sections of ruts and washboarding. It will take riders of beginning-to-intermediate riding ability and fitness about two hours to complete this route. The trail ends at the boundary to the wilderness area, which is off-limits to mountain bikes.

The views from this road into the Red Rock-Secret Mountain Wilderness Area are fantastic. You will skirt the western edge of Capitol Butte and Lost Wilson Mountain to your right, which provides views up to Devil's Bridge and into many alcoves along the way. To your left you will be looking up into the maze of canyons that run out from under Secret Mountain. Long Canyon, Earls Canyon, HS Canyon, Secret Canyon, and Sign Canyon all run toward you from the west. The scenic rating for this ride is high on the scale, and anyone who tours out this way won't be disappointed.

At the point where the trail ends, at the wilderness boundary, you can pick up a hiking trail that will take you about two miles up to Vultee Arch. Vultee Arch is named for Gerald Vultee, a famous pre-WWII aircraft designer, who was killed when his airplane crashed nearby in January of 1939. This is a great, short hike that is well worth a little extra time and effort.

General location: Just north and west of Sedona, Arizona.

Elevation change: From where you begin this ride, at the start of the dirt portion of Dry Creek Road, your elevation is approximately 4,600'. From there you will climb very gradually, rolling over small hills and through drainages, until you reach the elevation high on this ride of 4,800'. Elevation gain for this ride is a scant 200'.

Season: Spring through fall is the best time for riding out here, provided the road is dry. If the ground is saturated, or even if just the surface is wet, the fine clays in the soil turn this dirt into grease and it is extremely hard to get off your bike and shoes. Riding over this ground when it is saturated causes the deep ruts and scarring in the road surface, so it is a good time to steer clear of this area. In summertime the temperatures frequently rise well above the century mark.

Services: All services are available in Sedona.

Hazards: All the hazards of riding in a desert environment exist here. Make sure you stay covered up from the sun and drink plenty of water. Be aware of road traffic and watch out for those ruts.

Rescue index: This route gets a fair amount of traffic from tourists, bikers, hikers, and all kinds of sightseers. Help is not far away on this one.

Land status: Coconino National Forest.

Maps: The *Experience Sedona* map, published by Thorne Enterprises (this map

RIDE 33 *STERLING CANYON*

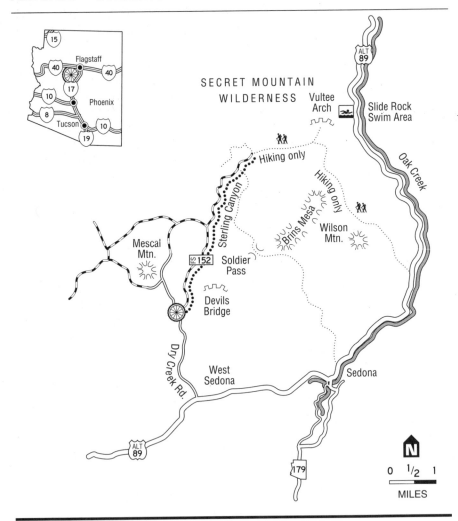

can be found in most Sedona area bookstores or at the Sedona Chamber of Commerce). The Coconino National Forest map is helpful, as are the USGS 7.5 minute quads of Sedona and Munds Mountain.

Finding the trail: From Sedona head west on US 89A to Dry Creek Road, about 3 miles from the "Y." Go right onto Dry Creek Road for approximately 2.5 miles, to where the dirt Dry Creek Road takes off to your right. This is also FS 152. Park here, just off the road after you turn off.

Sources of additional information: The Coconino National Forest address is listed in the introduction to this section.

Notes on the trail: You will ride this well-traveled dirt road in a north and northeasterly direction, rolling over mellow hills following the Dry Creek wash. You'll arrive at the boundary of the wilderness area just over 4.5 miles from where you began this ride. It's pretty hard to get lost on this one.

No real options for alternate routes exist out here, for you are surrounded by wilderness area. There are, however, several short spur roads taking off along the way that make for good exploring. None will take you more than a mile from the main road.

RIDE 34 *SCHEURMAN MOUNTAIN LOOP*

This ride is an eight-mile loop which will take riders of beginning riding ability, in good physical condition, about two hours to complete. Road surfaces include pavement and bladed dirt, the latter with several sections of washboarding. There is a great option here for about a two-mile single-track route up and over Scheurman Mountain, which will make this ride slightly more difficult. This is a somewhat technical trail, but I would encourage all riders looking for a challenge to give this route a try.

This route can be ridden from either direction, for the fantastic views of the red rock country (which have made this area so famous) are the same. You will be making a circuit of Scheurman Mountain via Upper Red Rock and Lower Red Rock Roads. To the east you'll be looking across Carrol Canyon to Table Top Mountain. Twin Buttes, Cathedral Rock, Bell Rock, and Courthouse Butte are some of the formations you can see to the east from the Upper Red Rock Road and Red Rock Crossing. To the south, House Mountain dominates the skyline.

General location: West and south of the town of Sedona.
Elevation change: From where you begin this ride, at the Red Rock Crossing Picnic Area, your elevation is approximately 4,000'. If you are riding this route in a clockwise direction you will climb gradually to where Lower Red Rock Road reaches US 89A, at 4,230'. You will continue to climb heading east on US 89A, to where Upper Red Rock Road leaves the highway at 4,480'. Elevation gain is 480'. If you choose to go up and over Scheurman Mountain you will reach a high elevation of 4,641'. This provides a total elevation gain of 641'.
Season: Spring through fall is the best time for riding out here. Summer temperatures frequently rise over 100 degrees. Dirt roads and trails are best avoided when wet, for the fine clays in the soil turn the dirt into a greasy mess which is very difficult to remove from bicycle parts, tires, and shoes.

RIDE 34 *SCHEURMAN MOUNTAIN LOOP*

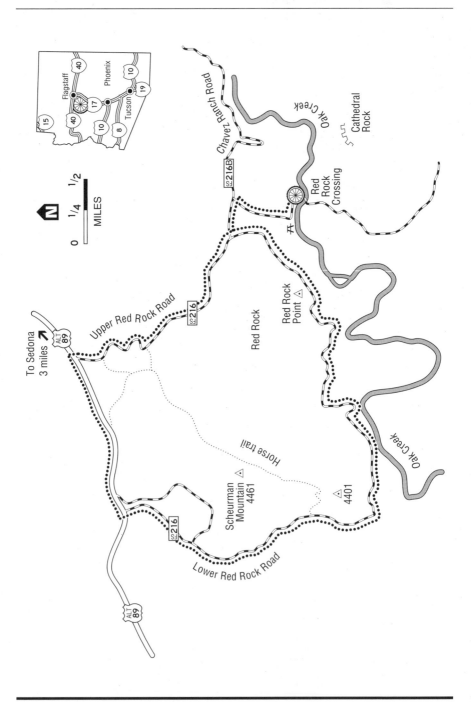

Services: All services are available in Sedona.

Hazards: All the hazards associated with riding in the desert exist here. Be aware of car traffic on this route.

Rescue index: This road receives a good amount of traffic from tourists and sightseers heading out to Red Rock Crossing. Help can be found easily along this route.

Land status: Coconino National Forest.

Maps: The *Experience Sedona* map, published by Thorne Enterprises (this map can be found in most Sedona area bookstores or at the Sedona Chamber of Commerce). The Coconino National Forest map is also helpful, as is the USGS 7.5 minute quad of Sedona.

Finding the trail: From Sedona you will want to head west on US 89A, just over 4 miles from the "Y," to the Upper Red Rock Road where you will go left. You will continue on this road for 1.7 miles to the Chavez Ranch Road, or Forest Service Road 216, which will take you to the Red Rock Crossing Picnic Area. Park here.

Sources of additional information: The Coconino National Forest address is listed in the introduction to this section.

Notes on the trail: You will probably want to ride this route in a clockwise direction, heading left onto the Red Rock Loop Road. This is a mild ride on a graded dirt road. You will climb steadily up to where the Lower Red Rock Road meets US 89A. Climb until you turn off the highway onto the Upper Red Rock Road, then head back to Red Rock Crossing where you left your car.

RIDE 35 ROBBER'S ROOST

This ride is a 20-mile out-and-back adventure which does not require a lot of technical skill. But an intermediate level of physical fitness will certainly make it more enjoyable. You will be riding on mostly level, hard-packed dirt roads which are rutted and washboarded in sections. The road surface deteriorates somewhat where you turn off on the spur road that takes you out to Robber's Roost. Allow three to four hours' riding time for this one.

This route will take you through beautiful, rolling, red sand hills, covered in prickly pear cactus and yucca with the occasional piñon and juniper tree along the way. You will enjoy sweeping views to the north and east, up to the red rock buttes and canyons of the Secret Mountain Wilderness Area. To the south and west you will be looking into the Verde Valley. A short trail at the end of this ride will take you up to the hideout carved into this enormous sandstone butte formation by wind and weather. Historically this cave was used as a lookout by cattle rustlers, horse thieves, and others on the run.

RIDE 35   *ROBBER'S ROOST*

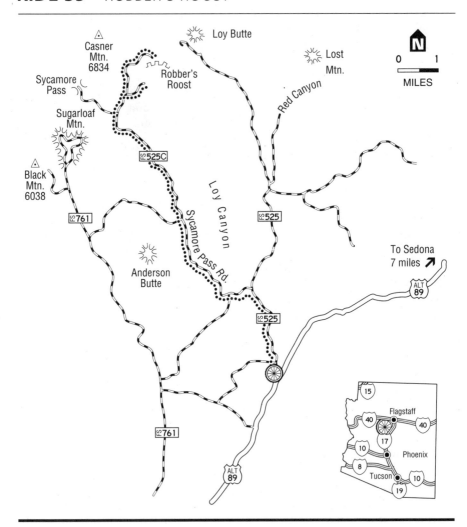

General location: West of the town of Sedona, in the Coconino National Forest.
Elevation change: At the point where Red Canyon Road leaves US 89A and where you will begin this ride your elevation is approximately 3,900′.
Season: This is a great ride to do year-round, provided roads are not wet and muddy.
Services: All services are available in Sedona.
Hazards: It can get pretty hot out here during the summer months; keep covered

up and drink as much water as you can hold. Watch out for those ruts, for they can be hard to negotiate when they get deep. Keep an ear out for car traffic. They're probably sightseers and they won't be looking for you.

Rescue index: Although this is empty country out here, you're likely to run into other tourists. The nearest help can be found on AZ 89 or in Sedona, 6 miles to the east.

Land status: Coconino National Forest.

Maps: The Coconino National Forest Map. The USGS 7.5 minute quads are Loy Butte and Page Springs.

Finding the trail: From Sedona you will head west out of town on AZ 89. You will continue heading west and south for approximately 6 miles until you reach Forest Service Road 525 leaving from the right side of the road. Turn off here and park your vehicle to the side of the road.

Sources of additional information: The Coconino National Forest address is listed in the introduction to this section.

Notes on the trail: Once on your bike you will continue on FS 525 for approximately 2.5 miles, until you reach a fork in the road. Go left onto FS 525C. Once you reach FS 525C you will see many side roads taking off to the right and left; keep going straight. Continue heading in a northerly direction on FS 525C for another 7 miles before reaching your next turn. This will be a right turn onto FS 9530, which will take you uphill on a rough jeep road. Stay to your left as you approach the butte and look for a trail up to the hideout, about a mile from where you started. Scramble on up. Have a good look around, eat some snacks (you did bring some, didn't you?), then head back the way you came.

There are lots of great possibilities for creating route options out here. Come prepared with maps and a compass if you plan to do some exploring.

The Mogollon Rim

Just north of Payson, Arizona, you'll find the cliffs and deep canyons that continue to define the Mogollon Rim, which stretches for more than 200 miles across Arizona's midsection. The Mogollon Rim is the southern boundary of the Colorado Plateau, a giant uplifted landmass that also covers portions of Utah, Colorado, and New Mexico. The rides in this section are grouped in an area above the rim that is referred to as the Mogollon Plateau. The eastern part of the Mogollon Plateau, which ranges between 7,000 and 8,000 feet in elevation, is heavily forested by ponderosa pine, like much of the country atop the rim. Several lakes in this area are stocked with trout, and on weekends draw large crowds of enthusiastic anglers who are seeking both recreation and cooler temperatures. Every now and then these forests reveal expansive meadows, rich in grasses and wildflowers. These grassy meadows, and the verdant forest floor, help to support a large population of Rocky Mountain elk and a number of other grazers. They make this a popular hunting spot in the fall.

The eastern section of the Mogollon Plateau, with its lakes and meadows, has always received the bulk of attention from fishermen, hunters, and all types of recreationalists. The special designation of Rim Lakes Recreation Area for this region was an attempt by the Forest Service to focus on, and more closely monitor and control, the human impact on wildlife and other forest resources. The Forest Service is now working to rehabilitate wildlife habitat disrupted by heavy logging and off-road vehicle use in the Rim Lakes Recreation Area. Their efforts have included the closing of many of the roads in this district to motorized traffic. Most of these roads, however, have remained open to mountain bikers. It is now possible to do some great deep forest cruising in this region without the disruption of motor vehicles. Excellent opportunities also exist for seeing wildlife while riding on these seldom-traveled back roads.

Gold first brought settlers to the Payson area in 1881, but those looking to make a profit soon realized that the real fortune to be made was in the straight, tall pines that blanket this area. By the end of the 1880s, the sawmills began to buzz, feeding the building needs of Arizona's growing cities to the south. Cattle ranching also became established in the surrounding area about this time. Although the saws have slowed a bit today, the town of Payson still thrives as a vacation community for city dwellers escaping to the cooler climes and the sweet smell of pines. The plateau has been heavily logged for over a century, and it is rare to find any large old growth still standing, even though the hills remain heavily wooded.

Like the rim above Sedona, in this area it is capped by a tough, weather-resistant layer of basalt that has clearly defined the rim and made for many dramatic canyons. The drainage pattern atop the Mogollon in this area is to the north, but there are several canyons along here with streams that have managed to erode the basalt and flow south. The Kaibab Limestone, the Supai Group, and the Redwall Formation all extend below the basalt cap here, but are most often obscured by vegetation and eroded soils from the top of the rim.

On fall evenings it is not uncommon to hear elk bugling and horns crashing as bulls compete to secure mates. The elk population along this part of the plateau shares its forage with white-tailed and mule deer, as well as pronghorn antelope. You may also see wild turkey, and even black bear, in the less traveled regions of this forest. Keep your eyes and ears open as you are cruising through the pines and you will likely spot any number of wild creatures.

The rim and plateau in this area receive almost twice as much rain per year as the cities and towns just a hundred miles to the south. During the monsoon season, which can run anywhere from mid-July to the first part of October, there is a moist, southerly flow that is forced upward, into cooler air at higher elevation, as it runs into the rim. As this moist, warm air collides with the colder air above, violent thunder and lightning storms and substantial amounts of rain and hail are generated. If this type of weather pattern persists, these storms can become a daily occurrence in the rim country. The weather is as wild here as any-where in the state. *Be prepared!* Start out early and try to be done riding before these storm buildups start rumbling. In the event you are caught out in one of these storms, leave your bike at a distance, split up from fellow riders, and seek shelter under low trees (*not* the tallest ones!) or bushes. Do not cluster together at the base of very tall or isolated trees. With elevations in the 6,000- to 7,000-foot range you can expect to find snow up here in winter and cool temperatures in summer. It is always a good idea to check in with Forest Service rangers to get an idea of current riding and weather conditions.

Apache-Sitgreaves National Forest
Supervisor's Office
309 South Mountain Avenue
U.S. Highway 180
P.O. Box 640
Springerville, Arizona 85938
(602) 333-4301

Willow Springs Area: Apache-Sitgreaves National Forest
Heber Ranger District
P.O. Box 968
Overgaard, Arizona 85933
(602) 535-4481

Woods Canyon Area: Chevelon Ranger District
HC 62, Box 600
Winslow, Arizona 86047
(602) 289-2471

RIDE 36 *WILLOW SPRINGS LAKE LOOP*

This ride is a very scenic six-mile loop that will be moderately easy for riders with beginning-to-intermediate riding skills, if they are in reasonably good physical condition. This route follows a rocky four-wheel-drive jeep road that is closed to motor vehicles. You may encounter some deadfall and new growth along the way. This ride will take only one to two hours to complete.

This route takes you through some really pretty country. The ground you will cover is mostly flat with a few rolling, rocky hills. Ponderosa forests surround beautiful Willow Springs Lake, where the trout fishing is excellent. You will find many spots along the shore of the lake to sit for awhile, take in your surroundings, and nibble on whatever goodies you brought along. This short ride is a good introduction to the area and gives a taste of what lies ahead.

General location: Thirty miles east of Payson, in the Rim Lakes Recreation Area of the Apache-Sitgreaves National Forest.

Elevation change: At the gate where you begin this ride your elevation is approximately 7,588' above sea level. You will gain and lose under 100' of elevation throughout the route.

Season: In summer the temperatures are ideal for riding. The days generally stay fairly cool, only rarely reaching up into the 90s. In winter you can expect snow. Watch out for thunder and lightning storms in late summer and fall.

Services: This is fairly remote country, so come prepared. Water is available at the Aspen and Canyon Point Campgrounds, on either side of Willow Springs Lake Campground along AZ 260. But water cannot be obtained at Willow Springs. Food, accommodations, and camping supplies are available in Payson. Bike shops are few and far between in this neck of the woods, so supply yourself with tubes and tools from shops in Phoenix or Flagstaff.

Hazards: This route is unmarked, and while it is hard to get really lost in this area, supplementary topographical maps are suggested. Topos will help you locate significant geographical markers and enhance your overall riding experience.

Watch out for those seasonal monsoon storms. They can be extremely violent. Start out early if thunderstorms and lightning are predicted.

Rescue index: Much of the country atop the rim here is remote wilderness. On this particular ride you will not be far from AZ 260 or the campground at Willow Springs Lake, where you will find campers and fishermen. You can find a ranger during business hours at the Visitor Information Trailer 2 miles west on AZ 260 from the Willow Springs Lake area.

Land status: Apache-Sitgreaves National Forest, Rim Lakes Recreation Management Area.

RIDE 36   *WILLOW SPRINGS LAKE LOOP*

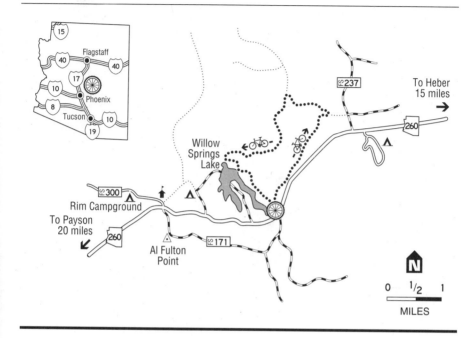

Maps: The scale of the Apache-Sitgreaves National Forest map is too large to show this short route. They do have a smaller map of the Rim Lakes Recreation Area, available by writing to them or by stopping by the Visitor Information Trailer 2 miles west of the Willow Springs Lake area on AZ 260. Because this Visitor Information Center is a trailer, and can be moved, you might check with the Forest Service on its location before you go. The USGS 15 minute quad is Woods Canyon and O W Point.

Finding the trail: From Payson take AZ 260 heading east. In about 30 miles you will see a sign for Forest Service Road 149 and Willow Springs Lake Campground. Pass this sign by continuing in the direction you are heading for another 1.5 miles, until you see a road to your right with signs for FS 181. Park on the opposite side of AZ 260 from this road.

Sources of additional information: Apache-Sitgreaves National Forest. Address and phone are listed in the introduction to this section.

Notes on the trail: There will be a gate across the dirt road you want to take. Once you cross the road and get around this gate you will be looking at a dirt road forking in two directions. You can go straight ahead, which means you will be riding this route in a clockwise direction. (If you go in this direction

The Willow Springs Lake Loop gives riders an opportunity to try their angling skills. A rod case packs easily onto a mountain bike and fishing is an excellent complement to a day's ride.

you will find yourself riding along the eastern shore of Willow Springs Lake.) Your other option is the road that takes off to your right, which will take you in a counterclockwise tour of this route. If you leave to your right you will proceed for approximately 2 miles before turning left, heading northwest. You will proceed along this road for 1 mile before turning left again. Travel for another 2 miles in this direction, ignoring roads leading off to the right. Then go left at about the 1-mile mark after your last left turn, and continue until you reach the northern end of Willow Springs Lake. At this point you will head south and east, following the shore, back to the point where you began this ride.

If you are interested in trying out options and doing a little exploring while visiting in this area, supplementary topographical maps are a must.

You may want to ride north on the road that leaves from the farthest point northwest in this loop. Or, when heading east, continue out to FS 237 where you will go right, intersecting with AZ 260, which you'll ride 2 miles back on pavement to where you left your car.

The General Crook Trail parallels the southeastern section of this route, with which you may become confused. This is a wide single-track that will eventually take you out to FS 237.

RIDE 37 *WOODS CANYON OVERLOOK RIDE*

This ride is an 8.5-mile out-and-back route. It will take bikers with beginning-to-intermediate riding ability, who are in good physical condition, two to three hours to complete. This trail consists of abandoned dirt roads which have become somewhat overgrown double-tracks. Sections will be slightly rocky, but most of the route is hard-packed dirt.

On this ride you will be rolling through ponderosa pine forests with a grassy, open forest floor. The route takes you back into the heart of the wildlife rehabilitation area, which is closed to motorized vehicles. Elk have reclaimed the region and exist in fairly healthy numbers. Mornings and evenings are the best time to catch them up and about. They are quite shy, however, as they are still hunted, so you'll have to be quiet if you want to catch a glimpse of them. The views into Woods Canyon and Chevelon Creek are wonderful.

General location: East of Payson some 26 miles, in the Rim Lakes Recreation Management Area of the Apache-Sitgreaves National Forest.
Elevation change: From where this ride begins, at the beginning of Forest Service Road 235, your elevation is approximately 7,500' above sea level. Elevation gains and losses will total less than 200' for the whole ride.
Season: In summer, temperatures are ideal for riding. The days are cool, rarely reaching up into the 90s. In winter you can expect snow. Watch out for thunder and lightning storms in late summer and fall.
Services: This is wilderness, so come prepared. Water is available at the Aspen and Canyon Point Campgrounds on either side of Willow Springs Lake Campground along AZ 260, but not at Willow Springs. Food, accommodations, and camping supplies are available in Payson, 26 miles away. Bike shops are few and far between in this neck of the woods, so supply yourself with tubes and tools from shops in Phoenix or Flagstaff.
Hazards: Watch out for those seasonal monsoon storms; they can be extremely violent. Start out early if thunderstorms are predicted.

It is not really possible to get lost on this route, for you are riding the ridge between Woods and Willow Springs Canyons.
Rescue index: Much of the country on the rim here is remote wilderness. On this particular ride you will not be far from AZ 260, or the campground at Willow Springs Lake where you will find campers and fishermen. You can find a ranger during business hours at the Visitor Information Trailer 2 miles west on AZ 260 from the Willow Springs Lake area.

RIDE 37 *WOODS CANYON OVERLOOK RIDE*

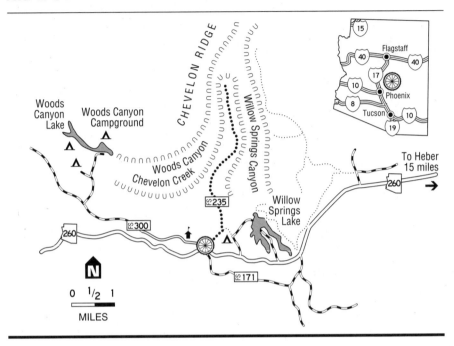

Land status: Apache-Sitgreaves National Forest, Rim Lakes Recreation Management Area.

Maps: The scale of the Apache-Sitgreaves National Forest map is too large to show this short route. They do have a smaller map of the Rim Lakes Recreation Area that you can obtain by writing to them or by stopping by the Visitor Information Trailer a little over a half mile west of the beginning of FS 235. The USGS 15 minute quad is Woods Canyon.

Finding the trail: Take AZ 260 from the town of Payson, Arizona for 26 miles east, to the junction with FS 300. This FS Road is paved at this junction where you will find signs for Woods Canyon Lake. Make a left turn (almost a "U") onto FS 300, and proceed for a quarter mile to the beginning of FS 235, which leaves from the right side of the road. Park there to begin your ride.

Sources of additional information: The Apache-Sitgreaves National Forest address is listed in the introduction to this section.

Notes on the trail: This is a straight out-and-back affair that needs few directions. There will be several less-used spur roads leaving from either side, but stay on the most well-worn road. On your return you will encounter a fork in the road near the end of the ride; if you mistakenly go left you will end up on the

Willow Springs Lake Road. Go back to FS 235 and ride it back out to where you left your car.

No real options exist here. There is the possibility of taking about a 1-mile spur that leaves one-half mile from the beginning of this trail, on the left side of the road. This takes you only a short distance and ends in a group of trees near the edge of the canyon.

RIDE 38 GENERAL CROOK'S TRAIL

The General Crook National Recreation Trail is a historic trail surveyed in 1871 by General Crook and a small group of his cavalry. Construction on the trail was begun the next year by the army, who needed the trail to move provisions and supply their forts as well as patrol the country for hostile Apache Indians. The trail, which took two years to build, originated at Fort Apache in eastern Arizona and wound its way for almost 200 miles to Prescott, which was then the territorial state capital. The trail was abandoned until the Boy Scouts cleared and marked the old trail in the mid-seventies. Almost 140 miles of this trail is now open to hikers, horseback riders, and bikers. The trail can be picked up and ridden for whatever distance is desired from the Rim Lakes Recreation Area. If you are the adventurous sort you may want to do your own research on the trail, fit your bike with panniers, and ride into the past.

Forest Service Road 300 traces substantial portions of General Crook's Trail and can be picked up from AZ 260 just as you reach the rim, about one mile before the Willow Springs Lake Campground heading west. Heading east you will need to pick up FS 300 and the General Crook Trail about nine miles east of the Willow Springs Lake Campground off AZ 260, where it turns south to Black Canyon Campground. At various points along FS 300 the General Crook Trail departs and travels along portions of the rim as a single-track. These sections of single-track, combined with FS 300, can take you as far as Horseshoe Lake to the west and the town of Show Low to the east, within the Apache-Sitgreaves National Forest. Beyond the boundaries of this national forest you can take this trail all the way to Prescott heading west.

This is gorgeous country, and once again, not what you'd expect to find in the desert state of Arizona. The rim is thickly forested with ponderosas, which give way to widely spaced piñon and juniper trees along certain stretches. Rolling grassy hills and open meadows often interrupt the consistency of the pines. Wildflowers bloom in the spring and then again in the fall after monsoonal rains. Traveling along the Mogollon Rim often feels like you are traversing the edge of the world. The earth drops away below you into dusky silhouettes of mountains upon more mountains. On the rim you remain high in your forested wonderland, where you can look out like a hawk perched on a high branch.

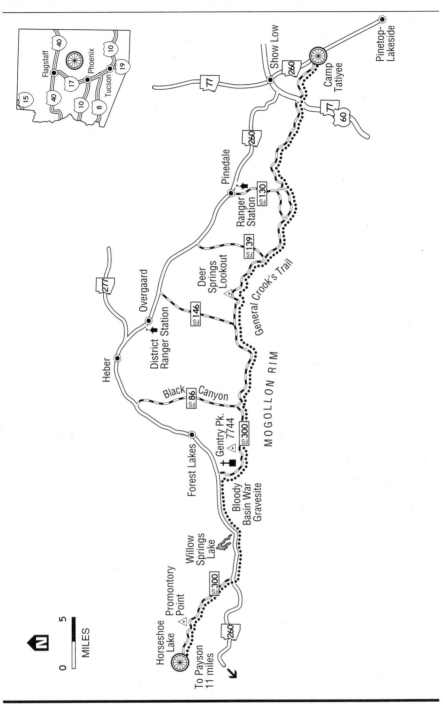

This route consists of wide (though seldom used) single-track and dirt roads that can become extremely muddy and rutted during and after wet weather. This trail is suggested not as a single ride, but as several. You can pack up your bike with panniers and all your gear and head out for some real adventure. Or, bring along a vehicle and driver and have a carefree supported ride. Or you could drive halfway in, establish a camp, and ride out for the day. If you are taking a vehicle, a high-clearance four-wheel-drive type is strongly suggested. Also, be sure to carry enough fuel and supplies with you, for you will not find any conveniences out here. Check in with the Apache-Sitgreaves Forest Service people at the Heber Ranger District office in Overgaard for route conditions before you go.

Any way you decide to do it, riding the General Crook Trail takes you into magnificent wilderness along the historic trail that helped settle Arizona.

General location: Apache-Sitgreaves National Forest in central Arizona.

Elevation change: The edge of the Mogollon Rim, along which the trail winds, fluctuates mainly between 7,000' and 7,800'.

Season: Dry times of year—late spring and early summer, and again in the late fall—are the best for heading out along General Crook's Trail. Temperatures are delightful for riding in spring, summer, and fall. Snow dominates the landscape during most of the winter. Beware of violent monsoonal thunderstorms that lash this country on a daily basis, starting as early as the middle of July and running through September.

Services: Food, water, accommodations, and camping supplies are available in the towns of Payson, Heber, and Show Low. Finding someone to help with your biking needs will be tough out in this area, so come prepared.

Hazards: FS 300 covers a long distance in a remote area. It is a good idea to carry extra fuel here, as well as more food and water than you think you'll need.

Be sure to check road and weather conditions with Forest Service rangers before you embark on this adventure.

Rescue index: Much of the country along this route is extremely remote wilderness. You may want to alert Forest Service rangers to your travel plans and establish contact times. Another option is to carry a two-way radio or an emergency transmitter with you when traveling in the outback like this. [Editor's note: A third option, especially appropriate for this historic trail, is to prepare your bike and yourself for real backcountry solo travel, and handling whatever situations arise. *Always* being "in touch" is a modern-day pain.]

Land status: Apache-Sitgreaves National Forest.

Maps: Apache-Sitgreaves National Forest map. The USGS 15 minute quads are Woods Canyon, O W Point, Brookbank, Heber, Clay Springs, Cibecue, and Show Low.

Finding the trail: If you wish to do a day's ride on the western section of FS 300 from the town of Payson, drive 26 miles east to the junction with the paved FS 300, which will have signs for Woods Canyon Lake. Make a left, almost a "U"

Breathtaking views to the south stretch away for miles all along the Mogollon Rim, a geologic feature that spans half the state of Arizona.

turn, onto FS 300, and proceed 9 miles to where the maintained graveled road ends at the intersection of FS 34. Park here and begin your ride heading west.

Heading east, FS 300 begins at the turnoff to Black Canyon Rim and the Bloody Basin War Gravesite. From here it heads east following the Mogollon Rim for almost 50 miles. Start your ride anywhere. Happy adventuring!

Sources of additional information: Apache-Sitgreaves National Forest. Address and phone are listed in the introduction to this section.

Notes on the trail: Many, many route options are possible from FS 300. If you are interested in exploring options from this route, supplementary Forest Service and topographical maps are a must.

If you are riding the western section of FS 300, the 2-mile spur on FS 76 out to Promontory Butte is a "don't miss" opportunity.

Alpine Area Rides

Just a stone's throw from the New Mexico border in central Arizona is the tiny town of Alpine. Alpine is perched high in the White Mountains at an elevation of 8,030 feet. Mid-summer highs reach only into the mid-80s in these mountains, which are covered by a thick layer of snow all winter long. This is gorgeous mountain country characterized by pine, spruce, fir, and aspen forests of the Canadian and Hudsonian Zones. The town of Alpine was founded and settled by Mormons in 1879, as were many of the communities along the rim. Today Alpine exists as a base for year-round recreational activities, including hiking, hunting, fishing, cross-country skiing, biking, and snowmobiling. The town of Alpine is surrounded by hundreds of thousands of Apache-Sitgreaves National Forest acres, which include the Blue Range Primitive Area. The enormous Fort Apache and San Carlos Indian Reservations border this expansive wilderness to the west.

The White Mountains are volcanic and are referred to, in geologic terms, as a volcanic field. The highest peaks in this area are at the center of this field, and are called strato volcanoes. Mt. Baldy, the highest point in the range, is a strato volcano that reaches an elevation of 11,490 feet. The surrounding mountains are made up of more than 200 cinder cones. The explosive volcanic activity that created these mountains completely dominates the landscape here, erasing all signs of the Mogollon Rim, which now lies below more than 4,000 feet of volcanic rock. These weather-grabbing peaks, which were once fiery volcanoes, receive enough snow and rain during the year to feed one of the few consistently flowing rivers in Arizona, the Blue River. The Blue River, which is also the most southern tributary to the Colorado River, traverses a wilderness area that supports healthy populations of elk, deer, black bear, mountain lion, and bobcat. Several species of rare southern raptors also make these mountains their home.

The White Mountains sit like an emerald on top of a crown of painted desert. At elevations of 7,000 feet and above, this area receives enough moisture to stay cool and green all summer long. These mountains are a welcome sight to hot and dusty desert travelers. Although some areas around Alpine receive heavy traffic from hunters during certain times of the year, there is some real wilderness out there, rough country that receives little traffic. Check with the Alpine Ranger of the Apache-Sitgreaves National Forest regarding the hunting schedules. If you are riding at all in this forest during hunting season it is a good idea to wear a flaming orange vest, or some piece of bright clothing, to alert anyone who might be out there to the fact that you are not a deer or an elk. A dark silhouette slipping quickly and quietly through the trees can be too much of a temptation for some hunters.

Here are a few addresses you will need to make traveling and riding plans for this area:

Alpine Chamber of Commerce
P.O. Box 410
Alpine, Arizona 85920
(602) 339-4330

Apache-Sitgreaves National Forest
Alpine Ranger District
P.O. Box 469
Alpine, Arizona 85920
(602) 339-4633

RIDE 39 *LUNA LAKE LOOP*

This ride is an easy eight-mile cruise through the forest and serves as a good introduction to this area. Riders in reasonably good physical condition, with beginning-to-intermediate riding skills, will be able to complete this route in about two hours. Route surfaces include pavement, grated gravel road, hard-packed dirt road, and single-track.

You will be riding through high alpine forests of mixed conifer and aspen on this route. Ride along the lake shore and enjoy the cool deep forests. Find a spot at the water's edge to take a break and eat lunch.

General location: Just east of Alpine, in the Apache-Sitgreaves National Forest.
Elevation change: From where you begin and end this ride, at the Luna Lake Campground, your elevation is approximately 8,000'. You will reach a high point of 8,200' in the northwestern corner of this loop. Elevation gain is approximately 200'.
Season: Spring, summer, and fall are all great times for riding in this region. Watch out for mud if the ground is saturated. Check with Forest Service rangers on hunting schedules in the area before you go out into these forests.
Services: All services are available in Alpine, although you probably won't have much luck finding a bike mechanic. Come prepared with bike parts, tools, and a do-it-yourself manual if you aren't experienced. Water is available at Luna Lake Campground.
Hazards: Although US 180 has a wide shoulder that serves as a bike lane, be careful of the traffic along here. A piece of bright clothing or a bright helmet cover always helps to alert motorists, and hunters, to your presence.
Rescue index: You are not far from a town or a main, paved road on this ride. Help is not far away.
Land status: Apache-Sitgreaves National Forest.
Maps: Apache-Sitgreaves National Forest map (this shows Luna Lake Camp-

RIDE 39 *LUNA LAKE LOOP*

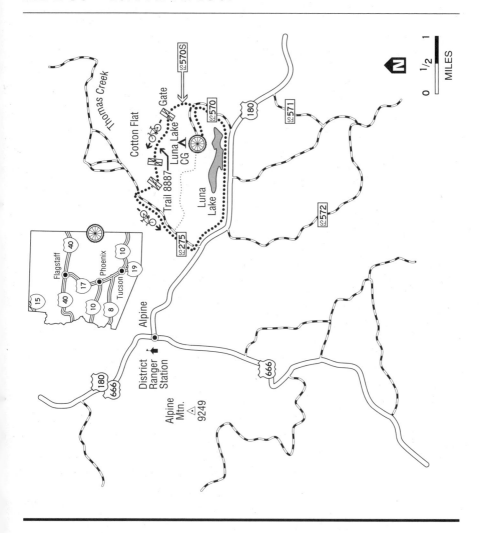

ground, and FS 275, but not the connecting route). The USGS 15 minute quad is Alpine.

Finding the trail: From the town of Alpine drive east on US 180 2.5 miles to FS 570, where you will go left to Luna Lake Campground. Park here to begin your ride.

Sources of additional information: The Apache-Sitgreaves National Forest, Alpine Ranger District, address is listed in the introduction to this section.

Notes on the trail: You can ride this loop in either direction, with no one direction being that much better than the other. I rode it in a counterclockwise direction, so that is the way I will describe it. Head out of the campground and go left, traveling north on FS 570S, which will dead-end at Trail #8887. Go left onto this trail, which will take you through 3 gates and over numerous water bars before it dead-ends at FS 275. Go left again, heading south on FS 275, which will take you into the town of Alpine and onto US 180 where you will go left. Head east along the shore of Luna Lake, looking for FS 570, which will take you back to Luna Lake Campground where you began.

If you would like to shorten this ride you can take FS 570, which leaves from the west end of the campground, and bisects this loop. If you would like to lengthen the ride, your only real possibility is taking FS 275 north, toward Cotton Flat. This spur can be lengthened to any distance, as this road continues for some 20 miles as it loops around Escudilla Mountain Wilderness before joining Route 666 10 miles south of Springerville.

RIDE 40 *TERRY FLAT LOOP*

This 12-mile ride includes an out-and-back section as well as a loop section. There are two good options for this ride, for total distances of 6 and 15 miles. This route will be moderately difficult for intermediate riders in good physical condition, and will take two to three hours to complete. Route surfaces include hard-packed dirt and gravel roads.

Mixed conifer and aspen, typical of high alpine environments, dominate this landscape. The extinct volcano called Escudilla Mountain (10,955 feet), and Profanity Ridge, which runs out to the south, rise in front of you as you approach Terry Flat. A wide, open grassy meadow is referred to as Terry Flat. The views of Escudilla Mountain Wilderness Area are great. This place is gorgeous! This is a good ride for acclimating to higher altitudes. Excellent campsites are here.

General location: North of Alpine some 6.5 miles, in the Apache-Sitgreaves National Forest.
Elevation change: From where Forest Service Road 56 leaves US 180/Route 666, your elevation is approximately 8,198'. At the point where you will go right, continuing on FS 56 (just past Hulsey Lake), your elevation will be 8,654'. From there you will climb steadily, skirting the wilderness boundary, until you come to a fork in the road where the Terry Flat Loop begins. Here your elevation is approximately 9,600'. The loop road then rolls along, reaching a high of 9,900'. Elevation gain is 1,700'.
Season: Spring, summer, and fall are all great times for riding in these moun-

RIDE 40   *TERRY FLAT LOOP*

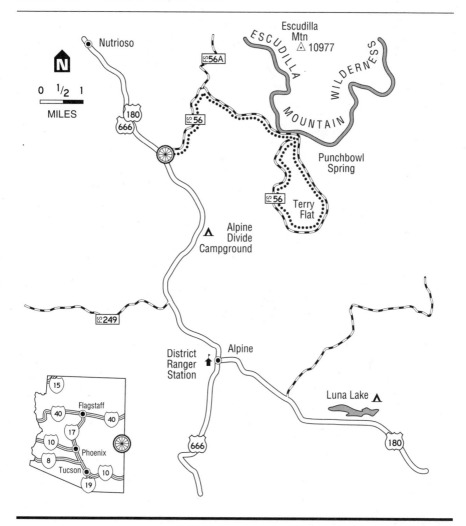

tains. Watch out for mud if the ground is saturated. Check with a Forest Service ranger on hunting schedules in the area before you go.

Services: All services are available in Alpine, although you probably won't have much luck finding a bike mechanic. Come prepared with bike parts and tools. There is no water available out here.

Hazards: Some of the hazards you might run into include rutted roads, mud,

The edge of an open meadow makes an excellent spot for a snack and a rest.

and hunters. If you are not used to these elevations they will probably take a toll on your aerobic strength and your energy.

Rescue index: You are in a fairly remote area on this ride, although US 180 (otherwise known as Route 666), the road you came out on, stays fairly busy and is not far away. A telephone and other assistance is available in Alpine just 6.5 miles away.

Land status: Apache-Sitgreaves National Forest.

Maps: Apache-Sitgreaves National Forest map. The USGS 15 minute quads are Alpine, Nutrioso, and Escudilla.

Finding the trail: From the town of Alpine head north on US 180/Route 666 for approximately 6.5 miles, at which point you will find FS 56 leaving from the right side of the road. Drive FS 56 as far as you want to adjust the length of this ride.

Sources of additional information: The Apache-Sitgreaves National Forest, Alpine Ranger District, address is listed in the introduction to this section.

Notes on the trail: This is a great ride in either direction. You will stay on FS 56, also labeled FS 8056, for the entire ride. Several less-used roads will branch from this main road, but the more traveled road will remain obvious.

If you are interested in exploring trail options, you should come equipped with supplementary topographical maps.

Several options exist for adjusting the length of this ride. You may want to begin this ride where FS 56 leaves US 666, which would give you a total mileage of 15 miles. The other option, which shortens this ride, is driving all the way to where the loop begins. Another possible option is to bear left at about the 2-mile mark, if you are riding this loop in a clockwise direction. Take this trail to Terry Lake, which affords good views into New Mexico and ELC Flat.

RIDE 41 *FOREST SERVICE ROAD 403 TO WILLIAMS VALLEY*

This ride can be done as an out-and-back, with a shuttle, or as a loop. Mileage in one direction is 11.5 miles. None of the options will result in distances higher than 25 miles. This ride will be moderately difficult for riders with intermediate-to-advanced riding skills, if they are in good physical condition. Route surfaces include pavement, grated gravel roads, and very rough, semi-abandoned jeep roads.

The scenery on this ride is high alpine. You will be riding the ridge, although it's hard to tell because of dense forests between Coyote and Luna Creeks. Tight canyons and small mountains surround you. Big water bars, ruts, rocks, and vegetation make navigating this route a lot of fun for the more advanced rider. It is also a good challenge for bikers looking to improve their skills.

General location: South and west of Alpine, in the Apache-Sitgreaves National Forest.
Elevation change: In Alpine your elevation will be 8,012'. FS 403 leaves US 180/ Route 666 at an elevation of 8,623'. You will go on to reach a high elevation of 9,450'. Elevation gain is 827'.
Season: Spring, summer, and fall are all great times for riding in these mountains. Watch out for mud if the ground is saturated. Check with a Forest Service ranger on hunting schedules in the area before you go.
Services: All services are available in Alpine, although you probably won't have much luck finding a bike mechanic. Come prepared with bike parts and tools. There is no water available out here.
Hazards: Water bars, rocks, and ruts make this ride slightly dicey. As always, you'll want to wear your helmet.

There are many, many old jeep roads heading off in all directions through here. It's a good idea to have supplementary maps and a compass so that you can double check your headings, and give yourself as many options as possible to explore.

RIDE 41 *WILLIAMS VALLEY ROAD*

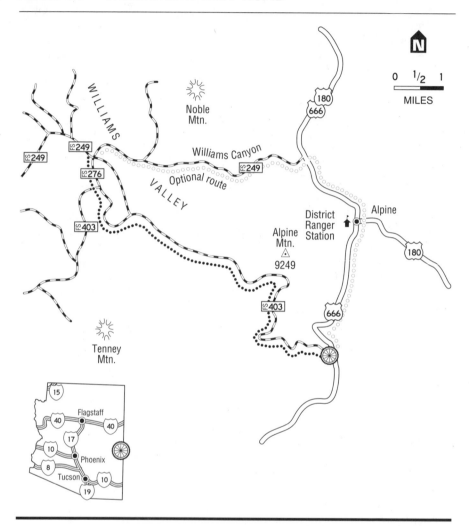

Rescue index: While this ride is somewhat remote, you are never far from well-traveled paved roads leading to Alpine. At the most, you will be no more than 11 miles from a town, some help, and a phone.

Land status: Apache-Sitgreaves National Forest.

Maps: Apache-Sitgreaves National Forest map. The USGS 15 minute quad is Alpine.

Finding the trail: Whichever way you have decided to do this ride, whether you are leaving your car in Alpine, or doing an out-and-back from the beginning of

FS 403, you will need to drive or ride south from the Alpine Ranger Station for approximately 2.7 miles, to where FS 403 leaves from the right side of the road. This is about a mile past the Alpine Civilian Conservation Center. Park just after you turn off onto FS 403, if you are doing an out-and-back.

Sources of additional information: The Apache-Sitgreaves National Forest, Alpine Ranger District, address is listed in the introduction to this section.

Notes on the trail: FS 403 leaves approximately 2.7 to 3 miles south of town from US 180/Route 666 on the right side of the road. Once on your bike you will wind through several tight canyons, with many side roads leaving FS 403 in all directions. Use your supplementary maps and compass to double check your heading if you are confused. The main route, which is the one you want, will remain obvious. Heading northwest at approximately mile 8, there will be a fork in the road. The right fork is a shortcut that can save you maybe a mile, and will take you directly to the intersection of FS 276 and 249. No big deal if you miss that, for you will end up at a "T" intersection with FS 276; go right. Go right again when you reach the intersection with FS 249 in another mile. You will meet your shuttle at this point, or you'll ride this road back to town. Good luck!

Riding this route as a loop is the same distance as riding it out and back. It can be ridden in either direction as a loop, or as an out-and-back. From Alpine you can ride south on US 180/Route 666, a distance of 2.6 miles to where FS 403 leaves on the right side of the road, heading west. At the end of FS 403 you will ride back to town heading east on FS 249, which will take you back to US 180/Route 666 just 1.5 miles from the ranger station.

RIDE 42   *BLUE RIVER / RED HILL ROAD*

This entire route, from where it begins three miles east of Alpine, to the junction of US 180/666 at the ranger station in Alpine, is a distance of approximately 40 miles. The Blue River Road and the Red Hill Road form a triangle-shaped loop with the town of Alpine. This route traverses some incredibly scenic and very remote country and can be ridden by ambitious riders in excellent physical condition in one day. Riders of varying abilities can enjoy this ride, however, by riding from a car parked anywhere along this route and just pedaling portions of the route, or by riding this route as a support trip with bikers taking turns at the wheel. You will encounter riding surfaces of pavement, grated gravel and dirt, and sections of fairly rough jeep roads.

For the first ten miles you will wind through gorgeous mountainous country before dropping down to the Blue River. You will then follow the Blue River, riding along its banks, for another nine miles before fording the river and climbing out of the drainage, heading up Red Hill Road. You will climb, climb, climb

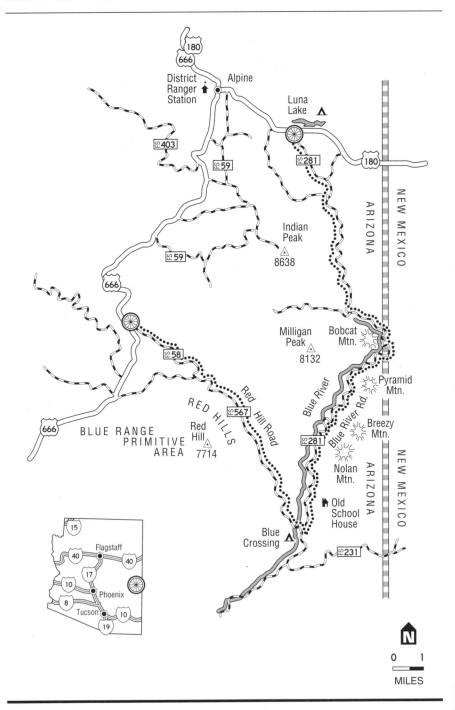

Riding deep into the mountainous wilds of eastern Arizona is easy on the Blue River Road. *Photo by Chip Thomas.*

up Red Hill Road, which travels ridge tops with excellent views. You will be skirting the edge of the Blue Range Primitive Area, some of the most remote and wild country Arizona has to offer.

This is considered one of Arizona's most scenic routes. The river, the views, and the country itself all combine to make this a memorable adventure.

General location: South of Alpine, in the Apache-Sitgreaves National Forest.
Elevation change: You will begin this ride from the town of Alpine at 8,012'. At the point where FS 281 leaves US 180 your elevation is about 8,000'. You will then descend, following Turkey Creek to where it hits the Blue River at an elevation of 6,544'. Continue heading downhill until you reach Blue Crossing at an elevation of 5,802'. You will climb from here, returning to an elevation of approximately 8,000', where Red Hill Road returns to the pavement of US Route 666. You will then return to the town of Alpine at 8,012'. Elevation gain is 2,210'.
Season: Spring, summer, and fall are all great times for riding in these mountains. Watch out for mud if the ground is saturated. Check with a Forest Service ranger on hunting schedules in the area before you go.
Services: All services are available in Alpine, although you probably won't have much luck finding a bike mechanic here. Come prepared with bike parts and

tools. No water is available out here. Excellent camping opportunities exist at the Upper Blue and Blue Crossing Campgrounds.

Hazards: This is remote country. Come prepared with enough fuel, food, and water for several days.

You will definitely want to check with the ranger for this district before you leave, to learn hunting schedules and road conditions. Bad weather can make this road impassable due to flooding. At certain times of year, high water at Blue Crossing Campground can make fording the river impossible.

Rescue index: The Blue River and Red Hill roads traverse some of the most remote country in Arizona. This may be a route where you will want to establish a trip schedule and check-in times with a district ranger in order to prevent becoming stranded due to vehicular breakdown. During certain times of the year, these roads get a fair amount of sightseer traffic, but during early spring and late fall they may remain relatively untraveled.

Land status: Apache-Sitgreaves National Forest.

Maps: Apache-Sitgreaves National Forest map. The USGS 15 minute quads are Luna Lake, Maness Peak, and Beaverhead.

Finding the trail: This route can be approached from either direction. From the town of Alpine head east on US 180 for approximately 3 miles to FS 281, on which you will turn right (heading south). To follow this route in a counterclockwise direction you will head south out of Alpine on US Route 666, continuing for approximately 10 miles, until you find FS 58 heading off in a southeasterly direction from the left side of the road.

Sources of additional information: The Apache-Sitgreaves National Forest, Alpine Ranger District, address is listed in the introduction to this section.

Notes on the trail: FS 281 is also Blue River Road, which you will follow south for 19 miles to Blue Crossing Campground. This is the intersection with FS 567, or Red Hill Road, which continues on in a northwesterly direction. At about mile 9 on Red Hill Road there will be a fork. FS 567 will branch to the left; FS 58 branches to the right. Both of these roads intersect US Route 666 in about 5 miles.

Flagstaff Area Rides

The town of Flagstaff is without a doubt the outdoor recreational capital of Arizona. Flagstaff rests at the base of the San Francisco Peaks, and at an elevation of 6,905 feet is high enough to receive the benefits of all four seasons. Just over 200 miles north of Phoenix, and 28 miles north of Sedona, the town of Flagstaff and the surrounding area is blanketed by ponderosa pine forests, which thrive in the cool temperatures and volcanic soils that distinguish this area. During the winter months, temperatures are cool enough to find snow in shadowy patches about town, while skiers can find plenty of snow up at the Fairfield Snowbowl Ski Resort on the west side of the San Francisco Peaks. The foothills and the volcanic peaks that rise just behind town, the Canadian and the Hudsonian forests that cloak the slopes of these mountains, and the Mogollon Rim that defines the southern boundary of the Colorado Plateau just to the south, all combine to make this a spectacular natural setting for some fantastic mountain biking.

The landscape of the Flagstaff area looked quite a bit different when the Sinagua people first settled here over a thousand years ago. The Sinagua, less sophisticated contemporaries of the Anasazi, undoubtedly witnessed and suffered the eruption of Sunset Crater in A.D. 1064–1065. Two sudden and very violent eruptions covered this region with 800 square miles of ash and lava flows. Evidence suggests the Sinagua first lived in primitive pit houses and canyon dwellings, like those at nearby Walnut Canyon. Initially fleeing the destruction brought on by the eruption of Sunset Crater, the Sinagua eventually returned to the Flagstaff area to farm the enriched soils and build free-standing stone pueblos like those of the Anasazi. Archaeologists believe that during this time of stress the Sinagua came under the influence of their more developed Anasazi cousins, adopting many of their building, artistry, and religious practices. These people flourished for well over a century after the eruption, but then suddenly disappeared like the ancients who vanished throughout the Southwest.

There are few clues as to what happened to these people, but theories include drought, exhaustive farming practices, disease, and pressure from invading tribes. Apache, Navajo, Yavapai, and Paiute tribes later moved through this general area, hunting, gathering, and trading. The Wupatki Basin, which lies to the northeast of the crater, is the site of several beautifully constructed ruins protected inside Wupatki National Monument. The Visitor Center there has many excellent displays and a good selection of books that provide a wealth of information on these primitive people, the ruins they left behind, and the land on which they lived and worshipped. Walnut Canyon, Sunset Crater National Monument, and Wupatki National Monument are definitely worth a visit while you are in the Flagstaff area.

In the early 1860s, the efforts of eastern commercial settlement companies to establish a community in the Flagstaff area failed, leaving the region unsettled until a sheepherder from California, named Thomas Forsythe McMillan, made the slopes of the San Francisco Peaks his permanent home. While water had to be drilled for and pumped, the lush meadows of these mountains provided ample forage for grazing animals. The lava, cinders, and limestone that covered the landscape around Flagstaff eliminated the hopes of fortune seekers for finding gold and other precious minerals. Many of the men who brought their families to this area during the settlement campaigns of the 1860s and 1870s were eventually lured west to California, after gold was discovered there. Only a few years later, in 1882, the railroad came to Flagstaff, bringing new opportunities for business, ranching, and other development. Cattle ranching and lumber were soon established as mainstays of the community's economy, and they continue to play a major role in supporting the area today. The many gas stations, fast-food restaurants, and hotels that line the main drag through town also help to support Flagstaff's economy, but perpetuate the undesired and undeserved reputation the town has had as nothing more than a gas stop along Interstate 40. While ranchers, settlers, travelers, and traders have passed through Flagstaff, using the town as a place to rest and refuel for years, the area has much, much more to offer to those who are willing to spend a few days, get off the beaten track, and have a look around.

The geology that distinguishes the Flagstaff area is one of its most intriguing features. From 75 miles west of Flagstaff, to Sunset Crater 15 miles northeast of town, the landscape is defined by volcanoes and cinder cones which have been erupting up until 900 years ago. Bill Williams Mountain, Kendrick Peak, Sitgreaves Peak, the San Francisco Peaks, Sunset Crater, Strawberry Crater, as well as numerous cinder cones and volcanic necks scattered around the region, have, over the last four million years, covered the area with the thick layer of lava and ash that hides the underlying geology. The layers of sedimentary rock exposed in Oak Creek Canyon, in the Sedona area to the south and in the Grand Canyon to the north, is what lies beneath the black cinders and grey volcanic rock surrounding Flagstaff. There are lava-free areas most easily identified as meadows. Beneath these meadows lies the Kaibab Limestone. Limestone (which is easily dissolved) and porous volcanic rock quickly absorb any surface water, leaving the geography of the area barren of drainages, lakes, and streams. The water that would normally pool on the surface trickles down through volcanic rock and sands, and through the Kaibab limestone, and is trapped in the Coconino sandstone, which serves as the city's aquifer and water supply. The Coconino sandstone, with its wind-designed crosshatched pattern and blond color, appears in the cliffs and ledges of small canyons draining toward the Mogollon Rim just south of town. You will see this on the Fisher Point ride.

The thick forests of straight, tall, red-barked ponderosa pines that populate much of Arizona's Transition and Canadian Zones dominate here, and have been the focus of lucrative logging efforts since the turn of the century. Oak, piñon, and juniper also make an appearance in spots surrounding town. The slopes of the San Francisco Peaks support stands of mixed conifers and beautiful, mature glades of aspen, which distinguish the Hudsonian Zone. Above 11,000 feet, toward the top of the San Francisco Peaks, you'll find the stunted evergreens and tundra-like vegetation which characterize the Alpine Zone. The wildflowers that bloom in the basins and on the slopes of these mountains in the spring, and again in the fall after summer's thunderstorms, are as colorful and luxuriant as those most people would associate with the peaks of the Rockies. Wildlife that make these mountains their home include elk, mule, white-tailed deer, antelope, black bear, mountain lion, and wild turkey. Wintering bald eagles, nesting osprey, several other raptor species, and a variety of songbirds are protected in this region as well.

Other forms of wildlife that inhabit the town of Flagstaff and outlying areas include a population of avid outdoor recreationalists. Northern Arizona University, a school with great strengths in the Forestry and Geology departments, does a lot to draw students who are interested in their natural surroundings. There is, as you might expect, a correspondingly high number of mountain bikers who exhibit all the benefits from riding at altitude in a mountain setting. Flagstaff also is home to several excellent bike shops with knowledgeable mechanics who support them. All of your biking and outdoor gear needs can be well taken care of while you are in Flagstaff.

Other points of interest you may want to check out while you are in Flagstaff include the Museum of Northern Arizona, which has excellent displays on natural history, archaeology, and Native American arts. Ancient and modern exhibits of Navajo, Hopi, and Zuni crafts are displayed and sold at this museum. You can view the stars at the Lowell Observatory, or learn about their geology and landforms at the USGS Flagstaff Field Center for the Study of Astrogeology. The Arboretum in town will give a good introduction to the wildflowers, shrubs, plants, and trees that thrive in and around Flagstaff, and has excellent exhibits on Native American traditional herbs and plants as well. Here are a few addresses to help you start planning your visit:

Flagstaff Chamber of Commerce and Visitor Center
101 West Santa Fe Avenue
Flagstaff, Arizona 86001
(602) 774-9541 or (800) 842-7293

Coconino National Forest
2323 East Greenlaw Lane
Flagstaff, Arizona 86004
(602) 527-3600

Absolute Bikes
18 North San Francisco Street
Flagstaff, Arizona 86001
(602) 779-5969

Cosmic Cycles
113 South San Francisco Street
Flagstaff, Arizona 86001
(602) 779-1092

Loose Spoke
1529 South Milton Street
Flagstaff, Arizona 86001
(602) 774-7428

RIDE 43   *FISHER POINT*

This short, 14-mile out-and-back excursion is close to town and can be done in a couple of hours. Little technical skill is required, although these dirt roads can become quite rough with deep ruts along certain sections. You may also encounter some sandy sections on this route. You will ride out of town on pavement and continue on hard-packed dirt roads. There are no steep hills. "Ramble" is a good description for this ride. Allow two to three hours to complete this route.

   You will traverse broad meadows and a few gently rolling hills forested with ponderosa pines, juniper, and Gambel oak. At the end of the ride you will encounter a buttress of sculpted, blond sandstone cliffs. This is the Coconino sandstone which is easily identifiable by its cross-hatched design, a result of its aeolian (wind) deposition. Two caves exist along the bottom of these cliffs, one at the bottom of Fisher Point itself and the other farther back in the canyon. Both can be reached by a short trail. Artifacts recovered from these caves point to use by the Sinagua people. This is the beginning of Walnut Canyon. The trail that begins here is one of the few places from which you can reach the canyon floor. This ride is a good introduction to the geography of the Flagstaff area.

General location: This ride is located just south and east out of Flagstaff, in the Coconino National Forest.
Elevation change: From where you begin this ride, in downtown Flagstaff, your elevation is 6,905'. The route is almost flat; there are two small hills that gain a maximum of 150'. Total approximate elevation gain is 300'.
Season: Early spring through late fall are the best times for riding out to Fisher Point, provided that the road is dry. Summer monsoons, as well as spring storms, can make this route a muddy bog.
Services: All services are available in Flagstaff.
Hazards: Wet weather can make this route miserably muddy and leave deep ruts. The ruts can be dangerous to the unwary or reckless rider.

   There are quite a few roads running in all directions back here. Supplemen-

RIDE 43   *FISHER POINT*

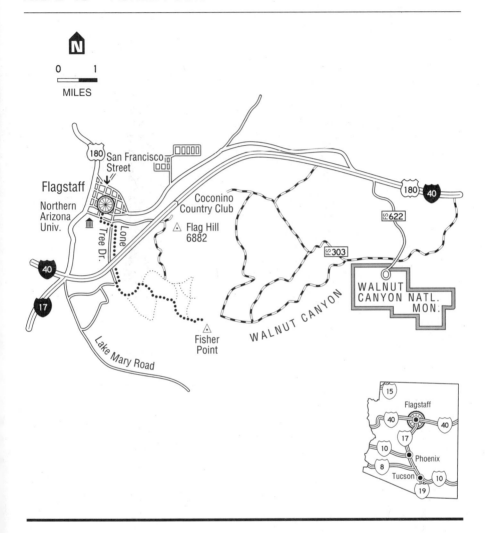

tary topographical maps will help both the easily confused and the adventurous riders.

Rescue index: This is an easy ride that does not take you far from town. The route is also well used by bikers and runners. Help and a telephone are never far away.

Land status: City of Flagstaff public lands, Coconino National Forest.

Maps: Coconino National Forest map (this does not show much detail). The

The buff-colored cliffs of Coconino Sandstone just south of Flag-staff are known as Fisher Point.

USGS 30 × 60 minute quad for Flagstaff and the 7.5 minute quad for Flagstaff East are of greater help.

Finding the trail: It is easy to do this ride right from town. From the corner of San Francisco and Santa Fe streets in downtown Flagstaff, head south on San Francisco Street. Continue heading south on San Francisco Street, through the Northern Arizona University campus, until this street intersects with Pine Knoll Street. Go left on Pine Knoll, then right in about a block on Lone Tree Street. You will still be heading south on Lone Tree when you go under a highway bridge and then encounter a sharp right turn. Go straight where the road makes this elbow turn. You will now be riding on a dirt road.

Sources of additional information: The Coconino National Forest address is listed in the introduction to this section.

Notes on the trail: Once you reach the dirt road head straight, past some junk cars and an old refrigerator riddled with bullet holes, and bear left at the first "Y." Go right at the next intersection, go left at the second, and left at the third. This combination of turns will take you directly to Fisher Point. If you missed your first turn you'll eventually hook up with an alternate route out to the point. If you miss any of these next turns it should be apparent to you rather quickly, as they branch off in the wrong direction. Remember, you will be heading in a southeasterly direction. There are no sign markers out here, so a compass is a handy tool to carry. You can't get too lost, and if you do you will be seeing other bikers out this way. Give 'em a holler and they'll be glad to get you going in the right direction.

RIDE 44 OBSERVATORY MESA TO A-1 MOUNTAIN

This ride is an incredibly scenic 14-mile loop that can be ridden from town. Allow two to three hours to ride this easy-to-moderate route, which climbs two short hills but otherwise rolls across wide open flats. You will be riding on well-maintained, hard-packed dirt roads, with a short stretch of pavement at the beginning and end of this ride.

You will climb up out of town onto Observatory Mesa, named for the Lowell Observatory perched at the mesa's edge, and find yourself riding in a thick forest of ponderosa pines. In less than a mile you'll emerge from the pines at the edge of an expansive meadow dotted with grazing livestock. The sweeping views across the meadow and up to the San Francisco Peaks are fantastic. The extinct cinder cone called A-1 Mountain rises beyond the northwestern corner of the meadow. It is your destination. Ride on!

General location: The loop out across Observatory Mesa to A-1 Mountain runs out of Flagstaff in a west to northwest direction, and lies within the Coconino National Forest.
Elevation change: From where you begin this ride in downtown Flagstaff your elevation is 6,905'. From there you will climb somewhat steeply for a short distance to get up onto the mesa, and then climb very gradually over mostly flat ground to a high elevation at the Radio Facility (at the base of A-1 Mountain) of 7,730'. Total elevation gain is 825'.
Season: Early spring through late fall are best for riding out here, provided roads are dry. Summer monsoons as well as spring storms can make these roads a muddy bog.
Services: All services are available in Flagstaff.
Hazards: Ruts and mud are something to be wary of on this ride.
There are many roads heading off in all directions. Supplementary maps are

RIDE 44 *OBSERVATORY MESA TO A-1 MOUNTAIN*

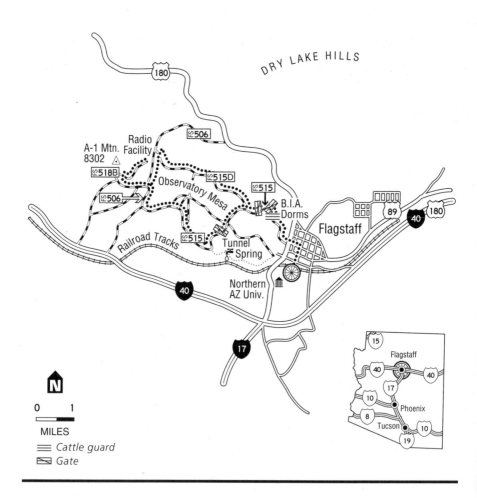

recommended, although geographical markers are easily identified. Gates need to be closed, if they are found closed, and livestock needs to be left alone to keep from angering ranchers.

Rescue index: You will see many other bikers and runners, for you are close to town on this ride. Town is never more than 6 miles away.

Land status: Coconino National Forest.

Maps: Coconino National Forest map (the scale of this map is small, and does not show much detail on this ride). The USGS 7.5 minute quad is Flagstaff West.

The San Francisco Peaks wear a coat of summer green as seen from Observatory Mesa in June.

Finding the trail: This is another good ride to start from downtown Flagstaff. Park anywhere. From downtown Flagstaff head north on San Francisco Street. Go left on Aspen Street and then right on Toltec Street. Continue on Toltec Street as it turns into Thorpe Street. You will continue straight onto the dirt road marked "BIA Dorms"; go past the dorms, then turn left over a cattle guard onto Forest Service Road 515.

Sources of additional information: The Coconino National Forest address is listed in the introduction to this section.

Notes on the trail: Shortly after you begin riding up FS 515 you will encounter 2 gates; make sure you close them behind you. You will also pass several roads branching off to either side of the main road you're on. Ignore them. You will continue on FS 515 as it winds south through pine forests, gaining elevation, and then turns, heading west and north as it starts to level out. You'll then emerge into a meadow cleared by ranchers to graze cattle. Across this wide open expanse you can see the San Francisco Peaks towering in the distance. You will continue heading in this direction until you come to an intersection with a graded dirt road heading due north toward A-1 Mountain. This is FS 506; go right. Follow this road for just under a mile to where you'll find FS 518B heading off to your left, uphill. This road will take you up to the radio facility on the slopes of A-1 Mountain. On your return, go left when you hit FS 506 and follow it north for about a mile to where the road forks. You want to bear right, onto FS 515D, heading in an east to southeast direction. In just over 3 miles this road will intersect with FS 515, which you can follow back past the BIA dorms into town.

You may want to consider riding this route in the opposite direction. Instead of following FS 515 all the way out, you can bear right onto FS 515D just over a mile after you pass the BIA dorms. You will then go left when you reach FS 506, and left again onto FS 515. You can follow FS 515 all the way back to town, or you can maintain your southeast heading where FS 515 turns and heads northeast at the edge of the meadow. This route will take you down a steep trail off the southern edge of the mesa, and then east along the railroad tracks past Tunnel Spring and into town. There are many, many possible options for exploring on top of this mesa. Supplementary maps and a compass will be a big help. With the San Francisco Peaks and A-1 Mountain markers, it is hard to get extremely lost.

RIDE 45 *SUNSET TRAIL*

This 15-mile loop belongs to a larger network of trails known as the Mount Elden/Dry Lake Hills Trail System. These trails offer some of the best riding opportunities close to a major town that I found anywhere in Arizona. The long climb up the Mount Elden Lookout Road can be accomplished easily by any rider in good physical condition; technical riding skills are not required. The ride down on the single-track, however, presents some substantial obstacles in the way of rocks and water bars, and should not be attempted by a beginning rider with little technical skill. You should allow three to four hours to complete this loop, and more if you'll be walking parts of the descent.

You will enjoy some gorgeous mountain scenery on this ride, for there are many great views in all directions. Ponderosas dominate up here, but you'll also find the occasional spruce and fir mixed in. Glades of aspen along this route will applaud your effort; they quake in the mountain breezes and turn a striking gold in fall. Atop Mount Elden, and for the first half mile of the descent on the Sunset Trail, you will be riding through a forest of dead snags left standing after a very hot, fast-burning fire scorched the area in 1977. This part of the ride is referred to as the "Hobbit Forest," for it gives a strange feeling and wild views as you whiz past heading downhill. This is mountain biking at its best!

General location: Mount Elden and the Dry Lake Hills Trail System are located just outside of town to the north, in the foothills behind Flagstaff. The area is maintained and managed by the Coconino National Forest Service.
Elevation change: From where you begin this ride, at the forked intersection of the Schultz Pass Road and Mount Elden Road, your elevation is approximately

RIDE 45 *SUNSET TRAIL*

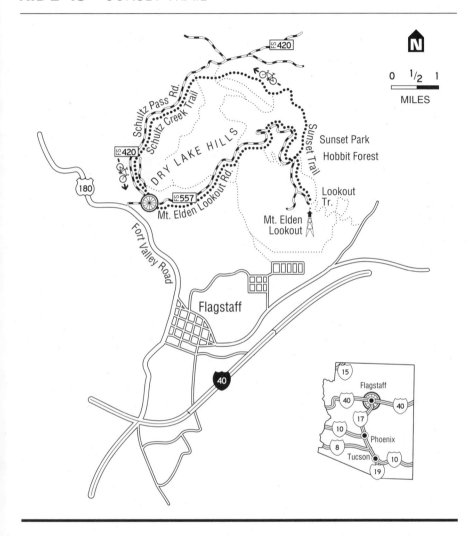

7,000'. From there you will climb to an elevation of 9,300' (!) at the Mount Elden Lookout Tower. Then you'll descend on the Sunset Trail, where you'll experience two more short climbs of 200' and 600'. Total elevation gain is 2,100'.

Season: Spring, summer, and fall are best for riding this loop, provided it is not wet. Watch out for those wild summer thunderstorms up high, for they can build in a hurry and leave you stranded in lightning and rain.

Services: All services are available in Flagstaff.

Hazards: The Mount Elden/Dry Lake Hills Trail System gets heavy use from

Riders begin their descent from the top of Mount Elden on the Sunset Trail, just outside of Flagstaff.

hikers, horseback riders, and mountain bikers. At one point most of these trails were closed to mountain bikers, but due to the responsible actions and lobbying efforts of the off-road biking community in Flagstaff they were reopened. Be courteous to other trail users in this area; say hello, smile, and give uphill riders and hikers the right-of-way. In the case of equestrians you need to dismount and pull your bike off the trail, unless the rider indicates otherwise. Horses can bolt away from bikes and toss their riders.

This is a steep, technical downhill single-track. Wear your helmet!

Don't get caught up here in a lightning storm. They can blossom quicker than you think.

Rescue index: This area gets a lot of traffic from all types of outdoor enthusiasts and sightseers driving up the road. You are not far from town and help on this ride.

Land status: Coconino National Forest.

Maps: A map of the Mount Elden/Dry Lake Hills Trail System can be obtained from the Flagstaff Chamber of Commerce. The Coconino National Forest map is not of an adequate scale for referencing this route. The USGS 7.5 minute quads are Flagstaff East, Flagstaff West, Humphrey's Peak, and Sunset Crater.

Finding the trail: From downtown Flagstaff head north on Fort Valley Road (US 180). You will proceed for just over 2 miles before taking a right onto the Schultz Pass/Mount Elden Road (FS 420). These 2 roads will fork in one-half mile. Park at this fork, taking care to stay clear of mailboxes.

Sources of additional information: The Coconino National Forest address is listed in the introduction to this section.

Notes on the trail: Begin riding by taking the right fork up Mount Elden Road. From here you will climb, climb, climb, all on the same road, almost 7 miles to the Mount Elden Lookout Tower. Have a look around and then head back down the road for approximately a quarter mile, looking for a single-track trail that takes off up the right side of the road. This is the Sunset Trail. There is a trail sign 5 yards or so up the bank indicating the beginning of the Sunset Trail. Scramble up the bank to this trail. Follow the Sunset Trail down, then up, then down, then up, and finally down to where it intersects the Schultz Pass Road. You will then cross over the drainage and get onto the Schultz Pass Road, which will take you back to the fork in the road where you left your car. The Schultz Creek Trail, which parallels the road on the opposite side of the drainage, is closed to downhill bike traffic. This trail looks very enticing for a fun, fast descent, but restrain yourself.

There are several options that exist as part of the Mount Elden/Dry Lake Hills Trail System. The first option you might consider taking is a short single-track trail that leaves from the parking lot adjacent to the lookout tower; it will take you down to the beginning of the Sunset Trail. And all the following rides in this section can be added to this route as options. One of these trails begins 2 miles after you start riding the Sunset Trail; this is the Brookbank Trail. It's a 2.5-mile trail that follows a drainage downhill and eventually crosses over the Mount Elden Lookout Road you pedaled up. Ride back down the Mount Elden Road to your car.

RIDE 46 *BROOKBANK TRAIL*

This trail is an 11-mile loop that gains over 2,000 feet in elevation, and belongs to the system of trails known as the Mount Elden/Dry Lake Hills Trail System. The long climb on the Mount Elden Road does not require much in the way of technical riding skills, but it does call for a good level of physical fitness. The descent on the Brookbank Trail will require some technical riding ability, how-

RIDE 46 *BROOKBANK TRAIL*

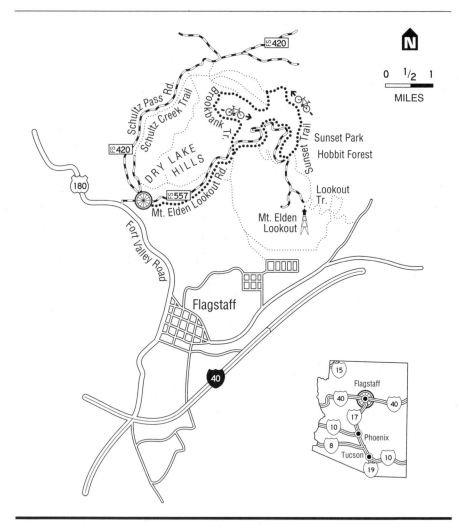

ever. Experienced riders with good technical skills, who are in good-to-excellent physical condition, should take somewhere between two and three hours to complete this ride. Other riders may take longer, but should not be discouraged from giving this excellent mountain biking route a try. Hard-packed dirt road and single-track, with sections of rock, root, and water bars for obstacles, should be anticipated.

You will be winding up the Mount Elden Road through healthy stands of ponderosa pine. Sweeping views of northern Arizona are to be had in all directions

Bikers crossing Brookbank Meadow in the Dry Lake Hills north of Flagstaff.

once you reach the Mount Elden Lookout Tower. Sunset Crater and Strawberry Crater rise to the east, and the town of Flagstaff lies quietly among the pines at the foot of the mountains to the south. You will head down the Lookout Trail to where it joins the Sunset Trail, which you'll follow for just about two miles to where you can pick up the Brookbank Trail. Check your speed, give hikers and equestrians the right-of-way, and give 'em all a big smile and a howdy! This is five-star mountain biking; do your part to keep it open to fat tires.

General location: Mount Elden and the Dry Lake Hills Trail System is located just outside of town to the north, in the foothills behind Flagstaff. These trails are maintained and managed by the Coconino National Forest.

Elevation change: From where you begin this ride, at the forked intersection of Schultz Pass Road and Mount Elden Road, your elevation is approximately 7,000'. From there you will climb and climb to an elevation of 9,300' at the Mount Elden Lookout Tower. From there you will descend on the Lookout, Sunset, and Brookbank trails, which eventually rejoin Mount Elden Lookout Road. This takes you back to your car. Total elevation gain is 2,100'.

Season: Spring, summer, and fall are best for riding this loop, provided it is not wet. Watch out for those wild summer thunderstorms up high. They can build in a hurry and leave you stranded in lightning and rain.

Services: All services are available in Flagstaff.

Hazards: The Mount Elden/Dry Lake Hills Trail System gets heavy use from hikers, horseback riders, and mountain bikers. Be particularly courteous to other trail users in this area. In the case of equestrians you need to dismount and pull your bike off the trail, unless the rider indicates otherwise.

This is a steep, technical downhill single-track, so wear your helmet!

Don't get caught up here in a lightning storm. They can blossom quicker than you think.

Rescue index: This area gets a lot of traffic from all types of outdoor enthusiasts and sightseers driving up the road. You are not far from town or other people on this ride. Flagstaff is just 5 miles away.

Land status: Coconino National Forest.

Maps: A map of the Mount Elden/Dry Lake Hills Trail System can be obtained from the Flagstaff Chamber of Commerce. The Coconino National Forest map is not of an adequate scale for referencing this route. The USGS 7.5 minute quads are Flagstaff East, Flagstaff West, Humphrey's Peak, and Sunset Crater.

Finding the trail: From downtown Flagstaff head north on Fort Valley Road (US 180). You will proceed for just over 2 miles before taking a right onto the Schultz Pass/Mount Elden Road (Forest Service Road 420). These 2 roads will fork in one-half mile. Park at this fork, taking care to stay clear of mailboxes.

Sources of additional information: The Coconino National Forest address is listed in the introduction to this section.

Notes on the trail: You will begin riding by taking the right fork up Mount Elden Road. From here you will climb, and climb, all the way up to the Mount Elden Lookout Tower. Have a look around and then find the single-track trail which leaves from the adjacent parking area. This is the Lookout Trail, which joins the Sunset Trail in about a quarter mile. You will follow the Sunset Trail down, then up, then down to where it meets the Brookbank Trail in the woods at a point where the Sunset Trail crosses a drainage. The Brookbank Trail heads off to the left, down the drainage. Soon the Brookbank Trail emerges at the edge of Brookbank Meadow, and skirts its edge for a quarter mile or so before disappearing back into the woods and heading downhill to where it meets Mount Elden Lookout Road. You can then ride back to where you left your car.

Several route options are possible here. You may want to combine this route with the Rocky Ridge Trail, the next ride covered in this section. Or, if you rode out to the start of this ride from town, you can take the Oldham Trail down the mountain to Buffalo Park and back to town that way. The Oldham Road takes off directly across the road from where the Brookbank Trail meets the Mount Elden Road.

RIDE 47 *ROCKY RIDGE TRAIL*

This route is a short 5.6-mile loop that will challenge even the most experienced riders. While elevation gain is negligible, the extremely rough and rocky section of this route (aptly called the Rocky Ridge Trail) makes this a ride tailored for the technical wizard and trials-type rider. It will take advanced riders in good physical condition one to two hours to finish this loop. It's worth checking this ride out even if you don't consider yourself a technical wizard, just to see what heights of technical riding skills can be achieved with practice. The first section of this ride is on the hard-packed dirt of Mount Elden Road.

Along this route you will be surrounded by deep, sweet-smelling ponderosa pine forests growing in the rocky, sandy slopes you'll be trying to negotiate on your bike. You may want to work this route into a longer ride including any of the Dry Lake Hills Trails listed in this section. Many route options are possible. Don't forget to wear your helmet and have a blast!

General location: Mount Elden and the Dry Lake Hills Trail System is located just outside of town to the north, in the foothills behind Flagstaff. These trails are maintained and managed by the Coconino National Forest.

Elevation change: From where you begin this ride, at the forked intersection of the Schultz Pass Road and Mount Elden Road, your elevation is approximately 7,000'. From there you will climb to an elevation of approximately 7,400'. You will descend only slightly to where you emerge onto the Schultz Pass Road at an elevation of 7,380'. Total elevation gain is 400'.

Season: Spring, summer, and fall are best for riding this loop. In the winter you will find snow on these trails.

Services: All services are available in Flagstaff.

Hazards: The Mount Elden/Dry Lake Hills Trail System gets heavy use from hikers, horseback riders, and mountain bikers. Be extra sensitive to other trail users in this area. In the case of equestrians you need to dismount and pull your bike off the trail, unless the rider indicates otherwise.

This is an extremely difficult, technical single-track. Wear your helmet and carry first-aid supplies for abrasions.

Rescue index: This area gets a lot of traffic from outdoor enthusiasts and sightseers driving up the road. You are not far from town and help on this ride. Flagstaff is just 2 miles away.

Land status: Coconino National Forest.

Maps: A map of the Mount Elden/Dry Lake Hills Trail System can be obtained from the Flagstaff Chamber of Commerce. The Coconino National Forest map is not of an adequate scale for referencing this route. The USGS 7.5 minute quads are Flagstaff East, Flagstaff West, Humphrey's Peak, and Sunset Crater.

RIDE 47   *ROCKY RIDGE TRAIL*

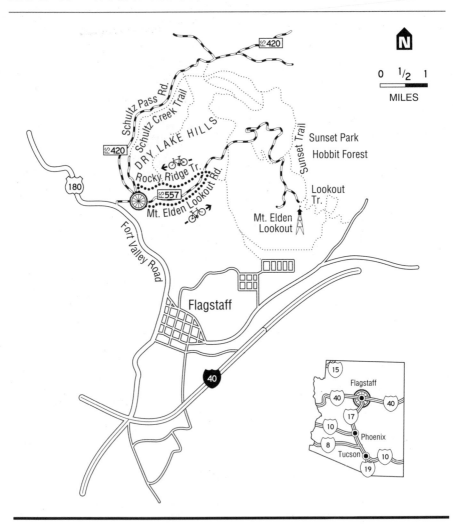

Finding the trail: From downtown Flagstaff head north on Fort Valley Road (US 180). You will proceed for just over 2 miles before taking a right onto the Schultz Pass/Mount Elden Road, also FS 420. These 2 roads will fork in one-half mile. Park at this fork, taking care to stay clear of mailboxes.

Sources of additional information: The Coconino National Forest address is listed in the introduction to this section.

Notes on the trail: You will begin riding by taking the right fork up Mount Elden Road. From here you will climb gently for approximately 1.8 miles, to where the Rocky Ridge Trail leaves the road on the left side. You will then ride as much as you can of the Rocky Ridge Trail to where it comes out on the Schultz Pass Road. Go left onto this road and follow it back to the intersection with the Mount Elden Road where you left your car.

Options for alternatives from this route are few, but many possibilities exist for incorporating Rocky Ridge Trail into longer rides. You may want to take Rocky Ridge Trail as an option toward the end of riding Brookbank Trail. About one mile past the point where you emerged onto Mount Elden Road, having finished Brookbank Trail, you will find Rocky Ridge Trail taking off on the right side of the road. Take Rocky Ridge Trail to Schultz Pass Road, which will take you back to the intersection with Mount Elden Road where you began your ride.

RIDE 48 *WATERLINE ROAD*

This ride follows the maintenance road for Flagstaff's main waterline, which brings water down from springs high up in the Inner Basin of the San Francisco Peaks. Round-trip from where this ride begins, at Schultz Tank on the Schultz Pass Road, is a distance of 23 miles. The road surface is hard-packed and does not suffer washboarded sections or heavy rutting because it is closed to motorized vehicles (except for the occasional maintenance truck). Allow four to five hours to complete this journey.

Along the way you will be cruising through beautiful alpine forests of mixed conifer and old aspen glades with some interesting rock formations along the way. This is a really fun middle-chainring climb for anyone who is in fairly good condition; little or no technical skill is required. In the fall this route is ablaze with the yellow glow of changing aspen leaves. The canopy overhead can be solid at times, providing precious shade and dappled lighting on the way up. Fill your water bottles, dunk your head, and drink heartily from Raspberry Spring when you make it to the top; the water is sweet and rejuvenating. (This is the water source for the Forest Service personnel whose cabins are nearby.) The short but rough ride down to Locket Meadow from Raspberry Spring can be an exhausting prospect after the ride up, but it is well worth the effort. This is a beautiful open meadow with a small lake and incredible views back to the peaks.

General location: This ride is due north of Flagstaff and is within the Coconino National Forest.
Elevation change: From where this ride begins, where the Waterline Road leaves the Schultz Pass Road, your elevation is approximately 8,000'. You will then

RIDE 48 *WATERLINE ROAD*

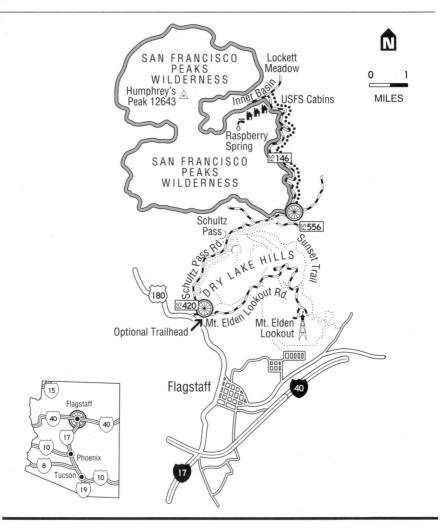

climb steadily to an elevation of 9,420' at the research cabins at Jack Smith Spring. It is a 620' drop if you are interested in the short ride down to Lockett Meadow (8,600') from here. Total elevation gain (without the trip down to Lockett Meadow) is 1,420'.

Season: This route can be ridden from spring through fall, provided the road is dry and free of snow. Look for icy patches on the road. Also, rapidly changing weather conditions and temperatures at high elevations are something to pre-

A rider climbs Waterline Road in the San Francisco Peaks beneath a canopy of quaking aspen.

pare for. A weatherproof shell and a thin (or thick) layer for warmth are good insurance for a comfortable ride down.

Services: All services are available in Flagstaff.

Hazards: Afternoon thunderstorms in the summer and fall can cause temperatures to drop rapidly. Storm clouds often build off the San Francisco Peaks during these times of year. Come prepared.

The descent on this ride tempts some into high-speed cruising. Watch for the occasional maintenance truck coming up the road, and other bikers.

Rescue index: Because of the distance gained on this ride you will get into some rather remote areas. You may find campers or picnickers down at Lockett Meadow.

Land status: Coconino National Forest.

Maps: The Coconino National Forest map will suffice here. The USGS 30 × 60 minute map for Flagstaff and the 7.5 minute quads for Humphrey's Peak and Sunset Crater West will also do the trick.

Finding the trail: From downtown Flagstaff drive north on Fort Valley Road (US 180). You will proceed for just over 2 miles before taking a right onto the Schultz Pass/Mount Elden Road (Forest Service Road 420). These 2 roads will fork in one-half mile; bear left onto Schultz Pass Road when you reach this fork. You will continue on Schultz Pass Road for 4.7 miles, to where Waterline Road (FS 146) leaves on the left side of the road. Park across the main road at Schultz Tank.

Sources of additional information: The Coconino National Forest address is listed in the introduction to this section.

Notes on the trail: Once you are on your bike you will go across the road from where you left your car, pick up FS 146, and begin climbing. You will climb this mellow grade at a consistent rate for about 11 miles. This is a great tour of some really gorgeous country. Have fun!

There aren't a lot of options up here as you are surrounded by Kachina Peaks Wilderness Area.

You may want to start this ride from back at the fork of Mount Elden and Schultz Pass roads. This adds about 10 miles and makes for a 32-mile round-trip day. It also adds about 1.5 hours to your riding time.

RIDE 49   *OLDHAM TRAIL*

This is a quick seven-mile out-and-back affair, with a short loop section, which offers some great intermediate single-track riding. This route will take riders of intermediate ability in good physical condition between two and three hours to complete. You will encounter both hard-packed road and single-track riding surfaces. Expect some rocky sections requiring technical maneuvers.

This trail starts at scenic Buffalo Park, a favorite spot for Flagstaff area runners, and then winds up through the pine-covered foothills below Mount Elden. You will find excellent cruising along some of these quiet forest trails, as well as fantastic views of Mount Elden. The trails in this area get quite a bit of use from hikers, so keep an eye out and yield the right-of-way.

General location: Mount Elden and the Dry Lake Hills Trail System are located just outside of town to the north in the foothills behind Flagstaff. These trails are maintained and managed by the Coconino National Forest.

Elevation change: Beginning elevation for this ride is approximately 7,140' at Buffalo Park. You will climb until you reach the Pipeline Road at about 7,200', and then emerge onto the Mount Elden Road at an elevation of 7,400'.

RIDE 49 *OLDHAM TRAIL*

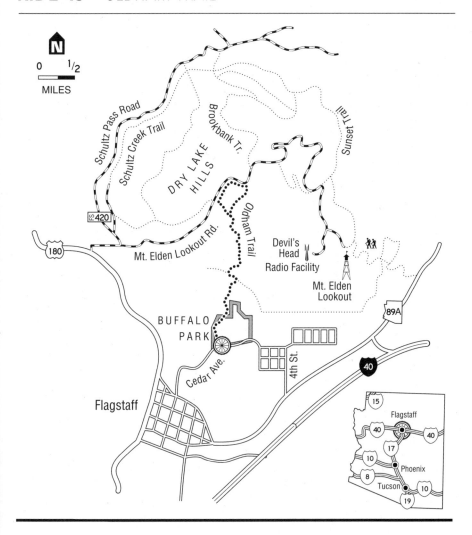

Season: Spring, summer, and fall are best for riding this trail. In the winter you may run into snow.

Services: All services are available in Flagstaff.

Hazards: The Mount Elden/Dry Lake Hills Trail System gets heavy use from hikers, horseback riders, and mountain bikers. Be courteous to other trail users in this area. In the case of equestrians you need to dismount and pull your bike off the trail, unless the rider indicates otherwise.

This can be a challenging technical single-track, so wear your helmet!

Heading up to the Oldham Trail from Buffalo Park in the early evening.

Rescue index: This area gets a lot of traffic from outdoor enthusiasts and sightseers. You are not far from town and help on this ride. Flagstaff is just 2 miles away.

Land status: Coconino National Forest.

Maps: A map of the Mount Elden/Dry Lake Hills Trail System can be obtained from the Flagstaff Chamber of Commerce. The Coconino National Forest map is not of an adequate scale for referencing this route. The USGS 7.5 minute quads are Flagstaff East, Flagstaff West, Humphrey's Peak, and Sunset Crater.

Finding the trail: To get to Buffalo Park from downtown Flagstaff take San Francisco Street north, past the hospital, to Cedar Street. Go right on Cedar Street and continue up to the top of the hill where you will find Buffalo Park. Park here.

Sources of additional information: The Coconino National Forest address is listed in the introduction to this section.

Notes on the trail: Ride around the perimeter of Buffalo Park on a dirt road looking for a small white house as you reach the top end of the park. Go through the gate behind the house onto the Oldham Trail and ride in a northerly direction. You will soon encounter Pipeline Road. Go left on Pipeline Road until you find a Forest Service sign reading "251." You need to go right onto a trail which actually leaves the road about 15 yards before that sign. You will continue on this trail following it until it emerges onto Mount Elden Road. Go right onto

Mount Elden Road, riding uphill for a little less than a mile, to a trail just beyond a cattle guard. Go right (downhill) onto this trail, and be prepared to react to rocks and other hazards on the way. You will once again encounter Pipeline Road. This time the trail should continue straight across on the other side of the road. You will soon emerge back at Buffalo Park.

There are not really any route options on this ride. There are several possibilities, however, for combining this ride with other rides in the Dry Lake Hills/Mount Elden Trails System. See the rides discussed above.

RIDE 50   *PIPELINE TRAIL*

This trail is accessed by the Oldham Trail that leaves from Buffalo Park. Total distance is close to eight miles for this out-and-back excursion that takes you in an easterly direction until it reaches the Mount Elden Trailhead on US 89A. This route is primarily a rough double-track (used only for maintenance of the pipeline), with some sections of single-track. Riders with an intermediate skill level, and who are in good physical condition, should take two to three hours to complete this ride.

You will be riding through sweet-smelling pine forests on the sometimes rocky Oldham Trail. This changes when you reach the Pipeline Trail or road. You will traverse the southern flank of Mount Elden as you cruise through the forest catching glimpses through tree branches of the grassy plains below. Soon you will see Sunset Crater to the north and east.

General location: Mount Elden and the Dry Lake Hills Trail System are located just outside of town to the north, in the foothills behind Flagstaff. These trails are maintained and managed by the Coconino National Forest.
Elevation change: From where you begin this ride, at the top of Buffalo Park, your elevation is approximately 7,140'. From here you will ride the Oldham Trail to where it meets the Pipeline Trail at an elevation of 7,200'. From here you will gain, and then lose, only slight amounts of elevation. You will reach a high elevation on this ride of almost 7,400'. You'll reach the Mount Elden Hiking Trail on Highway 89 at an elevation of approximately 7,100'. Total elevation gain is 360'.
Season: Spring, summer, and fall are best for riding this trail. You are likely to find snow during winter months, although it can sometimes be ridden during dry spells.
Services: All services are available in Flagstaff.
Hazards: The Mount Elden/Dry Lake Hills Trail System gets heavy use from hikers, horseback riders, and mountain bikers. The Pipeline Trail gets a lot of equestrian traffic, which will grow heavier as you near the Mount Elden Trail-

RIDE 50   *PIPELINE TRAIL*

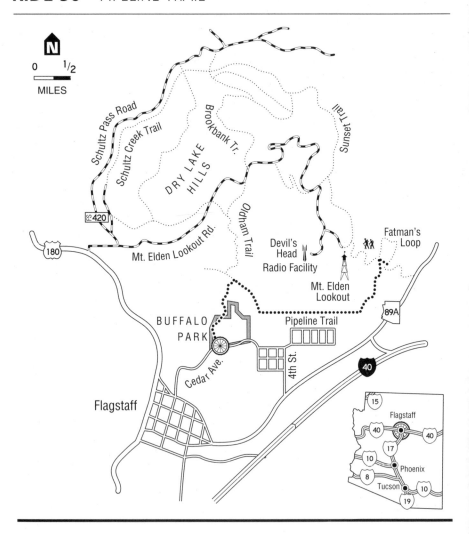

head. Be extra sensitive to other trail users in this area. In the case of equestrians you need to dismount and pull your bike off the trail, unless the rider indicates otherwise.

The Oldham Trail can be a challenging, technical single-track. Protect your head.

Rescue index: This area gets a lot of traffic from all types of outdoor enthusiasts and sightseers driving up the road. You are not far from town and help on this ride. Flagstaff is just 2 miles away.

Land status: Coconino National Forest.

Maps: A map of the Mount Elden/Dry Lake Hills Trail System can be obtained from the Flagstaff Chamber of Commerce. The Coconino National Forest map is not of an adequate scale for referencing this route. The USGS 7.5 minute quads are Flagstaff East, Flagstaff West, Humphrey's Peak, and Sunset Crater.

Finding the trail: To get to Buffalo Park from downtown Flagstaff, take San Francisco Street north, past the hospital, to Cedar Street. Go right on Cedar Street and continue up to the top of the hill, where you'll find the park. Park here.

Sources of additional information: The Coconino National Forest address is listed in the introduction to this section.

Notes on the trail: Ride around the perimeter of Buffalo Park on a dirt road, and look for a small white house as you reach the top end of the park. Go through the gate behind the house onto the Oldham Trail, and ride it in a northerly direction. You will soon encounter an open double-track or old abandoned road; this is Pipeline Road. Go right, following this rough double-track for approximately 3.2 miles to where it ends at the Mount Elden (hiking) Trailhead. Turn around and head on back the way you came.

There are several possibilities for combining this ride with other rides in the Dry Lake Hills/Mount Elden Trails System. Riding up to the top of Mount Elden from the Mount Elden Trailhead is not an option, for this trail is very steep and loose.

RIDE 51 *BILL WILLIAMS MOUNTAIN*

This ride features another long, middle-chainring climb that anyone in good physical condition will enjoy. The highlight of this ride, at least for more experienced riders, will be the technical downhill single-track. There are tight switchbacks, water bars, tree roots, and rocks. Beginning and even intermediate riders may choose to ride back down the road they came up. This ride is 19 miles round-trip and takes close to four hours to complete.

The views along this route are fantastic. The San Francisco Peaks rise to the north, while Sycamore and Oak Creek canyons, canyons which define the southern edge of the Colorado Plateau, stretch away to the east and south. Ponderosa pines eventually give way to pine, fir, and aspen as elevation is gained. The wildflowers in summer, including lupine, paintbrush, and penstamon, offer bright splashes of color. "Finger Rock," and accompanying rock formations, are worth a stop on your way up; look for the short trail leading out to them on the left side of the road at about the 5.5-mile mark. Fall colors are fantastic up here.

RIDE 51 *BILL WILLIAMS MOUNTAIN*

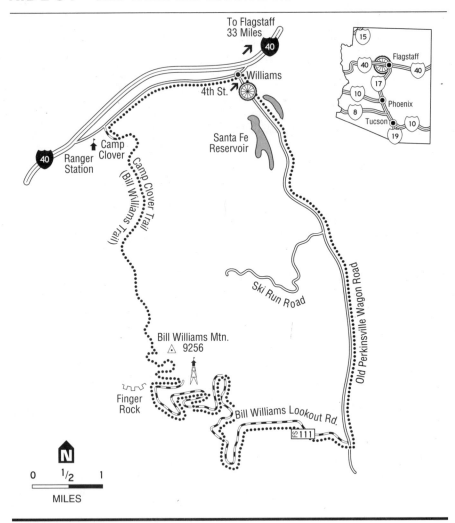

General location: Williams, and the nearby Kaibab National Forest.

Elevation change: From the town of Williams, where you begin this ride, your elevation is 6,770′. At the top of Bill Williams Mountain the elevation is 9,265′. Total elevation gain is 2,385′.

Season: This ride is great anytime from spring through fall, provided the road is dry and free of snow. Be aware of rapidly changing weather conditions and temperatures at high elevations. A weatherproof shell and a thin layer for warmth are good insurance for a comfortable ride down.

A rider near the end of his climb up to Bill Williams Mountain.

Services: You can get water and something to eat in Williams. All other needs, including those which are bike-related, can be met in Flagstaff.

Hazards: You are very high and quite exposed along much of this ride, and even more so when you reach the top of Bill Williams Mountain. Be aware of current weather conditions and forecasts. You don't want to get caught up here in one of those violent late summer monsoonal storms. Lightning *can* be deadly.

This is a technical downhill. Loose rock, tight switchbacks, water bars, and trail retention bars make this descent a real challenge. This is a good place to lower your seat.

Rescue index: This is a fairly remote area with little activity. The nearest place to find some help and a phone is in Williams. While in Williams, you may want to check in at the ranger station for the forecast and road condition information, and to let them know where you are riding and when you plan to return.

Land status: Kaibab National Forest, Williams Ranger District.

Maps: Kaibab National Forest, Williams, Chandler, and Tusayan Ranger District maps. The USGS 15 minute quads are Bill Williams Mountain and Ash Fork. **Finding the trail:** From Flagstaff you will drive west on old Route 666, or I-40 Business Loop, then take I-40 for 30 miles until you reach the exit for Williams. Park in the town of Williams near the intersection of 4th Street and Main.

Sources of additional information: Call the local operator for the current number of the Kaibab National Forest, Williams Ranger District. The long-distance operator can be reached at (602) 555-1212.

Notes on the trail: You will ride south, out of the town of Williams on 4th Street, which is also the Old Perkinsville Wagon Road. You will pass the Santa Fe Reservoir on your right, and then, a little farther down the road, the entrance to the Bill Williams Ski Area. Continue riding until you reach Bill Williams Lookout Road, which is also FS 111. You will climb, mostly in your middle chainring, up to the lookout. After you have had a good look around, climbed up to the top and said hello to the fire lookout, and had a good rest, you're ready to head down. Riding back down the road you will see signs for the Camp Clover Trail, which is also the Bill Williams Trail. This is it. You will head down the northern slope of Bill Williams Mountain, ending up at the Williams Ranger Station on I-40. Ride the frontage road that will take you back to Williams, where you can treat yourself and your buddies to a tasty snack at the Hot Dog Corral.

Once you are on top of Bill Williams Mountain your option is heading back down the road you came up, if you feel you are not up to the single-track descent. No other real options exist from up here.

The Kaibab Plateau Rides

The Kaibab Plateau, with its old quiet forests and broad green meadows, sits like a green cushion above the reds and browns of the desert below. From this perch there are astounding views in all directions. Sculpted sandstone pinnacles and rock formations guard the plateau's perimeter, beyond which a maze of canyons fall endlessly away. You can look down into the rumbling gorges that flow out to the Grand Canyon, across to the San Francisco Peaks over a hundred miles away, and up past the tops of 200-foot-high ponderosas into an enormous, deep desert blue sky decorated with towers of billowing cumulus during summer and fall afternoons. The spectacular beauty of the Kaibab Plateau is a unique and unforgettable experience, even amongst Arizona's many natural wonders.

"Kaibab" is a Paiute Indian word meaning "mountain lying down," a phrase which captures the essence of this place. Here deep forests of fir, pine, spruce, and aspen surround broad meadows filled with alpine wildflowers; it is a mountain scene that seems to float above the enormous abyss of the Grand Canyon and its tributaries. The Kaibab Plateau is an "island in the sky" in the biological sense as well. Species of flora and fauna have been held prisoner here, and intruders kept out, by a moat of hot, arid desert, for thousands of years. In their isolation several species of plants and animals on the Kaibab Plateau have developed characteristics different from those of their relatives that range freely beyond the yawning desert canyons. Elevations on and around the plateau extend from 9,000 feet at the highest point, to below 4,000 feet in the canyons that surround it, and include Lower Sonoran, Upper Sonoran, Transition, and Canadian life zones. The Kaibab Plateau forms the North Rim of the Grand Canyon. It is 1,500 feet higher, and receives 60 percent more moisture, than the South Rim of the canyon. The combination of elevation and moisture means substantial snowfall in the winter. Roads to the rim stay closed from first snowfall (sometime in late October or early November) to mid-May.

The earliest evidence of human activity on the plateau is dated sometime around 7,000 B.C. During this time, in what is called the Archaic Period, small bands hunted and gathered on the plateau, camping at the edges of meadows and in small caves. By A.D. 500 there emerged an identifiable group of area inhabitants who built permanent settlements, grew crops, and developed distinctive crafts, but lived mainly in the drainages surrounding the plateau. This group is known as the Anasazi. They flourished for centuries all across the Colorado Plateau and then, for reasons unknown by archaeologists, disappeared sometime around A.D. 1300. The Paiute Indians were next to make their living in the area. They passed through by season, hunting and gathering, but never took up permanent residence on the plateau. The Paiute still live nearby, on a reservation that is just west of Fredonia, Arizona, surrounding Pipe Springs National Monument.

195

The first non-Indian visitors to the area were the Spanish Friars Dominguez and Escalante, who led an expedition to the plateau and kept detailed accounts of their experiences and observations in the year 1776. The area remained unsettled until Mormon pioneers were sent to colonize this distant and unforgiving land in the mid-1800s. Most were able to eke out a living ranching, hunting, and lumbering, much as they do today. The astounding natural beauty of this plateau was recognized as early as 1893, when the federal government began administering the area within the establishment of the Grand Canyon Forest Reserve. In 1905 it came under the jurisdiction of the newly created National Forest Service, but gained special status the following year when it was designated as a game preserve by President Theodore Roosevelt. In 1908 the preserve was renamed as the Kaibab National Forest, and in 1919 much of the land was reallocated to Grand Canyon National Park, and managed by the newly created Park Service. The Kaibab National Forest boundaries were established as they exist today when the Tusayan National Forest was added in 1934.

The region that includes the Kaibab Plateau, the Grand Canyon, and what is referred to as the "North Rim" is considered one of the world's most spectacular geological formations. The creation of this formation began when the earth was still young, and now stands exposed by the work of erosion like a catalogue of time. The many layers of sandstones, limestones, shales, and toward the very bottom, schists, which are stacked upon each other for thousands of feet beneath a cap of Kaibab limestone, retell the story of how shallow seas, river deltas, sand dunes, marshes, deepening seas, and deserts periodically dominated this area's landscape. Encased in each layer are the creatures, sediments, and patterns of deposition that tell us about worlds much different than our own. These layers of rock have remained a stable, recognizable block in the earth's crust, a solidly built raft surrounded by a sea of moving faults that have tilted and squeezed the earth around it for more than 600 million years. This raft of rock, or plateau, which provides us with the most complete geological record in the world, is named for its most dominant feature—the Colorado River.

There are more than 50 species of mammals, 90 species of birds, and several species of reptiles living in the wide variety of life zones identified in the Kaibab region. Among the most notable is the Kaibab squirrel, which is found only here and is identified by its distinctive black and white markings and tasseled or tufted ears. Black bear haunt some of the more remote areas of the plateau, and the mountain lion has started to make a comeback after being almost entirely exterminated in the first decade of the century.

Hunting has always been one of the area's biggest attractions, which results in heavy hunter traffic during the fall. The reputation that the plateau has for great hunting developed right after the turn of the century, when Theodore Roosevelt established the area as a game preserve. The biological isolation that species experience on the plateau has made it an interesting place for the study of the effects of man's activities on nature. During the 1800s, hundreds of thousands of cattle and sheep overgrazed the plateau, causing much of the grass to be replaced by broad-leafed shrubs and other woody plants. While forage decreased for livestock it increased for deer, whose numbers began to increase rapidly. At this point the area was set aside as a game preserve and all predators were destroyed, including the grey wolf, which has never recovered. The combination of the absence of predators and increased forage resulted in a population explosion of deer. From the estimated 3,000 deer that existed on the plateau in 1906, over 100,000 struggled to survive there in 1924. The deer soon overgrazed the plateau, and died off in enormous numbers due to starvation. These events, isolated atop the plateau, gave invaluable insight to land managers on the necessity of controlling the grazing, hunting, and other human practices that until this point had largely gone unchecked.

The mixed conifer and aspen forests, and the wide meadows brimming with wildflowers at mid-summer, carpet the plateau in luxuriant greens, which are a stunning contrast to the barren red rock walls of the canyons that fall away around it. Along the edge of the plateau, and throughout its lower elevations toward the north, you will find piñon, juniper, Gambel oak and sage. Logging has long been practiced on the plateau in the National Forest, and one of the most productive mills in the southwest, fed with trees from the plateau, supports the community of Fredonia. Grand Canyon National Park protects some of the oldest trees to be found on the plateau, or anywhere in Arizona and the Southwest. These ponderosa pines, many of which bear the scars of numerous lightning strikes, reach more than four feet in diameter.

The North Rim of the Grand Canyon, indeed the entire Kaibab Plateau, is host to extremely violent weather at certain times of the year. A very moist monsoonal flow (which dominates the weather throughout the Southwest, starting in mid-July and running through the end of September) can lash this region with a daily barrage of hailstones, lightning, and rain. While this unstable weather pattern persists, the day can go from cloudless blue, to a few fluffy clouds, to angry dark towers of storm clouds within a couple of hours. Be prepared for all types of weather up here, and check with the ranger for weather forecasts. Temperatures can drop in a hurry as well. It is also a good idea to check with the nearest ranger for scheduled hunts during the spring and fall. A bright piece of clothing or helmet cover should be worn at this time of year.

There is lodging at the Grand Canyon Lodge at the North Rim and at the Jacob Lake Inn at Jacob Lake and at the Kaibab Lodge 25 miles south of Jacob Lake. Backcountry permits need to be obtained for camping in the park, but they are free. You can camp anywhere in the National Forest. You can get gas, groceries, and water at Jacob Lake and near the campground at the rim. You will not find camping supplies, bike supplies, or a bike mechanic within a hundred miles of here, so come prepared. Here are a few addresses to help you start planning your trip:

Kaibab National Forest Headquarters
800 South 6th Street
Williams, Arizona 86046
(602) 635-2681

North Kaibab Ranger District
P.O. Box 248
Fredonia, Arizona 86022
(602) 643-7395

Grand Canyon National Park
Superintendent
P.O. Box 129
Grand Canyon, Arizona 86023
(602) 638-7864

RIDE 52 BUCK RIDGE POINT

On this short five-mile ride you will get an introduction to the Kaibab Plateau's beautiful forests and spectacular views. Little technical skill is required for cruising out to Buck Ridge Point on this seldom-used dirt road that has a grassy median and a few soft, sandy spots. Give yourself a couple of hours to ride out and back to this point. This will also give you time to take in the scenery.

Buck Ridge Point is on the northwestern edge of the Kaibab Plateau. Views from here stretch out across a desolate strip of desert between here and the Utah border, which is referred to as the "Arizona Strip," one of the wildest and most remote areas in the Southwest. Broken mountain ridges, twisting canyons, and the distant Vermillion Cliffs form a beautiful and nearly empty landscape. The pink and amber buttes of Bryce Canyon, and the buff-colored walls of Zion National Park can be seen along the distant northern horizon. Snake Gulch and Kanab Creek Canyon are main drainages, forming the northwestern and western boundaries of the Plateau. Kanab Creek Canyon appears to be a miniature of that grandest of canyons, which it joins several miles downstream.

General location: The Snake Gulch/Kanab Canyon Area, Kaibab Plateau, Kaibab National Forest, is 30 miles south of Fredonia, Arizona, and 166 miles north of Flagstaff.
Elevation change: At the intersection of Forest Service roads 461 and 264 your elevation is 7,822' above sea level. From there you will be heading gradually downhill until you reach Buck Ridge Point at 7,555'. Total elevation gain is 267'.
Season: Because this is not as high as the southernmost reaches of the plateau,

RIDE 52 *BUCK RIDGE POINT*

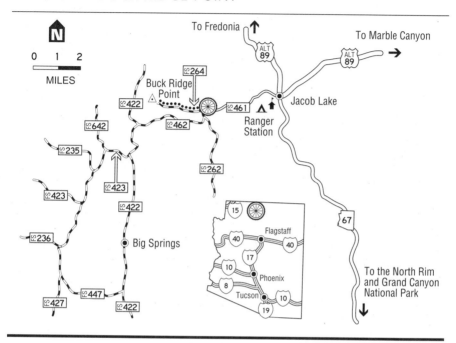

riding is excellent from April through November. Beware of violent summer thunderstorms.

Services: Water, groceries, prepared meals, and accommodations are available at Jacob Lake, at the Grand Canyon Lodge, and the North Rim campground grocery store.

Hazards: This road receives little use, but keep an eye (and ear) out for the occasional jeep. Hunters in the spring and fall pose a serious hazard. Violent thunder and lightning storms in summer and fall are also hazards you should be aware of. Check in with the ranger for hunting seasons and weather forecasts at the Jacob Lake Ranger Station before you go.

Rescue index: Because this is such remote country it is a good idea to establish a schedule and contact times with the district ranger or someone by a phone, who has local emergency numbers. Or at least be prepared to handle whatever situation may arise.

Land status: Kaibab National Forest.

Maps: The Kaibab National Forest map is not of an adequate scale to show this ride. The USGS 15 minute quad for Warm Springs Canyon is preferable.

Finding the trail: From the Jacob Lake intersection drive one quarter-mile south

Looking north from Buck Ridge Point on the Kaibab Plateau, across the Arizona Strip, to the cliffs and buttes of Zion National Park in southern Utah.

on AZ 67 to FS 461. Turn right onto FS 461, a gravel road. Head west for 4 miles to the beginning of FS 264, the Buck Ridge Point Road. Park here to begin your ride.

Sources of additional information: The Kaibab National Forest, North Kaibab Ranger District, address is listed in the introduction to this section.

Notes on the trail: You will follow this jeep road, FS 264, out to the point where it ends in a stand of juniper trees. There is an abandoned mine site nearby and you will see a steep, rocky road heading down the west side of the plateau. Don't go down there unless you are up for a grueling ride and/or push to get back up. Take a minute to have a bite to eat and to familiarize yourself with the landmarks of the area. Go back the way you came.

There are many, many options here. Supplementary maps and a compass are a necessity if you are planning some exploring. The best option here is for extending the length of this ride to 13 miles by riding from the Jacob Lake Inn and ranger station.

You will encounter several side roads taking you to overlooks off Buck Ridge. Roads off to your right will leave at a quarter of a mile, 1 mile, 2.3 miles, and 3.8 miles. These are short spurs that make for good adventuring but won't get you lost. There are actually two main points extending from Buck Ridge. The most obvious will take you out to the point described in the trail description. If you want to head out to the other point, also commonly referred to as Buck Ridge Point, turn around and go right at the first intersection you hit on your return.

RIDE 53 WILLOW POINT

The ride out to Willow Point is an easy-to-moderate 12 miles that take you to more fantastic views off the western edge of the Kaibab Plateau. This is a seldom-used jeep track with a vegetated median, also called a double-track by mountain bikers. There are a few negotiable rocky spots requiring basic technical skills. But beginning mountain bikers will have little difficulty. Allow at least two hours' riding time on this one.

You are still in the lower reaches of the plateau here, so you'll be rolling along through piñon, juniper, and the occasional clump of Gambel oak. The ever-present ponderosa pine is easy to identify here. From Willow Point you will have great views into Upper Snake Gulch, across to Kanab Creek Gulch, and into surrounding rock formations. Both these canyons hold numerous Anasazi sites but are designated as wilderness areas, and are therefore off-limits to mountain bikes. Several hiking trails access the canyon bottoms, however, and are worth checking out if you are going to be in the area for several days.

General location: The Snake Gulch/Kanab Canyon Area, Kaibab Plateau, and Kaibab National Forest are located 30 miles south of Fredonia, Arizona, and 166 miles north of Flagstaff.
Elevation change: Elevation at Oak Corral in Nail Canyon is 6,375'. Where you bear left onto Forest Service Road 423 your elevation will be 6,137'. Where you make a right turn onto FS 235 your elevation will be 6,600'. At the intersection of FS 235 and FS 237 you will have come back down to 6,171'. You will then descend to a low elevation of 5,600' at Willow Point. Elevation gain is approximately 1,240'.
Season: Riding out here is great from early spring through late fall.
Services: Water, groceries, prepared meals, and accommodations are available at Jacob Lake, at the Grand Canyon Lodge, and at the North Rim campground grocery store.
Hazards: This road is rarely used, so traffic is not a problem. Hunters and lightning storms will be your biggest concern. Check with the ranger for hunting seasons and weather information either before your visit, or when you arrive.

The roads that access this ride are gravel, all-weather roads, but they may become impassable during the winter or after spring and fall storms.
Rescue index: Because this is such remote country it is a good idea to establish

RIDE 53   *WILLOW POINT*

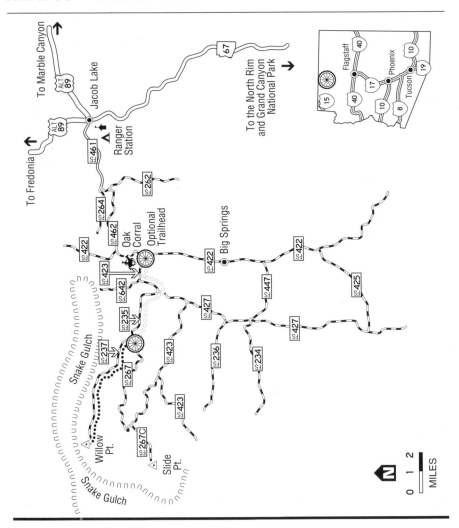

a schedule and contact times with the district ranger or someone with a phone who has local emergency numbers. Or at least be prepared to handle whatever problems may arise.

Land status: Kaibab National Forest.

Maps: The Kaibab National Forest map for the North Kaibab District is adequate here. The USGS 7.5 minute quads are Big Springs and Toothpick Ridge; the Jump Up Canyon quad is the 15 minute series.

Looking into Snake Gulch on the way out to Willow Point, on the Kaibab Plateau in northern Arizona.

Finding the trail: Follow AZ 67 south from the Jacob Lake Intersection one quarter mile to FS 461. Turn west on FS 461 and drive about 6 miles to FS 462. Continue west on FS 462 to the intersection with FS 422. Turn south on FS 422 to Oak Corral Road (FS 423). Follow FS 423 2 miles to FS 235. Turn northwest on FS 235; it is 4 miles to Willow Point Road (FS 237). Park at this intersection.

Sources of additional information: The Kaibab National Forest, North Kaibab Ranger District, address is listed in the introduction to this section.

Notes on the trail: This ride rolls along on a good double-track, descending as you progress toward Willow Point. This is a straight out-and-back with little possibility of getting lost. Strap on that helmet and enjoy!

This is an isolated road with no real options for alternate routes once you are out at the point. You may want to lengthen this ride, however, which can be done by leaving your vehicle at Oak Corral in Nail Canyon. This will almost double the mileage on this ride, adding 11 miles.

RIDE 54 *JUMPUP POINT*

This 20.6-mile ride, which takes you out and back to Jumpup Point, requires some technical skill as well as a good base of physical fitness. There are several side roads that are good for exploring, for those who are up to it. This route follows a curving, rolling, graded dirt and gravel road that has some steep pitches. Allow three to four hours' riding time to get out to Jumpup Point and back, and another hour of driving to reach the trail.

You will be riding through tall stands of ponderosa pine for about the first half of this ride, before dropping into healthy stands of piñon pine and juniper. The scenery is outstanding all along the way, but nothing can beat the view that awaits you at Jumpup Point. Jumpup Point is at the end of a long finger of the plateau suspended over a breathtaking maze of sculpted buttes and canyons. Looking out you will see Fishtail Mesa to your left, and to your right Kanab Creek Canyon and Kanab Point. Across the Colorado you will be looking at Matkatambia Mesa, the Kangaroo Headlands, Gatagama Terrace, and Tahuta Terrace. Great names, huh? The view is big out here, spectacular, unmistakably the Grand Canyon.

General location: Snake Gulch/Kanab Canyon Area, Kaibab Plateau, Kaibab National Forest, which is 30 miles south of Fredonia, Arizona, and 166 miles north of Flagstaff.
Elevation change: At the intersection of Forest Service roads 423, 201, and 236, where this ride begins, your elevation is 5,489'. Where you reach the road to Jensen Point your elevation will be 5,971'. When you reach Jumpup Point your elevation is 5,800'. Elevation gain is approximately 650'.
Season: Riding is fantastic out here from spring through late fall.
Services: Water, groceries, prepared meals, and accommodations are available at Jacob Lake, at the Grand Canyon Lodge, and at the North Rim campground grocery store.
Hazards: This road attracts a good deal of vehicular traffic and there are a sufficient number of blind corners and loose, steep grades to warrant caution. A bright piece of clothing or helmet cover will help to alert motorists to your presence. This also helps to let hunters know you are in the area.

Check with the ranger before your visit, or when you arrive, for hunting schedules and weather information. The roads that access this ride are gravel, all-weather roads, but they may become impassable during the winter and after spring and fall storms.

Watch out for those dark billowy clouds that grow quickly on summer afternoons, for they'll scare the daylights out of you when they bust open. You are very exposed out here. Get off your bike and take shelter if you are caught in a lightning storm.

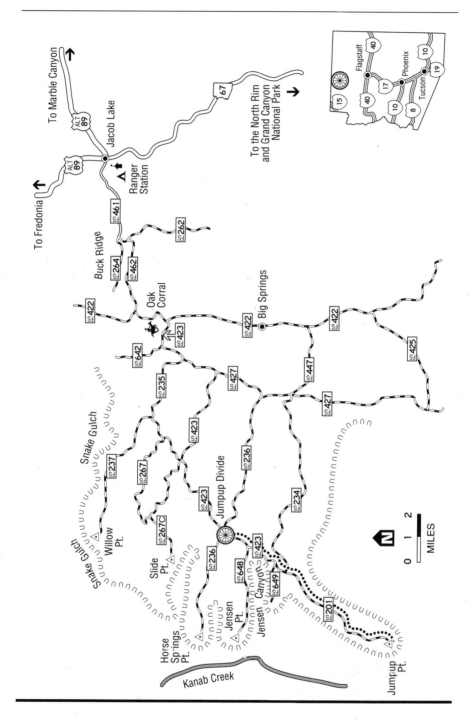

Rescue index: Because this is such remote country it is a good idea to establish a schedule and contact times with the district ranger or someone by a phone who has local emergency numbers. Or at least be prepared to handle whatever situations may arise.

Land status: Kaibab National Forest.

Maps: The Kaibab National Forest map for the North Kaibab District is adequate here. The USGS 15 minute quad is Jump Up Canyon.

Finding the trail: Follow AZ 67 south from the Jacob Lake Intersection a quarter mile to FS 461. Turn west on FS 461 and drive about 6 miles to FS 462. Continue west on FS 462 to the intersection with FS 422. Turn south on FS 422 to Oak Corral Road (FS 423). Follow FS 423 past FS 235 to where it bends to the left and continues in a westerly direction up Slide Canyon. Continue on 423 until you reach the intersection with FS 236 and 201. Park at this intersection to begin your ride.

Sources of additional information: The Kaibab National Forest, North Kaibab Ranger District, address is listed in the introduction to this section.

Notes on the trail: From where you parked go straight ahead onto FS 201 and ride it all the way to Jumpup Point. You will roll gently through hilly country, gaining elevation as you go. As you near Jumpup Point you will find yourself in distinctly desert-like country. Views through the branches are distracting, but there are many places to stop and gander along the way.

If you are interested in extending the length of this ride, there is about an 8.5-mile spur that will take you out to Jensen Point and reveal more fantastic views. Here the deep red sandstone of the Supai Group first makes its appearance. To reach this spur take a left off FS 201A. Bear left at the "Y" for the best views along the plateau rim.

Another short 3-mile spur is possible by taking FS 649, which takes you out to Jensen Trick Tank. This is a nice, short option with beautiful scenery and some good views.

You may want to shorten this ride to 17 miles round-trip by starting at the intersection of FS 649 and 201.

RIDE 55 *CRAZY JUG POINT*

Crazy Jug Point is another fantastic destination on the Kaibab Plateau. This out-and-back route accesses Crazy Jug Point from the east and gives a total distance of 20 miles. If you are staying in or near Jacob Lake you can ride a route option from the north, for a distance of 28.5 miles. This is a sparsely traveled jeep road that is really a double-track. Some short sections will be steep and somewhat loose. Riders with beginning-to-intermediate riding skills, who are in good-to-

RIDE 55 *CRAZY JUG POINT*

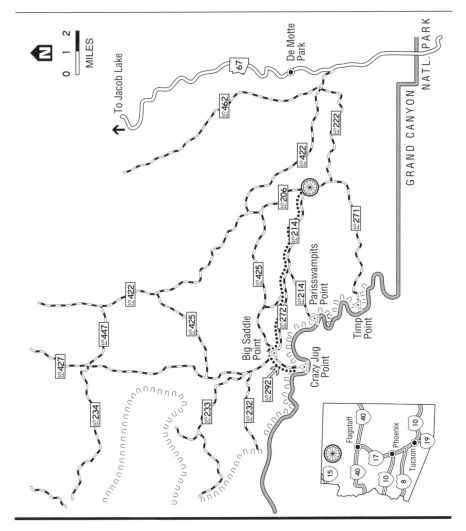

excellent physical condition, should allow three to four hours' riding time. A shuttle or vehicle-supported ride is also a good option here.

The northern route option will take you down the narrow, winding, densely wooded Sowats Canyon. The route from the east winds through Indian Hollow, which also is densely forested by Gambel oak, ponderosa pine, and aspen. You will find wide, grassy meadows sometimes filled with wildflowers along either route. Because this area is fairly remote and not well traveled it is a good opportunity to see wildlife. Once you reach Crazy Jug Point you will be looking south at fantastic Grand Canyon scenery. The Tapeats Amphitheater, carved out by a network of drainages including Tapeats Creek, surrounds you from this point. Further to the south you will be looking across to Arrowhead Terrace, Steamboat Mountain, and beyond to the Powell Plateau. You'll need a little while to sit on the rocks at Crazy Jug Point and take this all in. Plan your ride so you won't have to rush.

General location: This ride is on the Kaibab Plateau, in the Kaibab National Forest, 30 miles south of Fredonia, Arizona, and 166 miles north of Flagstaff.

Elevation change: At the intersection of FS 425 and 422, where this ride begins, your elevation is 6,375'. You will roll along, gaining in elevation, until you reach Crazy Jug Point at an elevation of 7,449'. If you choose to continue the extra distance to Monument Point you will descend to an elevation of 7,206'. Elevation gain is 1,074', or 1,280' with the option out to Monument Point.

Season: The only times Crazy Jug Point is accessible is late spring through fall. During winter and early spring most of these roads remain closed due to snow.

Services: Water, groceries, prepared meals, and accommodations are available at Jacob Lake, at the Grand Canyon Lodge, and at the North Rim campground grocery store.

Hazards: These roads are rarely used and may have some rough spots and overgrown vegetation. Hunters and lightning storms will be your biggest concern when you're out this way. Check with the ranger before your visit or when you arrive for hunting schedules and weather information.

The roads that access this ride are gravel all-weather roads, but they may become impassable due to severe thunderstorms or unexpected snowstorms.

Rescue index: Because this is such remote country it is a good idea to establish a schedule and contact times with the district ranger or someone with a phone who has local emergency numbers. Or at least come prepared to handle whatever situation may arise.

Land status: Kaibab National Forest.

Maps: The Kaibab National Forest map for the North Kaibab District is adequate here. The USGS 15 minute quad is Jump Up Canyon.

Finding the trail: The east-to-west route that accesses Crazy Jug Point begins at the intersection of FS 206 and 214. You will again leave AZ 67 when you reach signs for De Motte Park. This will be FS 422, which you will take for just over 8 miles to where it intersects FS 206. Go left onto FS 206 and continue for 4 miles to the intersection with FS 214. Park when you reach this intersection.

Sources of additional information: The Kaibab National Forest, North Kaibab Ranger District, address is listed in the introduction to this section.

Notes on the trail: Beginning at the intersection of FS 206 and FS 214 you will ride just over 3 miles, at which point you'll bear right onto FS 272. Another 3 miles along FS 272 the route forks again. The left side of the fork remains

A maze of buttes and drainages known as Tapeats Amphitheater lays beneath you at Crazy Jug Point.

FS 272, while the right fork becomes FS 425. You want to bear left on FS 272, although the right fork, FS 425, takes you within a half mile of where FS 272 intersects FS 292—which will take you the 2 miles to Crazy Jug Point. You may want to take one route out and the other back.

To reach this ride from the north follow AZ 67 south from the Jacob Lake intersection for 25 miles. Turn right when you reach signs for De Motte Park; you are now on FS 422. You will continue on FS 422 for almost 15 miles to the intersection with FS 425. Park when you reach this intersection. You will follow FS 425 for almost 12 miles before bearing right onto FS 292, which will take you out to Crazy Jug Point after 2 miles.

There are many options for alternative routes and spurs on your way out to Crazy Jug Point. I strongly suggest supplementary Forest Service and topographical maps for riding in this area. They will not only help you create your own routes, but will help you to identify the many distinctive landmarks in the region.

RIDE 56 *TIYO POINT*

This is a 22-mile out-and-back excursion which highlights some of the most beautiful country on the Kaibab Plateau. For bikers with intermediate riding skills and good-to-excellent physical condition this ride will take about five hours to complete. Add more for taking in the view from Tiyo Point. This route is a rough jeep road that is really a double-track. You will find a riding surface of hard-packed dirt most of the time, but there will be sections that are rocky.

From where you begin this ride at the Widfross Trailhead parking lot (elevation 8,163 feet) you will be in alpine forests of mixed conifer and aspen. You will reach the turnoff out to Tiyo Point in a large meadow known as The Basin. In another six miles you will be perched above the Grand Canyon with a hawk's eye view of one of the world's great wonders.

General location: North Rim of the Grand Canyon, Grand Canyon National Park, Kaibab Plateau.
Elevation change: At the spot where the Point Sublime Trail/Road begins, at the Widfross Trail parking lot, your elevation is 8,163'. From here you will traverse several short climbs and descents before arriving at The Basin, a meadow where you pick up Tiyo Point Road (8,147'). After you make your turnoff you will climb gradually until you begin to descend to Tiyo Point, at an elevation of 7,762'. Total elevation gain is 400'.
Season: This ride is not accessible until the road to the North Rim opens in mid-May. Even then you may find substantial amounts of snow lingering in pockets of cool forest shade. Deadfall from winter storms is another obstacle you may run into on this route when it first opens. If the ground becomes saturated, due to heavy rains or snowmelt, it can be a muddy bog. Be prepared for anything. This route should stay rideable until the road is closed again sometime in October.
Services: Water, groceries, food, and accommodations are available at Jacob Lake, at the Grand Canyon Lodge, and at the North Rim campground grocery store.
Hazards: This road can be very rough and receives light use. Generally the route becomes impassable when the ground is saturated due to snowmelt or heavy rains.

Your biggest concern out here is weather, especially violent monsoonal thunderstorms, which can lash this plateau with cold rain, hail, and lightning in August and September. Be sure to check in with the park ranger for weather forecasts before you head out.
Rescue index: Because this is such remote country it is a good idea to establish a schedule and contact times with park rangers, or at least let them know your plans before you go.

RIDE 56 *TIYO POINT*

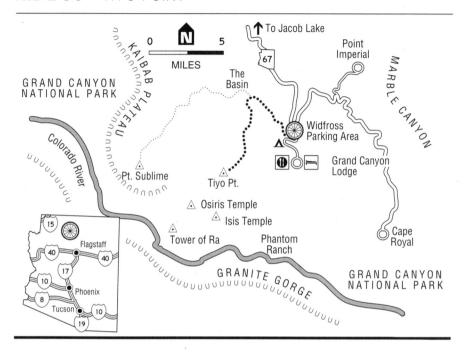

Land status: Grand Canyon National Park.

Maps: The Kaibab National Forest map for the North Kaibab Ranger District is adequate for this ride. The USGS 15 minute quads are De Motte Park and Powell Plateau.

Finding the trail: The road to Point Sublime and Tiyo Point begins 2.7 miles north of Grand Canyon Lodge. Turn west onto the road marked "Widfross Trailhead." You can park here and begin your ride, or adjust the length of your ride by driving down the road if you have a high-clearance, four-wheel-drive vehicle.

Sources of additional information: You will want to stop in at the information desk at the Grand Canyon Lodge and talk to one of the park rangers about road conditions out to Point Sublime. If you are interested in camping out at Point Sublime you will need to secure a backcountry permit from the park ranger's office near the entrance to the campground. Other information about visiting and riding in the park is available by contacting the Grand Canyon National Park. The address is listed in the introduction to this section.

Notes on the trail: Leave the Widfross Trailhead parking lot riding the road that takes you up a gentle grade to the garbage dump. Bear right when you reach the dump and head into the woods. You will make several short climbs and descents as you ride through the woods before reaching a large meadow area at mile 4. This meadow is referred to as The Basin. You will ride down a hill into the meadow and begin climbing gently. Keep an eye out over your left shoulder for your turn onto the Tiyo Point Road. Where this road forks off to the left is not very distinct, but you will see the road heading off to the south, up and over a rise. That's your turn. It's the only left turn in the meadow. Come prepared as this ride can be a long day. Make sure you carry plenty of water and high-energy snacks, and an extra layer of clothing. Enjoy!

RIDE 57 *POINT SUBLIME*

The ride out to Point Sublime is a long 35-mile round-trip excursion for the adventurous who are in excellent physical condition. This route follows a four-wheel-drive jeep road that is often rutted and muddy in spots. Passenger cars should not attempt driving on this road. There are many short climbs and descents on this ride as you roll over successive ridges and valleys. The length and elevation make the route difficult; it will take most of a day to complete.

This ride begins near the Grand Canyon Lodge at the North Rim, at the Widfross Trailhead parking lot. For the next ten miles you will be riding through alpine forests of mixed conifers, dominated by ponderosa and aspen. These deep cool forests give way at times to open, sunny meadows, which are a favorite hangout for browsers, fellow bikers, and other wildlife.

General location: North Rim of the Grand Canyon, Grand Canyon National Park, Kaibab Plateau.
Elevation change: At the point where the Point Sublime Trail/Road begins, at the Widfross Trail parking lot, your elevation is 8,163'. From there you will experience many short gains and losses in elevation before reaching a high elevation of 8,400' on Crystal Ridge. From Crystal Ridge you will drop steadily to Point Sublime, which is at an elevation of 7,458'. There are many short, sometimes steep climbs and descents along this route. You will be gaining roughly 1,180' in elevation.
Season: This ride is not accessible until the road to the North Rim opens in mid-May. Even then you may find substantial amounts of snow lingering in pockets of cool forest shade. Deadfall from winter storms is another obstacle you may run into in the spring. If the ground becomes saturated due to heavy rains or snowmelt it can be a muddy bog. Be prepared for anything. This route should stay rideable until the road is closed again sometime in October.
Services: Water, groceries, prepared meals, and accommodations are available at Jacob Lake, at the Grand Canyon Lodge, and at the North Rim campground grocery store.

RIDE 57 *POINT SUBLIME*

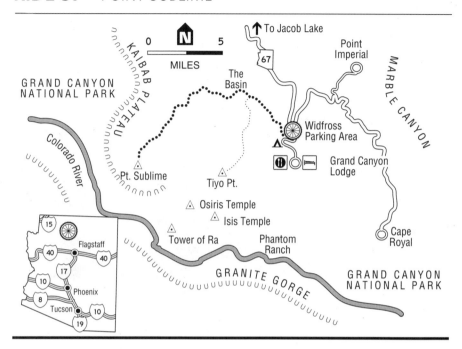

Hazards: This road can be very rough and receives light use. Generally the route becomes impassable when the ground is saturated due to snowmelt or heavy rains.

Your biggest concern out here is weather, especially violent monsoonal thunderstorms, which can lash this plateau with cold rain, hail, and lightning in August and September. Be sure to check in with the park ranger for a weather forecast before you head out.

Also, this is a long day, so make sure you are in adequate physical condition before you begin. Bring lots of extra fluids and high-energy foods. No water is available along the trail.

Rescue index: Because this is such remote country it is a good idea to establish a schedule and contact times with a park ranger, or at least let them know your plans before you go.

Land status: Grand Canyon National Park.

Maps: The Kaibab National Forest map for the North Kaibab Ranger District is adequate for this ride. The USGS 15 minute quads are De Motte Park and Powell Plateau.

Finding the trail: The road to Point Sublime begins 2.7 miles north of Grand Canyon Lodge. Turn west onto the road marked "Widfross Trailhead." You can

The view into the Crystal Creek drainage and the Grand Canyon on the way out to Point Sublime.

park here and begin your ride, or adjust the length of your ride by driving down the road—if you have a high-clearance, four-wheel-drive vehicle.

Sources of additional information: You will want to stop in at the information desk at the Grand Canyon Lodge and talk to one of the park rangers about road conditions out to Point Sublime. If you are interested in camping out at Point Sublime you will need to secure a backcountry permit from the park ranger's office near the entrance to the campground. Other information about visiting and riding in the park is available by contacting the Grand Canyon National Park. The address is listed in the introduction to this section.

Notes on the trail: You will leave the Widfross Trailhead parking lot on the road that takes you up a gentle grade past a refuse dumping area and then bears right, taking you into the woods. There are several less-used roads taking off from the main Point Sublime Road, which is easy to follow as it shows signs of more use. You will ride through densely forested rolling terrain for most of the way out, emerging at times into meadowy areas. You'll encounter a large meadow referred to as The Basin at about mile 4. You will climb and descend across several short, steep hills before reaching the overlook to Crystal Drainage just past mile 8. There is a short road taking off to your left; grab your camera and be prepared for a tremendous view.

From here you will begin to lose elevation. Ponderosas soon give way to piñon and juniper, and by the time you arrive at Point Sublime, 8.5 miles later, the scenery becomes more of what you'd expect to find in the desert. This ride is a day-long odyssey that takes you through incredible country. Come prepared! Make sure you carry plenty of water and high-energy snacks and an extra layer of clothing. Enjoy!

Few options exist on this route, except that you may want to drive in a distance to adjust the length of your ride. Do not attempt this without a high-clearance four-wheel-drive vehicle.

You may also want to head out to Tiyo Point instead of going the whole distance to Point Sublime. You can reach the Tiyo Point Road by forking to the right 4 miles from the start of the Point Sublime Road.

RIDE 58 *THE ARIZONA TRAIL*

The Kaibab National Forest has recently cut and cleared a route across the Kaibab Plateau from north to south, which includes existing dirt roads, abandoned jeep roads, and single-track. While many parts of this route existed previously, they had gone unused for many years. Other sections of trail had to be created to connect existing trails. This entire route, called the Arizona Trail, will eventually span the entire state from north to south and someday connect with a cross-state trail traversing Utah. The portion of the Arizona Trail which traverses the Kaibab Plateau is called the Kaibab Plateau Trail, and was used historically for travel in the area. Later portions of it became the Moqui Stage Line. The trail was relocated and resurrected by members of the Arizona State Hiking and Equestrian Committee and the Sierra Club, with help from the Forest Service.

The Arizona Trail is open to mountain bikes on the Kaibab Plateau from where it emerges from the park in the south, to where it exits the Northern Kaibab Ranger District as Forest Service Road 248 near Rock Canyon Reservoir. The total distance between these points is almost 60 miles. For most cyclists it will be best to ride the Arizona Trail which occasionally crisscrosses the Kaibab Plateau. The Kaibab Plateau Trail becomes the Arizona Trail once again when it leaves the national forest and continues northward. This section of the trail is BLM land which is also open to mountain bikes, though it is not regularly maintained. For the adventurous this trail holds limitless possibilities.

The Arizona Trail, or Kaibab Plateau Trail, traverses some of the most beautiful country in Arizona. Deep stands of alpine conifers mixed with aspen shade long portions of this route. At other times you will emerge into enormous meadows, sometimes called dry lakes. The chance of seeing deer, elk, and many other types of wildlife is excellent along this route.

RIDE 58 *THE ARIZONA TRAIL*

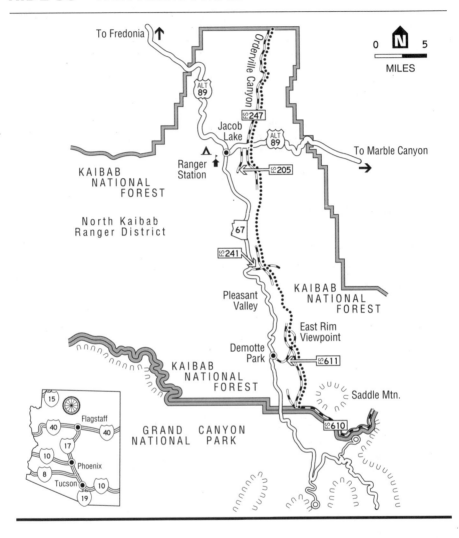

General location: Kaibab Plateau, Kaibab National Forest, North Kaibab Ranger District in northern Arizona.

Elevation change: Elevations along this route range from just over 9,000' in the south, where the trail merges from the park, to just over 6,600' in the north where the trail exits the national forest boundary. For the most part this is rolling, hilly country providing riders with many short climbs and descents.

Season: The section of the Arizona Trail that traverses the Kaibab Plateau is not

Forests of mixed conifers and aspen cover most of the Kaibab Plateau, which rises to elevations over 9,000 feet.

accessible until the road to the North Rim opens in mid-May. Even then you may find substantial amounts of snow lingering in pockets of cool forest shade. Deadfall from winter storms is another obstacle you may run into along this route. If the ground becomes saturated due to heavy rains or snowmelt it can be a muddy bog. Be prepared for anything. This route should stay rideable until the road is closed again sometime in October.

Services: Water, groceries, prepared meals, and accommodations are available at Jacob Lake, at the Grand Canyon Lodge, and at the North Rim campground grocery store.

Hazards: This route can be rough and somewhat overgrown since it receives light use. Generally the route becomes impassable when the ground is saturated due to snowmelt or heavy rains. In some places the trail surfaces become soft and spongy due to layers and layers of pine needles and other forest debris. This condition makes for tough pedaling. Large pine cones strewn along the trail can also be a hazard. Meadow crossings can be a challenge due to the efforts of ground squirrels and moles. The holes and mounded tunnels these little guys leave behind can make for some rough riding, and can knock the unsuspecting rider out of the saddle.

You will want to be aware of the weather out here. Violent summer and fall thunderstorms are a common occurrence. Besides scaring the daylights out of you they can leave you wet and cold. It's a good idea to check in with the forest rangers before heading out. They can tell you which sections of trail are going to be in the best shape and what the weather has in store.

Rescue index: Because this is remote country you may want to establish a schedule and contact times with a park ranger, or at least let them know your plans before you go.

Land status: Kaibab National Forest, North Kaibab Ranger District.

Maps: The Kaibab National Forest map for the North Kaibab Ranger District is adequate for this ride.

Finding the trail: There are many places where you can access the Arizona, or Kaibab Plateau, Trail from AZ 67, the paved road that traverses the plateau. One of the best is toward the south, just south of De Motte Park, where you can find the Kaibab Lodge, Rim Store, and De Motte Campground. One mile past De Motte Park, as you are heading south, you will find FS 611 leaving from the left side of the road. Turn off onto this road and follow it to the East Rim Viewpoint. You can park here and pick up the Arizona Trail as a single-track from where it leaves on the right side of the road, a quarter mile past the East Rim Viewpoint Turnout. Or you can ride back out on FS 611 for 1.25 miles to where the Arizona Trail leaves from the left side of the road and heads in the opposite direction. This trail can be ridden until you reach FS 610, which skirts the edge of Grand Canyon National Park, heading in an east and southeast direction.

Another place you can pick up the trail is off FS 241, which leaves from the left side of the road and heads east off AZ 67, 13 miles south of Jacob Lake. Three miles in on FS 241 you can pick up the Arizona Trail heading north, or continue another .6 miles to where the trail heads south up Cane Canyon. An alternate loop route of the Arizona Trail leaves less than one-tenth of a mile up FS 241 and heads south, paralleling AZ 67.

You can pick up the Arizona Trail heading either north or south off FS 224, which is 6.5 miles south of Jacob Lake. The trail leaves FS 241 just under one-quarter mile from where it leaves AZ 67.

The last most convenient place to reach the Arizona Trail on the Kaibab Plateau is approximately 3.3 miles east of Jacob Lake off AZ 89. The Arizona Trail leaves AZ 89 as FS 247 to the north, and joins AZ 89 from the south just parallel to FS 205.

Sources of additional information: The Kaibab National Forest, North Kaibab Ranger District, address is listed in the introduction to this section.

Notes on the trail: It is not possible to give a detailed description of this route for the entire 60 miles. I strongly suggest carrying detailed USGS topographical maps along with you on this ride, and talking to a forest service ranger about current route conditions before you go.

There are literally hundreds of options for riding sections of the Arizona Trail and combining them with other routes and trails on the plateau. Besides a desire for adventure you will need a Forest Service map, topographical maps, and knowledge of how to use a compass if you are going to navigate the Kaibab backcountry effectively.

Monument Valley

Finally, no Arizona guidebook of any kind would be complete without including Monument Valley. The beautiful polished red rock, sage-covered sands, rippling dunes, and massive sandstone formations of this valley form one of America's most celebrated landscapes. The features and landforms of Monument Valley were first brought to the public eye through the lenses of Hollywood cameras. Since it was discovered by the American public at the turn of the century the landscape of Monument Valley has served as inspiration, subject, and backdrop for photographers, filmmakers, painters, and many other artists. The images of this place, the sky, the weather, the light and its shadows, dance magnificently around towering buttes and spires as the sun moves overhead. An afternoon spent gliding across this enchanted valley on your mountain bike will provide images and sensations not soon forgotten.

At an elevation of just over 5,500 feet, Monument Valley is high enough to receive snow throughout the winter. The snowstorms that move through will dust mesa crowns and sagebrush for a day or two, but will not accumulate over the season. Snow will linger, however, in deep shadowy pockets, in narrow canyons, and along northern slopes. Summers in this red rock desert are hot, as you might expect, with days frequently reaching 100 degrees and higher.

Although there is no consistent water source in the valley, evidence of occupation by the Anasazi has been discovered at more than 100 different sites throughout Monument Valley. Like their counterparts all across the Colorado Plateau, the Anasazi who lived here vanished mysteriously around A.D. 1300. While it is uncertain when the Navajo first settled in Monument Valley, they have herded sheep and other livestock in the area for many generations. One account has the valley settled by the Navajo in the years following 1863–64, when Kit Carson was campaigning against the Navajo at Canyon de Chelly. Chief Hoskinini and his people fled to the safety of the open country in and around Monument Valley. Today the valley is home to several Navajo families and is cherished as sacred land by the tribe as a whole. Monument Valley is a Navajo Tribal Park, comprising of almost 30,000 acres. The park was established in 1958. The park is administered and protected by the Parks and Recreation Department within the Division of Natural Resources. You must check in at the Visitor Center and pay a fee before entering the park.

The history of the creation of the fantastic red rock buttes, pinnacles, and mesas of Monument Valley began with the birth of the Colorado Plateau. Materials from the ancient Rocky Mountains were eroded and deposited over this area by wind and water, and then cemented into sandstone. As the plateau uplifted and bulged, the sandstone cracked, assisting the wind and rain in the work of erosion. The softer Cutler Formation sandstone eventually eroded away from the harder, vertical slabs of de Chelly Sandstone, leaving the towers and buttes of red rock that one sees here. Both these types of sandstone are 160 million year-old Precambrian Rock, commonly found in this part of the Colorado Plateau upwarp. These rocks distinguish the landscape throughout northern Arizona and Southern Utah. Agathla Peak and Chastla Butte, at the southern end of the valley, are old volcanic necks that now stand out among the red sandstone as dark, rough, igneous rock. Fifteen to twenty million years ago these volcanic necks fed volcanoes that are now completely eroded away. The beautiful peach and crimson sands of the sweeping dunes in this valley are another remarkable geological feature of this area.

The open and arid nature of this country makes it unsuitable for any large type of mammal, except for those which are tended as livestock. Some cattle, sheep, and goats are raised by Navajo families in the valley. A flourishing variety of rodents, birds, and reptiles are superbly adapted to this desert and are able to thrive here.

Monument Valley Navajo Tribal Park is located on the border of northeastern Arizona and southeastern Utah. To get there from Arizona take US 163 north from Kayenta for 24 miles. From Utah, take US 163 south from Mexican Hat for 25 miles. A four-mile all-weather access road heads east from US 163 to the Monument Valley Visitor Center. Weather permitting, the 17-mile loop through the park is open from 7 A.M. to 7 P.M. during the summer months (May–September), and 8 A.M. to 5 P.M. in winter. Here are the information sources you need to check with before heading down this way:

Monument Valley Navajo Tribal Park
Parks and Recreation Department
Division of Natural Resources
P.O. Box 308
Window Rock, Arizona 86515
(602) 871-6645 or 6646

Superintendent
P.O. Box 360289
Monument Valley, Utah 84536
(801) 727-3287

RIDE 59   VALLEY DRIVE

This 17-mile loop around Monument Valley Tribal Park is an easy-to-moderate ride on a hard-packed dirt road. This road receives a substantial amount of traffic at certain times of year and can become rutted and washboarded. Heavy rains

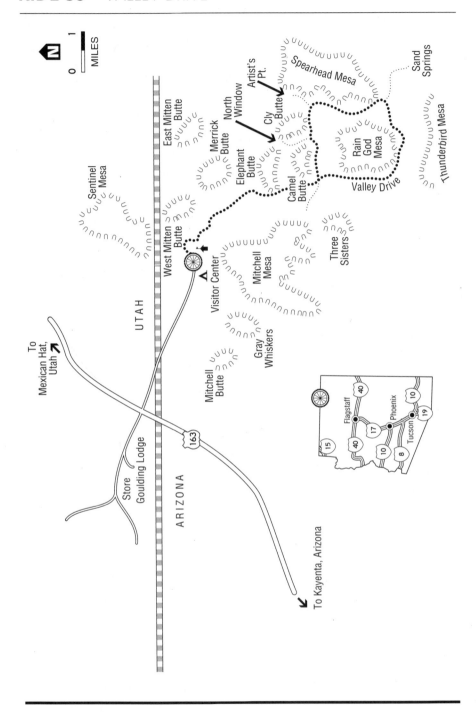

The author in Monument Valley. *Photo by Dennis Coello.*

can also make this road extremely muddy. Little technical skill is required for negotiating this route, but a moderate level of physical fitness is recommended. Allow two to three hours' riding time.

On this scenic loop road you will find eleven numbered posts which correspond to marked points on a map of the valley available at the Visitor Center. This map will help you to identify the various rock formations at each stop along the way. Red rock buttes and spires, such as Mitten Buttes, Elephant Butte, The Three Sisters, and Camel Butte, are just a few of the fantastic natural sculptures you will see. Give yourself some time to take in the view at Artist's Point, or at North Window, where you can listen to the quiet.

General location: On the Utah/Arizona border.

Elevation change: At the Visitor Center, on Lookout Point, the elevation is 5,564′. From here you will drop into Monument Valley to an elevation of 5,200′. Your elevation will vary only a hundred feet or so as you roll along the valley floor.

Season: Provided the road surface is dry, this route makes for excellent riding year-round.

Services: The Gouldings Trading Post complex, located about 6 miles west of the Visitor Center, has food and accommodations. There is a campground next to the Monument Valley Visitor Center. All services, except those which are bike related, can be obtained in the towns of Kayenta, Arizona, or Mexican Hat in Utah.

Hazards: When these desert soils become mixed with water they can produce a type of greasy mud that adheres like glue and is very hard to remove. This mud will quickly clog tire treads, derailleurs, and brakes, and will take hours and a lot of patience to clean off. Be aware of fast-growing summer thunderstorms which can darken the sky to a steely gray and spike the desert with brilliant forks of lightning.

Rescue index: You are in a fairly remote part of the country here. However, the park itself receives quite a lot of tourist traffic, and there is always someone on duty at the Visitor Center during business hours. In case of emergency contact the Park Superintendent.

Land status: Navajo Nation Tribal Park.

Maps: The handout available at the Park Visitor Center has a map showing the route as well as points of interest; the map is all that is necessary for finding your way. The USGS 15 minute topos are Agathla Peak and Dinnehotso, Arizona. The 7.5 minute quads are Goulding, Monument Pass, and Halgaith Spring.

Finding the trail: See my introductory remarks for access information.

Sources of additional information: You will find the address of the Tribal Park in the introductory paragraphs of this ride.

Notes on the trail: From the Visitor Center you will follow the road well marked as Valley Drive heading downhill into the valley. After a short descent you will begin to roll gently up and down along the one-way route that will take you on a tour of the Monument's buttes and pinnacles. There is no possibility of getting lost on this road.

There are no options possible here. Riding off of established roadways is prohibited. You are on the private property of the Navajo Nation. Be respectful.

Glossary

This short list of terms does not contain all the words used by mountain bike enthusiasts when discussing their sport. But it should be sufficient as an introduction to the lingo you'll hear on the trails.

ATB
all-terrain bike; this, like "fat-tire bike," is another name for a mountain bike

ATV
all-terrain vehicle; this usually refers to the loud, fume-spewing three- or four-wheeled motorized vehicles you will not enjoy meeting on the trail—except of course if you crash and have to hitch a ride out on one

bladed
refers to a dirt road which has been smoothed out by the use of a wide blade on earth-moving equipment; "blading" gets rid of the teeth-chattering, much-cursed washboards found on so many dirt roads after heavy vehicle use

blaze
a mark on a tree made by chipping away a piece of the bark, usually done to designate a trail; such trails are sometimes described as "blazed"

BLM
Bureau of Land Management, an agency of the federal government

buffed
used to describe a very smooth trail

catching air
taking a jump in such a way that both wheels of the bike are off the ground at the same time

clean
while this can be used to describe what you and your bike *won't* be after following many trails, the term is most often used as a verb to denote the action of pedaling a tough section of trail successfully

deadfall
a tangled mass of fallen trees or branches

diversion ditch
a usually narrow, shallow ditch dug across or around a trail; funneling the water in this manner keeps it from destroying the trail

double-track
the dual tracks made by a jeep or other vehicle, with grass or weeds or rocks between; the mountain biker can therefore ride in either of the tracks, but will of course find that whichever is chosen, no matter how many times he or she

changes back and forth, the other track will appear to offer smoother travel

dugway a steep, unpaved, switchbacked descent

feathering using a light touch on the brake lever, hitting it lightly many times rather than very hard or locking the brake

four-wheel-drive this refers to any vehicle with drive-wheel capability on all four wheels (a jeep, for instance, as compared with a two-wheel-drive passenger car), or to a rough road or trail which requires four-wheel-drive capability (or a *one*-wheel-drive mountain bike!) to traverse it

game trail the usually narrow trail made by deer, elk, or other game

gated everyone knows what a gate is, and how many variations exist upon this theme; well, if a trail is described as "gated" it simply has a gate across it; don't forget that the rule is if you find a gate closed, close it behind you; if you find one open, leave it that way

Giardia shorthand for *Giardia lamblia,* and known as the "backpacker's bane" until we mountain bikers appropriated it; this is a waterborne parasite that begins its life cycle when swallowed, and one to four weeks later has its host (you) bloated, vomiting, shivering with chills and living in the bathroom; the disease can be avoided by "treating" (purifying) the water you acquire along the trail (see "Hitting the Trail")

gnarly a term thankfully used less and less these days, it refers to tough trails

hammer to ride very hard

hardpack used to describe a trail in which the dirt surface is packed down hard; such trails make for good and fast riding, and very painful landings; bikers most often use "hardpack" as both a noun and adjective, and "hard-packed" as an adjective only (the grammar lesson will help you when diagramming sentences in camp)

jeep road, jeep trail a rough road or trail which requires four-wheel-drive capability (or a horse or mountain bike) to traverse it

kamikaze while this once referred primarily to those Japanese fliers who quaffed a glass of saki, then flew off as human bombs in suicide missions against U.S. naval vessels, it has more recently been applied to the idiot mountain bikers who, far less honorably, scream down hiking trails, endangering the physical and mental safety of the walking, biking, and equestrian traffic they meet; deck guns were necessary to stop the Japanese kamikaze pilots, but a bike pump or walking staff in the spokes is sufficient for the current-day kamikazes who threaten to get us all kicked off the trails

multi-purpose   a BLM designation of land which is open to multi-purpose use; mountain biking is allowed

out-and-back   a ride in which you will return on the same trail you pedaled out; while this might sound far more boring than a loop route, many trails look very different when pedaled in the opposite direction

portage   to carry your bike on your person

quads   bikers use this term to refer both to the extensor muscle in the front of the thigh (which is separated into four parts), and to USGS maps; the expression "Nice quads!" refers always to the former, however, except in those instances when the speaker is an engineer

runoff   rainwater or snowmelt

signed   a signed trail is denoted by signs in place of blazes

single-track   a single track through grass or brush or over rocky terrain, often created by deer, elk, or backpackers; single-track riding is some of the best fun around

slickrock   the rock-hard, compacted sandstone which is *great* to ride and even prettier to look at; you'll appreciate it more if you think of it as a petrified sand dune or seabed, and if the rider before you hasn't left tire marks (through unnecessary skidding) or granola bar wrappers behind

snowmelt   runoff produced by the melting of snow

snowpack   unmelted snow accumulated over weeks or months of winter, or over years in high-mountain terrain

spur   a road or trail which intersects the main trail you're following

technical   terrain that is difficult to ride due not to its grade (steepness) but because of obstacles—rocks, logs, ledges, loose soil . . .

topo	short for topographical map, the kind that shows both linear distance *and* elevation gain and loss; "topo" is pronounced with both vowels long
trashed	a trail which has been destroyed (same term used no matter what has destroyed it . . . cattle, horses, or even mountain bikers riding when the ground was too wet)
two-wheel-drive	this refers to any vehicle with drive-wheel capability on only two wheels (a passenger car, for instance, compared to a jeep), or to an easy road or trail which a two-wheel-drive vehicle could traverse
water bar	earth, rock, or wooden structure which funnels water off trails
washboarded	a road with many ridges spaced closely together, like the ripples on a washboard; these make for very rough riding, and even worse driving in a car or jeep
wilderness area	land that is officially set aside by the Federal Government to remain *natural*—pure, pristine, and untrammeled by any vehicle, including mountain bikes; though mountain bikes had not been born in 1964 (when the United States Congress passed the Wilderness Act, establishing the National Wilderness Preservation system) they are considered a "form of mechanical transport" and are thereby excluded; in short, stay out
wind chill	a reference to the wind's cooling effect upon exposed flesh; for example, if the temperature is 10 degrees Fahrenheit and the wind is blowing at 20 miles per hour, the wind-chill effect (that is, the actual temperature to which your skin reacts) is *minus* 32 degrees; if you are riding in wet conditions things are even worse, for the wind-chill effect would then be *minus 74 degrees!*
windfall	anything (trees, limbs, brush, fellow bikers) blown down by the wind

SARAH BENNETT grew up in Salt Lake City, biking and skiing in the Rockies and hiking southern Utah's desert canyonlands. She took her BA degree in English literature at the University of Colorado, and combined her love for the West and the written word into an occupation of writing sports, outdoor, and environmental articles for a wide variety of publications. An avid sportswoman, Sarah competes in national and international telemark skiing contests. She worked as a cook on a sailboat in the Caribbean for a year, and for twice as long mountain biked the mountains and deserts of Arizona and New Mexico for her two books in this series. "I've toured the Roman ruins in southern France," says Sarah, "as well as those in Greece and Italy. They're fascinating. . . a real thrill. But there's *nothing* more exquisite than pedaling or hiking up to the ancient Indian dwellings in our own Southwest." Not surprisingly, her favorite author is Wallace Stegner.

Dennis Coello's America By Mountain Bike Series

Happy Trails

Hop on your mountain bike and let our guidebooks take you on America's classic trails and rides. These "where-to" books are published jointly by Falcon Press and Menasha Ridge Press and written by local biking experts. Twenty regional books will blanket the country when the series is complete.

Choose from an assortment of rides—easy rambles to all-day treks. Guides contain helpful trail and route descriptions, mountain bike shop listings, and interesting facts on area history. Each trail is described in terms of difficulty, scenery, condition, length, and elevation change. The guides also explain trail hazards, nearby services and ranger stations, how much water to bring, and what kind of gear to pack.

So before you hit the trail, grab one of our guidebooks to help make your outdoor adventures safe and memorable.

Call or write
Falcon Press or Menasha Ridge Press
Falcon Press
P.O. Box 1718, Helena, MT 59624
1-800-582-2665
Menasha Ridge Press
3169 Cahaba Heights Road, Birmingham, AL 35243
1-800-247-9437

FALCONGUIDES *Perfect for every outdoor adventure!*

FISHING
Angler's Guide to Alaska
Angler's Guide to Minnesota
Angler's Guide to Montana
Beartooth Fishing Guide

FLOATING
Floater's Guide to Colorado
Floater's Guide to Missouri
Floater's Guide to Montana

HIKING
Hiker's Guide to Alaska
Hiker's Guide to Alberta
Hiker's Guide to Arizona
Hiker's Guide to California
Hiker's Guide to Colorado
Hiker's Guide to Hot Springs
    in the Pacific Northwest
Hiker's Guide to Idaho
Hiker's Guide to Missouri
Hiker's Guide to Montana
Hiker's Guide to Montana's
    Continental Divide Trail
Hiker's Guide to Nevada
Hiker's Guide to New Mexico
Hiker's Guide to Oregon
Hiker's Guide to Texas
Hiker's Guide to Utah
Hiker's Guide to Virginia
Hiker's Guide to Washington
Hiker's Guide to Wyoming
Hiking Softly, Hiking Safely
Trail Guide to Glacier National Park

MOUNTAIN BIKING
Mountain Biker's Guide to Arizona
Mountain Biker's Guide to
    Central Appalachia

Mountain Biker's Guide to
    Northern New England
Mountain Biker's Guide to
    Southern California

ROCKHOUNDING
Rockhound's Guide to Arizona
Rockhound's Guide to Montana

SCENIC DRIVING
Arizona Scenic Drives
Back Country Byways
California Scenic Drives
Oregon Scenic Drives
Scenic Byways
Scenic Byways II
Trail of the Great Bear
Traveler's Guide to the Oregon Trail

WILDLIFE VIEWING GUIDES
Arizona Wildlife Viewing Guide
California Wildlife Viewing Guide
Colorado Wildlife Viewing Guide
Idaho Wildlife Viewing Guide
Indiana Wildlife Viewing Guide
Montana Wildlife Viewing Guide
North Carolina Wildlife Viewing Guide
North Dakota Wildlife Viewing Guide
Oregon Wildlife Viewing Guide
Texas Wildlife Viewing Guide
Utah Wildlife Viewing Guide
Washington Wildlife Viewing Guide

PLUS—
Birder's Guide to Montana
Hunter's Guide to Montana
Recreation Guide to
    California National Forests
Recreation Guide to
    Washington National Forests

Falcon Press Publishing Co. • *Call toll-free 1-800-582-2665*